Racial and Ethnic Politics in American Suburbs

Racial and Ethnic Politics in American Suburbs examines racial and ethnic politics outside traditional urban contexts and questions the standard theories we use to understand mobility and government responses to rapid demographic change and political demands. This study moves beyond traditional scholarship in urban politics, departing from the persistent treatment of racial dynamics in terms of a simple black-white binary. Combining an interdisciplinary, multi-method, and multiracial approach with a well-integrated analysis of multiple forms of data including focus groups, in-depth interviews, and census data, *Racial and Ethnic Politics in American Suburbs* explains how redistributive policies and programs are developed and implemented at the local level to assist immigrants, racial/ethnic minorities, and low-income groups – something that given earlier knowledge and theorizing should rarely happen. Lorrie Frasure-Yokley relies on the framework of suburban institutional interdependency (SII), which presents a new way of thinking systematically about local politics within the context of suburban political institutions in the United States today.

Lorrie Frasure-Yokley is an Associate Professor of political science at UCLA. Some of her recent work appears in *Urban Affairs Review* and *National Political Science Review*. She is the co-principal investigator of the Collaborative Multi-racial Post-election Survey (CMPS) 2008 and 2012, a multistate, multiracial, multilingual postelection study of racial and political preferences and behavior among registered voters in the United States. She is the recipient of several local and national awards, including the Ford Foundation Postdoctoral Fellowship from the National Research Council of the National Academies and the Clarence Stone Young Scholars Award of the American Political Science Association's Urban Politics Section.

Racial and Ethnic Politics in American Suburbs

LORRIE FRASURE-YOKLEY
University of California, Los Angeles

CAMBRIDGE
UNIVERSITY PRESS

32 Avenue of the Americas, New York NY 10013-2473, USA

Cambridge University Press is part of the University of Cambridge.

It furthers the University's mission by disseminating knowledge in the pursuit of education, learning and research at the highest international levels of excellence.

www.cambridge.org
Information on this title: www.cambridge.org/9781107446922

© Lorrie Frasure-Yokley 2015

First published 2015
First paperback edition 2016

A catalogue record for this publication is available from the British Library

Library of Congress Cataloguing in Publication data
Names: Frasure-Yokley, Lorrie.
Title: Racial and ethnic politics in American suburbs / Lorrie Frasure-Yokley, University of California, Los Angeles.
Description: New York, NY : Cambridge University Press, [2015] | Includes bibliographical references and index.
Identifiers: LCCN 2015021717 | ISBN 9781107084957 (hardback)
Subjects: LCSH: Washington Suburban Area – Immigration and emigration – Political aspects. | Washington Suburban Area – Ethnic relations – Political aspects. | Washington Suburban Area – Race relations – Political aspects. | Immigrants – Washington Suburban Area – Social conditions. | Washington Suburban Area – Social conditions.
Classification: LCC JV6940 .F73 2015 | DDC 305.6/0691209753–dc23
LC record available at http://lccn.loc.gov/2015021717

ISBN 978-1-107-08495-7 Hardback
ISBN 978-1-107-44692-2 Paperback

To the loving memory of Shirley and John Frasure
For Gabrielle Elise Yokley

With permission of the artist, this page displays the full panel 1 of the mural on the book cover.
"Celebration to Food plants of the World." 2004.
Acrylic paint on Viroc panels, 20 ft. X 8 ft. - Silver Spring, Maryland, USA
Artist: Designed and created by Jorge Luis Somarriba
Photographed by Janelle Wong, Ph.D.

Contents

Figures

Tables

Acknowledgments

The enthusiastic support and sound direction of my advisor and dissertation chair, the late Linda Faye Williams, was immeasurable to the advancement of this project. I am grateful for the lasting influence her advice and guidance have had on my career. From the project's inception, I was fortunate to work with a supportive and insightful committee that included Michael Jones-Correa, Bart Landry, Irwin Morris, and Joe Oppenheimer. As Jones-Correa's research assistants at the Woodrow Wilson International Center in Washington, DC, we conducted field research and data collection that made this project possible. I am thankful he allowed the use of these data for this project and for his continued support as a colleague, coauthor, and friend.

Field research is impossible without those who graciously agree to be interviewed. Special thanks to each elected official, bureaucratic administrator, and community-based organization leader for his or her time and informative insight. I thank each focus group member for sharing personal stories and listening to those of others. Thank you to Ivonne Rivera and Rivera Qualitative Research for their assistance in the participant selection and facilitation of the native-language focus group discussions.

This research was made possible by generous support from the University of Maryland-College Park, the Ford Foundation Dissertation Fellowship through the National Research Council (NRC) of the National Academies, and the Cornell University Department of Government's Visiting Graduate Student Fellowship, as well as the Cornell University Provost's Academic Diversity Postdoctoral Fellowship and the American Political Science Association's Fund for Latino Scholarship. I am also thankful to Dr. Ansley Abraham and the Southern Regional Education Board (SREB) for funding my doctoral studies and providing an outlet for professional support and development.

At UCLA, I am grateful for funding from several sources: the Faculty Research Grant from the Academic Senate Council on Research, the UCLA

Center for American Politics and Public Policy (CAPPP) Faculty Fellowship, the Faculty Career Development Award, the Office of Faculty Diversity and Development, the Institute of American Culture's Research Grant Program in Ethnic Studies, the UCLA, Ralph J. Bunche Center for African American Studies, and the Academic Senate Travel Award. Thank you to the Ford Foundation Postdoctoral Fellowship through the National Research Council (NRC) of the National Academies, which provided much needed funding for my sabbatical year. I am thankful to Taeku Lee and to the University of California, Berkeley, Department of Political Science, where I served part of my sabbatical.

This project was greatly improved by the opportunity to give research talks at various workshops and colloquia. I would like to thank participants in the Politics of Race, Immigration, and Ethnicity Consortium (PRIEC); the Washington Institute for the Study of Ethnicity, Race, and Sexuality (WISER) at the University of Washington; the Ethnicity and Democratic Governance Project in the Department of Political Studies at Queen's University; the National Center for Suburban Studies at Hofstra University; the Women of Color Policy Network at the Wagner Graduate School of Public Service, New York University; the Black-Latino Relations Conference at the University of California; and the University of Notre Dame's Program in American Democracy. I am thankful to Kerry Ann Rockquemore and the National Center for Faculty Development and Diversity for providing an outlet for professional development and support.

I was introduced to the study of racial and ethnic politics during my freshman year at the University of Illinois, Urbana-Champaign. I am thankful for the long-standing mentorship and friendship of Louis Desipio, Dianne Pinderhughes, and Todd Shaw, who first modeled a research scholar, teacher, and mentor in the field of race, ethnicity, and politics and American politics more broadly. I am thankful to Louis and Dianne as well as Steven Erie and Jane Junn, who read chapters of this manuscript, and whose feedback, and encouragement were invaluable.

This project benefited greatly from the advice, critique, and support of my UCLA colleagues Ray Rocco, Ed Keller, and Mark Sawyer. Mark read several drafts of this manuscript and provided the resources and encouragement for my UCLA book workshop in 2011. I am also grateful for the support and insightful conversations concerning my research from colleagues at UCLA: Richard Anderson, Michael Chwe, Frank Gilliam, Jr., Jeff Lewis, Tom Schwartz, David Sears, Mike Thies, Lynn Vavryck, the late Victor Wolfenstein, and John Zaller; as well as the broader UCLA community, including Leisy Abrego, Scot Brown, Ally Fields, Gabrielle Grey, Celia Lacayo, Mignon Moore, Gary Orfield, Belinda Tucker, Abel Valenzuela, Roger Waldinger, and Yael Warshel. I am thankful to Dean of Social Sciences Alessandro Duranti and to Vice Provost for Diversity & Faculty Development Christine Littleton for their support and encouragement. I also express my gratitude to several UCLA students who provided research assistance at various stages of this project, including Stephanie Garcia, Stacey Greene, Lacey Johnson, Carrie LeVan, Green Son, Jessica Steward, and Drew Wegner.

The completion of this project would have been impossible without finding an intellectual home in various scholarly communities and across different methodologies and research paradigms. I am grateful to be a part of a strong community of scholars through the National Conference of Black Political Scientists (NCOBPS) and the Western Political Science Association (WPSA), as well as the Racial and Ethnic Politics (REP) and the Urban Politics Sections of the American Political Science Association (APSA). I appreciate the friendship and support of colleagues whose conversations about immigrant and racial/ethnic politics, the political economy of metro areas, and/ or state and local governance were invaluable, including Tony Affigne, Matt Barreto, Adolpus Belk, Nadia Brown, Ruth Nicole Brown, Niambi Carter, Megan Francis, John Garcia, Andrea Gillespie, Ange-Marie Hancock, Tyson King-Meadows, Pei-Te Lien, Sylvia Manzano, Sherry Martin, C. Nicole Mason, Natalie Masuoka, Naomi Murakuwa, J. Eric Oliver, Marion Orr, Micheal Leo Owens, Chris Parker, Karthick Ramakrishnan, Ricardo Ramirez, Boris Ricks, Reuel Rogers, Gabe Sanchez, Christine Sierra, Wendy Smooth, Clarence Stone, Alvin Tillery, Tamelyn Tucker-Worgs, Ali Valenzuela, Sophia Jordán Wallace, Dorian Warren, Chris Whitt, David Wilson, and Donn Worgs. Special thank you to artist Jorge Luis Somarriba for permission to use his "Celebration to Food Plants of the World" mural as cover art for this project. I am grateful to Janelle Wong for her support of this project, and contributing a high-resolution photograph of the mural (just in the nick of time).

Thank you to Cambridge editor Robert Dreesen and the editorial team, who were a pleasure to work with, for their patience, insightful advice, and encouragement. I am also especially grateful for the anonymous reviewers for Cambridge whose feedback helped to strengthen and bring this book to fruition.

Thank you to Kirsteen E. Anderson, who provided excellent edits and comments for drafts of this manuscript. Wonderful friends and loved ones helped provide laughter, encouragement, and support during this journey: May Bourjolly, Andrea Brown, Erica Burroughs, Karyn C. Coleman, Akua Cleveland, Maria Davidis, Chris (Chevez) Frazier, Monica Horton, Frank and Barbara Jordan, Tiffany Jordan, Demetria Malloy, Senta and Felton Newell, Sang and Alma Park, Nicoli Richardson, Michelle Rush, Sammia Saeed, Mona and Wade Smart, Karen Stern, Heather Tarlington, and Tamara Witherspoon. I am forever grateful to my parents, the late John and Shirley Frasure, and my siblings, Deborah, Carolyn, Rose, Sheri, and Marvin, as well as my in-laws, Mattie, Henry, Chad, and Christie, for their love and support. Finally, to my husband and best friend, Dedric D. Yokley, thank you for your love, big-picture thinking, advice, patience, encouragement, and unyielding support. Together, we are so excited to welcome little Gabrielle Elise to our family. All errors and omissions in the following pages are, of course, my own.

Introduction

On January 31, 2005, a group of Montgomery County, Maryland, elected officials, bureaucrats, and community leaders held a press conference at the site of a new day labor center, located in Wheaton, a suburb situated just north of Washington, DC. All the groups praised their collective efforts in opening this, the second formal worker center paid for, in part, by county tax dollars. The county leases the center space, while the day-to-day operations of the center are contracted through and managed by a long-standing local nonprofit organization named CASA de Maryland, which serves the Latino and immigrant populations in metropolitan Washington, DC, and Baltimore, Maryland. Unlike the informal hiring sites – such as street corners or parking lots of convenience stores or home improvement stores – where day laborers gather each morning hoping to sell their labor, formalized day laborer centers are designated as job pick-up sites. At these locations workers also receive shelter, job assistance, and the means to report unscrupulous employer practices and receive advocacy support, and if necessary restitution through legal channels.[1]

Standing with representatives of both public and nonprofit institutions at the construction site in Wheaton, county executive Doug Duncan announced, "I am confident that this center will build on the success of the county's first day-laborer site in Langley Park.... New immigrants have an entrepreneurial spirit and the thirst to work and be productive members of our community, and I am proud to help them help themselves to earn a living and support their families."[2] Gustavo

---

[1] Parts of this chapter first appeared in my doctoral dissertation, Frasure (2005) "We Won't Turn Back: The Political Economy Paradoxes of Immigrant and Ethnic Minority Settlement in Suburban America," University of Maryland-College Park. Portions of the opening narrative first appeared in Frasure and Jones-Correa (2010) "The Logic of Institutional Interdependency: The Case of Day Laborer Policy in Suburbia." *Urban Affairs Review*, 45: 451–482, and are used here with the permission of *Urban Affairs Review*.

[2] Doug Duncan served as Montgomery County executive from 1994 to 2006.

Torres, executive director of CASA of Maryland, responded, "Doug Duncan has made Montgomery County into a national model in responding sensitively and intelligently to the needs of day laborers." Tom Perez, a former member of CASA's board of directors and Montgomery County Council's first Latino president, further noted, "This center renews our commitment to include everyone in Montgomery County's economic development.... The successful partnership between business, government and CASA of Maryland has shown that matching employers and employees in a safe and organized environment benefit families, small businesses, and the community. The rising tide of ... redevelopment must lift all boats to succeed."[3] Maryland State Delegate Ana Sol Gutierrez added, "This new Wheaton day laborer employment center demonstrates clearly that Montgomery County values all its workforce and recognizes the contributions that all hard-working individuals make to the growth and strength of our state's economy.... I applaud the exemplary efforts of our County Executive and Council members for finding a solution that serves the growing workforce in the Wheaton area. We are helping to make Wheaton and my District 18 a great place to live" (Montgomery County News Release, 2005).

The range of political and nonprofit leaders present at this groundbreaking indicates a significant degree of political backing in Montgomery County for joint public-nonprofit initiatives and coalitions that address newly pressing public policy issues in suburbia, such as day labor. Such initiatives are neither uncontroversial nor costless. The rise of both informal and regulated or institutionalized day labor sites funded by public dollars violates perceived suburban norms regarding the use of public space and public funds, in addition to raising public safety, health, and other concerns among suburban residents. Day labor sites are a very visible appropriation of public space by people who many residents believe have no right to lay claim to suburban space. Informal day labor sites often raise the ire of local business owners and residents, spurring them to petition their local representatives to ban these sites or at least relocate them away from their vicinity. Adding fuel to the fire are charges by undocumented immigration watchdog groups, such as the Minutemen Civil Defense Corps and the Federation for American Immigration Reform (FAIR), that local governments that regulate day labor centers are misappropriating public dollars to fund services for undocumented immigrants.

On August 17, 2005, just across the Potomac River in Fairfax County, Virginia, Mayor Michael O'Reilly and the city council of the suburb of Herndon approved a publicly funded, institutionalized day labor hiring center

[3] Perez is a civil rights lawyer. He was elected to the Montgomery County Council in 2002, where he served as council president from 2005 until the end of his tenure in 2006. He was appointed by Governor Martin O'Malley to serve as the secretary of the Maryland Department of Labor, Licensing, and Regulation (DLLR) in 2007 until his confirmation to serve as U.S. assistant attorney general for the Civil Rights Division in 2009. He was confirmed as the secretary of labor for the Obama administration in July 2013. His affiliation with CASA de Maryland will be discussed in greater detail in Chapter 4.

called the Herndon Official Worker (HOW) Center, which quickly attracted national attention. The local government, in collaboration with local churches and leaders of community-based organizations, contracted Project Hope and Harmony to facilitate the setup and operation of the center inside a former police station. In September 2005, the conservative political watchdog group Judicial Watch filed a lawsuit against the town of Herndon and Fairfax County for using taxpayer funds to establish the day labor center. Less than a year following the opening of the center, Herndon voters voted out of office the local officials who supported it, including the city mayor and several council members, replacing them with candidates who openly opposed the center's establishment (Osterling & McClure, 2008).

In the face of persistent local and national public outcry surrounding the center, coupled with strong opposition from anti-immigrant groups such as Help Save Herndon and the Herndon chapter of the Minutemen, as well as lobbying from 2006 Republican gubernatorial candidate Jerry W. Kilgore, the day labor center closed in September 2007, after operating for only twenty-one months. Thus, two suburbs undertook similar projects with similar public-private partners but experienced very different outcomes.

The preceding narrative reveals both how suburban jurisdictions are tackling issues not generally considered suburban concerns and how divergent local responses can be. To understand the new racial and ethnic politics in the United States and the policy responses of local governments to racially and economically marginalized communities we must turn our lens to the suburbs. This book is about the unprecedented rise of immigrant and ethnic minorities in American suburbs, and specifically, the development and implementation of the policy responses of local governments to these recent mobility patterns. For the purposes of this study a suburb is broadly defined as the remainder of a metropolitan area outside a primary city.[4] However, in this study I move beyond the traditional suburb-versus-central-city dichotomy and toward an examination of the racial/ethnic, cultural, economic, and political differences contained within various types of American suburbs, particularly those in multiethnic areas.

Today, most blacks, Latinos, and Asian Americans reside in the suburbs. Yet scholars continue to rely on models developed when these groups were primarily urban dwellers to understand the politics of redistribution in the United States. To be clear, this book does *not* examine why certain suburban actors initially choose to provide controversial programs and services to immigrant, minority, and low-income groups in suburbia. Instead, I examine how public-nonprofit partnerships are developed, maintained, or dismantled through the implementation of controversial policies/programs that use, at

---

[4] Although a crude typology, this definition is consistent with the U.S. Census Bureau and the Office of Management and Budget (OMB) geographic classifications and is "easy to compute and readily understood" (Massey & Denton, 1988b, p. 596).

least in part, local tax dollars. I examine what actors such as elected officials, bureaucrats, and nonprofit leaders gain by developing partnerships toward policy development and implementation.

The Changing Face of Suburban America

This study serves as a corrective to the conventional wisdom of the urban politics and racial/ethnic politics literatures, which represent immigration and racial/ethnic diversity as concentrated in America's inner cities. Popular characterizations of American suburban life – ranging from 1950s and 1960s "feel good" family sitcoms such as *Father Knows Best* and *Leave It to Beaver*, to more contemporary films such as *Pleasantville* (1998) and *Revolutionary Road* (2008) – often portray suburbia as a bland, homogenous place. These depictions suggest suburbs are made up largely of white, upper-middle-income dwellers of Levittown-style tract homes. These residents are assumed to hold conformist ideals regarding family life and the domestic roles of women, to be politically conservative, and to be generally concerned with issues such as schools, low taxes, and maintaining small, localized, autonomous government. Yet most suburbs hardly fit this stereotype of tree-lined neighborhoods populated with "all-American" families like the Cleavers.

Despite the persistent stereotype that American suburbs are white and affluent, more than half of all racial/ethnic minority groups now reside in the suburbs of large metropolitan areas with populations exceeding 500,000. By 2000, 94 percent of immigrants lived in metropolitan areas, and of those immigrants, 52 percent lived in suburbs (Singer et al., 2001). Whites still reside in suburban areas in larger proportions than any other racial/ethnic group, growing from 74 percent in 1990 to 78 percent in 2010, but by 2010, 62 percent of Asians and 59 percent of Latinos also lived in suburbs (up from 54 percent and 47 percent, respectively, in 1990). In contrast, African American suburbanization grew little during that period, increasing by just 7 percent between 1990 and 2000 (from 37 to 44 percent). Black suburbanization finally crossed the 50 percent mark by 2010 (Frey, 2011). According to Frey, "Nearly half (49 percent) of growth in suburbs in the 2000s was attributable to Hispanics, compared to just 9 percent for whites. This contrasts with the 1990s, when Hispanics accounted for 38 percent of suburban growth, compared to 26 percent for whites and 36 percent for other groups" (2011, p. 4).

Many suburban school districts have been transformed from largely white to majority minority; so-called international corridors housing a variety of ethnic restaurants and other specialty shops have replaced nostalgic suburban "bedroom communities"; and increasing numbers of minority candidates have won election to local office. There is good reason to welcome these recent trends in suburban multiethnic diversity whereby heterogeneous groups of racial/ethnic minorities more readily make their way out of central cities, and some immigrants choose to bypass residence in the urban core altogether. However,

Nicolaides and Wiese offer evidence that by the late nineteenth century, American suburbs were already places of significant economic and class diversity, albeit what they term *segregated diversity*. As factories and other employers migrated to the suburbs so too did white, immigrant, and African American working-class families – although these groups settled in their own enclaves, separate from affluent suburbs (2006, p. 99). Nicolaides and Wiese write, "While the suburban periphery diversified, elite and middle-class Americans sought to maintain the exclusivity of their own communities. Through statutory, ideological, and cultural means, they reinforced both the barriers and internal meaning of their own elite suburbs. Neighborhood associations and restrictive covenants became the tools of segregation, operating at the local level" (p. 4).

Fueled by rising immigration from Asia, Latin America, Africa, and the Middle East, many U.S. suburbs, in particular those closest to urban cores and developed during or shortly after World War II, are shifting racially, ethnically, and economically at an unprecedented pace. These demographic changes are no longer simply from predominantly white to majority black; increasingly suburbs house a mix of native-born racial/ethnic migrants from central cities and international migrants, who move directly to American suburbs, bypassing the traditional ethnic succession process of initially residing in urban enclaves. However, the contemporary rise in minority representation in U.S. suburbs has not yielded substantial declines in residential segregation. Some suburban areas are paradoxically faced with increasing minority segregation and isolation rather than racial/ethnic diversity (Charles, 2003; Logan, 2003, p. 238).

Despite these developments, scholarship has been slow to recognize these demographic shifts and to analyze the dynamics of new population inflows of immigrants and ethnic minorities into suburbs and the implications for local politics. There remains little written on the politics of suburban government responsiveness to racial/ethnic minorities and immigrant newcomers (but see Graauw, Gleeson, & Bloemraad, 2012; Singer, 2012; Singer, Hardwick, & Brettell, 2008; Varsanyi, 2010; Walker & Leitner, 2011; Winders, 2012). We know very little about how recent suburbanization among immigrants and ethnic minorities is reshaping American political life and the exercise of American democracy (Oliver, 1999, 2001, 2003; Oliver & Ha, 2007; Singer et al., 2008). Unprecedented relocation of racial/ethnic minorities to American suburbs since the 1980s has resulted in close physical proximity among various racial/ethnic groups in these settings, with a host of social and public policy implications: How do "new neighbors" of varying cultural backgrounds (beyond the black-white binary) interact with and perceive their suburban environment? How do their local governments perceive and treat them? How do local institutional actors – such as elected officials, bureaucrats, and leaders of community-based organizations – in suburban jurisdictions address issues important to immigrant and ethnic minority groups (e.g., English as a second language in public schools, translation services at public facilities, employment opportunities for low-skilled laborers)?

As immigrants and racial/ethnic minorities move to U.S. suburbs in unprecedented numbers, government actors in these jurisdictions increasingly find themselves balancing the allocation of local public goods and services between long-standing residents' and newcomers' interests. The persistent debates about the proper role of governmental and nongovernmental actors in the provision of local public goods and services only become more heated when the needs and demands of immigrants enter the mix, particularly if these immigrants are (or are perceived to be) undocumented. Given that suburbs face local budgetary constraints and a political environment likely to be averse to a change in the status quo, the reasons some immigrant and ethnic groups choose to move to certain suburban jurisdictions and the ways local institutions respond to these influxes are increasingly important to understand. Elected officials and the public at large have voiced their opposition to undocumented immigration through contested legislation such as California's Proposition 187 and Arizona's S.B. 1070.[5] Other groups, such as the Minutemen, target local communities more directly, setting up local branches in suburbs to deter local municipalities from funding organizations that provide social services to immigrants, both documented and undocumented.

This book sets forth theoretical and methodological goals important to the study of metropolitan governance, American racial/ethnic politics, and public policy. I use literature from political science, sociology, economics, and demography to develop a theoretical road map for advancing the study of immigrant and ethnic minority suburbanization. This book examines four factors related to new patterns of immigrant and ethnic minority suburbanization: why some racial/ethnic groups move to certain types of suburbs, how they interact with their neighbors, how they perceive their local governments' responsiveness to their needs and concerns, and finally, local governments' policy responses to demographic change.

Theoretically, this book challenges interpretations of constraints on local politics emanating from the traditions of public choice (Bish, 1971; Buchanan, 1971; Fischel, 2001; Peterson, 1981; M. Schneider, 1989a; Tiebout, 1956) and urban regime theories (Sanders & Stone, 1987b; Stone 1989; Swanstrom 1988). On one hand, public choice theorists suggest that when localities attempt redistributive programs (and pay for them through local taxation), suburban businesses and individuals will move to a jurisdiction with lower taxation

---

[5] Proposition 187 was a 1994 ballot initiative designed to bar undocumented immigrants' access to state-level social services including nonemergency health care and public education. The referendum passed but has since been declared unconstitutional. S.B. 1070 requires law enforcement officers to detain any individuals suspected of being in the country illegally, unless those individuals can produce documentation proving they are U.S. citizens or legal immigrants. It also bars state or local officials or agencies from restricting enforcement of federal immigration laws.

(with higher-income residents being more likely to move); hence, residents in local jurisdictions will sort out by class according to local taxation regimens. Therefore, redistributive programs of any kind are unlikely in the fragmented, competitive contexts of U.S. metropolitan areas, and are even less likely since the cuts to intergovernmental transfers from the federal government to states and localities during the 1980s. On the other hand, urban regime theorists argue that both economic imperatives *and* electoral politics matter. Local governments are constrained not only by tax burdens, but also by a political logic whereby public officials need to build and maintain electoral coalitions sufficient both to win office and to govern (Sanders & Stone, 1987b; Stone, 1989; Swanstrom, 1988). In other words, voters matter not necessarily because they will exit, but because they may choose to stay and exercise their voices at the ballot box, in which case public officials would like them to sing a tune in their favor. Therefore, any redistribution that occurs would be the result of electoral pressures as elected officials seek to maintain their governing coalitions.

I argue that both public choice and regime theories fail to explain the mechanisms that drive some suburban jurisdictions to work with nonprofit organizations in an effort to provide goods and services to lower-income, foreign-born, or racial/ethnic minority residents in the absence of either outside funding to underwrite redistributive spending (as public choice theorists would predict), or electoral pressures from voters acting as part of electoral coalitions (as regime theorists would predict).

In this book, I address what I refer to as the *suburban political economy dilemma* facing suburban institutions. This dilemma concerns how local actors address mounting redistributive concerns in the face of rapidly changing demographics in suburbia. I refer to the new suburban policy landscape as a dilemma because the provision of government services to immigrants and ethnic minorities goes counter to the predictions of the classic literature in local governance whose models require some reexamination. For decades public choice theorists suggested that the proper role of municipalities is the provision of local public goods and services that meet their economic development interests and the interests of their upper-income populations. They cautioned local governments to refrain from redistributive policies, which could perceivably raise taxes and induce flight. Such models were developed during the postwar period, when much greater flows of federal dollars served to develop and maintain the economic and racial/ethnic homogeny of suburban neighborhoods and concentrate minorities in the urban areas. During that era the practice of economic sorting across politically fragmented suburban areas was aided by exclusionary zoning, racial covenants, and other de jure and de facto policies that largely exempted suburban jurisdictions from dealing with the redistributive concerns their more diverse urban counterparts were facing.

Indeed, many suburban jurisdictions face a dilemma following the unprecedented exit of the non-Hispanic white population (either back to gentrified central cities or farther into exurbia) and a subsequent influx of lower-income immigrant and racial/ethnic minorities, many who are noncitizens, ineligible to vote, or disinterested in voting. The increasingly heterogeneous context of many suburban jurisdictions arguably leads to the greater likelihood of redistribution. Today, by implementing programs to address the needs of struggling segments of their demographically diverse populations, institutional actors in these suburban jurisdictions are seemingly acting counter to their locality's economic development interests and the interests of the upper-income residents who are *still* their principal electoral constituents.

I examine the new political economy of fiscal austerity and the need to leverage or stretch scarce resources. I parse the institutional logic behind partnerships of local institutional actors that form to enact redistributive programs and policies benefiting immigrant and racial/ethnic minority newcomers in their increasingly diverse suburban jurisdictions. I argue that to get things done in the "new suburbia," local suburban bureaucracies often resort to outsourcing to nonprofit organizations to mitigate some of the cost of meeting the needs of immigrant and racial/ethnic minority newcomers in their jurisdiction. These collaborative efforts lead to a type of selective inclusion for actors otherwise kept away from the decision-making table. What is more, this form of selective inclusion in suburbia shines a light on the age-old question of politics: "Who holds the power?"

The political processes in post-1980s suburbia differ from those in force during past waves of European migration and the Great Black Migration to Northern cities during the early to mid-twentieth century. Yet new immigrants and racial/ethnic migrants such as African Americans enter a suburban space deeply stratified by race, ethnicity, and class and shaped through decades of systemic, institutional, and structural discrimination in American suburbs. The persistence of the American racial hierarchy, an ordering of political power among groups classified by race (Masuoka & Junn, 2013), further complicates who gets what, when, and how in suburban space. Moreover, the introduction of immigrant and ethnic minority issues into suburban politics often requires some redistribution of public resources. However, political machines and the political parties attached to them play lesser roles in incorporating suburban newcomers than was true for earlier waves of immigration and migration to urban areas.

Underscoring the institutional logic behind collective action to address controversial issues that require redistributive policy solutions, I argue that demographic shifts and fiscal austerity change how politics operates at the local level. Each suburban sector – elected officials, bureaucrats, and community-based organizations – has certain tangible and intangible resources at its disposal but also has constraints on these resources. Local bureaucracies may bring select nonprofit organizations into the fold in order to facilitate the incorporation of newcomers into the social, economic, cultural, and political life of suburbia. I examine the extent to which collaborations are formed and remain stable among unlikely partners. In order to explain how some suburban institutional actors (particularly electoral, bureaucratic, and nonprofit) form unlikely alliances to advance policies and programs benefiting immigrants and racial/ethnic minorities, I advance a framework called *suburban institutional interdependency* (SII).[6] SII explores the intersection of suburban institutions and contemporary immigrant and ethnic minority incorporation in the United States. The fundamental logic of SII is simple and practical: through repeated interactions, some local public and nonprofit institutions build partnerships based on reciprocity and the exchange of selective incentives for cooperation. The institutional interdependency in suburbia also includes a division of labor and scarce resources that facilitates "getting things done" in the face of rapidly changing demographics and tightening local budgets. These symbiotic relationships between local suburban institutional actors are dynamic. Whereas some collaborative efforts are enduring and last beyond the specific public policy concern that precipitated the formation of the coalition, other alliances are volatile and can be disrupted by changes within the local environment, such as the strength of an opposition group or a regime change resulting from a local election. Haus and Klausen contend that

we should avoid the harmonistic notions often connected with governance rhetoric, which suggest that 'common' problem solving and 'partnership' are keys to new modes of governance. Governance networks can be understood as a reaction to the crisis of traditional modes of governing, and there is no reason to believe that their creation and operation are free of conflicts and hegemonic strategies. In the end, some type of solution must be found in order to address the complexities of current problems, though it may well be that conflict and contestation play a productive role in the struggle for governance (2011, p. 458).

This research is influenced by the interdisciplinary work of scholars of local governance and public-nonprofit partnerships. The cooperative relationship between public and nonprofit organizations to respond to and solve municipal concerns spans decades (see de Graauw 2008; Marwell 2004; Salomon 1995). However, with few exceptions, this relationship has largely been understood from an urban or central city perspective. So what makes the framework of institutional interdependency appropriate for understanding local politics and governance in suburban areas, and perhaps distinct from its urban counterpart? The central tenets of institutional interdependency may prove generalizable in a variety of urban or rural settings. There are three factors related to centralized (city) versus fragmented/decentralized (suburban) government structures, which make SII particularly applicable (and important) to an American suburban context. First, distinct political jurisdictions and local (government) autonomy are, in many ways, the essence of suburbanization and the basis of local suburban politics (Oliver, 2003; M. Schneider, 1989a). Once a suburban municipality incorporates, the local government assumes

[6] Frasure and Jones-Correa, "The Logic of Institutional Interdependency."

control over the physical and social environment and may also become largely responsible for providing its own local goods and services, such as fire and police protection, libraries, parks, and public schools. Thus, the local market for public goods in suburbia is, to some degree, driven by a political economy that links the structure of local government to decisions about service and tax packages offered to residents (M. Schneider, 1989a). During the 1950s, amid rapid post–World War II suburbanization, public choice scholars argued that if government intervention occurred at all at the local level, it should be restricted to ensuring efficient allocation of local public goods (e.g., police and fire protection) with low taxes and a resistance to income redistribution, which could potentially raise taxes and induce (white) flight. The suburban jurisdictions developed around the country during the post–World War II era, from Levittown, PA, to Orange County, CA, served as a testing ground for such theories (Schneider 1989a).

Second, historically, the political incorporation of immigrant "consumer-voters" in urban centers was inextricably tied to their electoral incorpora-tion (e.g., urban political machines). Unlike during earlier eras of immigration to urban centers, during the post-1980s wave of immigrant suburbaniza-tion, institutional responsiveness to newcomers' needs often preceded their political incorporation, at least in terms of their likely electoral mobilization (Frasure & Jones-Correa, 2010; Marrow, 2009). Many of the interdependent public-nonprofit partnerships examined in this book developed within a politi-cal environment but outside of traditional mainstream (urban) electoral poli-tics framework: the most direct beneficiaries are often nonvoters, legal and undocumented residents.

Third, what makes the recent wave of immigration and racial/ethnic spatial mobility to suburbs and local responsiveness to these patterns unique from earlier waves in urban areas is the lack of federally funded redistributive pro-grams to address the needs of newcomers to suburban areas. Scholars and practitioners in general are not optimistic about a great resurgence of feder-ally funded redistributive programs, akin to the 1960s Great Society or War on Poverty programs, to address affordable housing or greater employment and educational opportunities for new immigrants, minorities, and low-income residents. This is despite the changing demographics of poverty or the grow-ing "suburbanization of poverty" in the United States. As Kneebone and Garr contend, "Suburbs saw by far the greatest growth in their poor population and by 2008 had become home to the largest share of the nation's poor" (2010, p. 1). A study of poverty levels among U.S.-born and foreign-born residents in the nation's ninety-five largest metropolitan areas in 2000 and 2009 finds that foreign-born suburban dwellers experienced higher poverty (14.1 percent) than their U.S.-born counterparts (9.8 percent). Of the 2.7 million foreign-born poor in the suburbs, one of every five lived in poverty (Suro, Wilson, & Singer, 2011). However, as this book will underscore, many suburban initiatives to address the concerns of newcomers are funded, at least in part and not without controversy, by *local* tax dollars and often do not screen clients for their citizenship status.

Each of these factors seem to fundamentally upset the perceived suburban social compact of low taxes and high-quality local public goods and services like public education, between long-standing residents and their local governments. These factors make the application of SII an appropriate framework for explaining how public-nonprofit partnerships are formed to implement programs and policies to serve immigrants, racial/ethnic minorities, and low-income groups.

Arguably, no single methodological framework can grasp all the dynamic processes at work in rapidly changing suburbs. This book is unique in that the underlying research uses a mixed-methods approach combining census data with qualitative data from face-to-face, semi-structured, in-depth interviews with a variety of government and nonprofit leaders.[7] Specifically, using data from more than 100 face-to-face, semi-structured, in-depth interviews with elected, bureaucratic, and nonprofit officials, I apply SII to explain how local institutional actors respond to several recently developing policy issues in suburbia, including the provision of public education programs to immigrant and ethnic minority children, the siting of formal day laborer pickup sites, and language access services at public facilities in suburban Washington, DC.

In order to explain how suburban institutional actors respond to the needs and concerns of immigrant and ethnic groups, it is important first to understand the factors influencing one's residential choice or constraints when selecting a destination in a multiethnic metro area.[8]

There are numerous "decision to move" studies of the "push and pull factors" regarding international and domestic migration (Abramitzky, Boustan, & Eriksson, 2012; Berube et al., 2009; Boustan, 2007; Cohn & Morin, 2008; Frey, 1995, 2003b; Ihrke & Faber, 2012; Koles & Muench, 2002; J. P. Schachter, 2004; P. Taylor, 2008). However, beyond one's initial decision to move, few contemporary studies examine what factors influence or constrain residential *choice of destination*, specifically to American suburbs. Given rapidly changing demographics in metropolitan areas and the greater mobility to suburban destinations for newcomers, it is important to examine the extent to which the classic theories of spatial assimilation and place stratification (in sociology), and economic sorting models (in political economy) explain recent residential choice, preferences, and constraints.

---

[7] The author conducted these interviews, together with Michael Jones-Correa of Cornell University and Junsik Yoon of George Washington University (see in-depth interview protocols in appendixes).

[8] Following demographer William Frey, in this study I use the terms *multiethnic* and *melting pot* interchangeably to describe such metropolitan statistical areas (urban or suburban) where least 35 percent of residents are nonwhite. In 2010, 36 of the 100 most populous metropolitan areas nationwide (i.e., with populations exceeding 500,000) fit this demographic classification. See Frey, "Melting Pot Cities and Suburbs."

The sociology literature often clings to models developed to explain the nineteenth-century immigration and spatial assimilation of ethnic whites. The traditional spatial assimilation model predicts that immigrant groups would typically spend a generation or more in central-city enclaves, while second- or third-generation descendants would subsequently relocate outward to suburban jurisdictions.[9] However, 2010 census estimates are that 40 percent of new immigrants move *directly* to American suburbs from abroad. Recent waves of immigrants to the United States are less likely to undergo the "ethnic succession process" of initially settling in urban areas. The recent phenomenon of immigrant groups bypassing the traditional ethnic succession process via the urban core undermines the individual-level processes predicted by spatial assimilation theory.

Place stratification theory, also emanating from the sociology field, suggests that racial preferences or other structural and institutional discriminatory practices restrain mobility opportunities for certain groups. I argue, however, that proponents of this theory have largely failed to move beyond a black/white or Latino/white binary to examine patterns from a multiethnic perspective, particularly as pertains to immigrant and ethnic minorities in U.S. suburbs (but see Alba & Logan, 1991; Charles, 2000, 2001; Zubrinsky & Bobo, 1996).

In the 1950s and 1960s, public choice theorists proposed economic sorting models predicting that individuals would move to those communities whose tax and expenditure policies matched their preferences (Peterson, 1981; Schneider, 1989a; Tiebout, 1956). I argue that a fundamental problem with these models is their persistent disregard for issues of race and class, which they often treat as exogenous factors. In the American political economy, class dynamics and racial dynamics are inextricably linked. The two cannot be viewed as mutually exclusive, particularly not in suburbia. Thus, the forces shaping recent immigrant and ethnic minority preferences toward suburban living are largely missing from the political economy literature.

I use census data from 2000 to 2010 to provide a national snapshot of recent movers to American multiethnic suburbs. To gain deeper insight into residential selection decisions and its implications from the perspective of individual residents, I supplement census data with the results of five separate focus group discussions conducted in suburban Washington, DC, one of the largest multiethnic metro areas in the United States, and present a case study of recent immigrant and ethnic minority suburbanization in three counties surrounding the DC area.

Unlike the post–World War II era of mass American suburbanization, the post-1980s wave is marked by a notable absence of case study research on suburban demographic shifts and their implications (for early suburban community case studies, see Dobriner, 1958; Gans, 1967; Whyte, 1956; Wood, 1959).

---

[9] See Alba & Logan, 1991; Alba et al., 1999; Frey & Speare, 1988; Massey, 1985; Massey & Denton, 1988a, 1988b, 1993.

Baldassare makes a strong case for the significance of qualitative case studies of suburbia, observing:

field studies of suburban communities have been largely absent in recent times. The early observational reports on suburbs were influential in developing theories about the effects of suburban living. They were critical in the rejection of several myths, including the lack of suburban diversity. They helped place into perspective the effects of suburban community structure on individuals, compared with other factors such as social class and life cycle ... empirical knowledge about the suburban industrial region [is] limited by the lack of in-depth, qualitative community studies. (1992, p. 490)

Case study research enables researchers to carefully build a theoretical framework of suburban migration and government response by describing the actors, strategies, rules of the game, payoffs, and plausible outcomes. For example, the late Nobel laureate Elinor Ostrom, in *Governing the Commons* (1990), provides an outstanding example of the use of qualitative data to build a model, present conjectures, make predictions, and later develop a testable theory. Similar classic case studies of American urban governance and politics include Robert Dahl's (1961) *Who Governs* study of New Haven, Ira Katznelson's (1982) *City Trenches* study of Washington Heights, and Clarence Stone's (1989) *Regime Politics* study of Atlanta. Similar to this study, each used single or a select few cases to develop their theories or frameworks. These studies sparked a cottage industry of interdisciplinary work in political science, economics, sociology, urban affairs, and public policy, often expanding the frameworks to other metropolitan contexts. Unlike these studies, my research focuses on various racial/ethnic groups residing in American suburbs.

Overview of this Book

Chapter 1 places American suburbanization within a theoretical and historical context by reviewing federally backed exclusionary programs that promoted economic and racial inequality in suburban jurisdictions. In this chapter, I also link three of the dominant theoretical frameworks used in this study (spatial assimilation, place stratification, and public choice theory) to suburban political fragmentation and its historic and contemporary influence in shaping American metropolitan areas. I underscore the ways suburban residential patterns were preserved and shaped by government-sponsored discriminatory housing loan programs and exclusionary fiscal zoning policies.

Postwar federal housing and urban development policies sought to "renew" urban America by underwriting single-family home purchases for millions of white suburbanites, constructing an elaborate interstate highway system to shuttle them from their bedroom communities to their jobs in the central cities, and subsidizing the construction of infrastructure such as hospitals and sewage plants – all outside of the urban core (Danielson, 1976; Dreier, Mollenkopf, & Swanstrom, 2004; Haynes, 2001; Jackson, 1985; Massey &

Denton, 1993; Ross & Levine, 2005; Williams, 2003). The "helping hand" of these government interventionist policies played a crucial role in exacerbating metropolitan inequalities by making substantial investments in American suburbs with consequent disinvestments in central cities (Dreier et al., 2004; Ross & Levine, 2005; Williams, 2003).

Then, I examine how public choice and urban regime scholars have traditionally addressed the relationship between local government actors and residents, as well as interpreted these actors' strategies and subsequent outcomes at the local level. As an alternative approach, I advance the SII framework, which I use to examine the formation of coalitions of local actors – specifically elected officials, bureaucratic service and regulatory employees, and community-based organization leaders – who implement policies and programs to address the needs of immigrant and ethnic minority newcomers in suburban jurisdictions. I argue that public-nonprofit partnerships emerge and actors engage in coalition formation beyond what might ordinarily be expected not only to simply "get things done" but because doing so enhances legitimacy and reduces transaction costs (financial, political, cultural) of incorporating newcomers to rapidly changing American suburbs.

The bulk of this analysis of suburban governments responsiveness does not occur until Chapters 3–5. However, Chapter 2 is an important part of the overall story of this book, setting the stage and aiding the development of the SII framework by providing a view of the contemporary demographic and dynamic political environment of suburban Washington, DC. This chapter examines the extent to which spatial assimilation and place stratification literatures in sociology and economic sorting models in the political economy literature explain recent residential choice or constraint. I argue that some central tenets of these theories present an outdated picture of life in the metropolis, and an even less complete picture of its suburban periphery. These existing literatures leave us with significant limitations in our understanding of the dynamics of new residential patterns and the socioeconomic, cultural, and political implications thereof in American suburbs.

Chapter 2 presents a qualitative case study of recent immigrant and ethnic minority suburbanization to the fourth largest multiethnic metro area in the United States, suburban Washington, DC. Specifically, I focus on Prince George's and Montgomery Counties in Maryland, and Fairfax County in northern Virginia. To examine residential selection decisions within this large multiethnic metropolitan area and among various racial/ethnic groups, I also use data from a unique series of five separate focus groups with adult immigrant or minority suburban residents in their native languages: African Americans (English), Chinese (Mandarin), Iranians (Farsi), Koreans (Korean), and Latinos (Spanish).[10] The data from Chapter 2 help to explain residential choice decisions, and to examine which factors promote or deter neighborhood interactions

---

[10] These focus groups were funded by the Russell Sage Foundation and conducted with Michael Jones-Correa in 2005 (see the focus group protocol in Appendix A).

among racial and ethnic groups. The focus group data that animate Chapter 2 provide the foundation for group-based coalitions discussed in the case study in Chapters 3–5, and without this background, the forthcoming analysis would lack the context for which coalitions and partnerships may be formed.

In Chapters 3, 4, and 5, I examine the extent to which SII explains how local institutional actors respond to several policy issues in suburbia. I use the SII framework to examine the logical and practical reasons some suburban institutional actors (particularly electoral, bureaucratic, and nonprofit) form unlikely alliances to advance policies and programs that provide goods and services to immigrants and ethnic minorities. I focus on three issues in suburban Washington, DC: *public education:* the provision of support services for limited-English-proficient (LEP) children and parents in suburban public schools (Chapter 3); *day labor:* the establishment of several formal, institutionalized (local government-funded) day laborer employment sites (Chapter 4); and *language access at public agencies:* access to government services for adults with limited English proficiency (LEP) (Chapter 5). I use a combination of census data and qualitative data from more than 100 face-to-face, semi-structured, in-depth interviews and participant observations among state and local elected/appointed officials, bureaucratic service and regulatory agency administrators, and leaders of community-based organizations in Prince George's, Montgomery, and Fairfax Counties. These three counties make up the so-called national capital suburbs surrounding the District of Columbia. The bulk of the analysis in Chapters 3, 4, and 5 compare and contrast the local responses of leaders in the two counties with the most similar demographics – Montgomery County, MD and Fairfax County, VA.

The concluding chapter synthesizes the findings of the preceding chapters and describes their implications for the study of local politics and government responsiveness, as well as of civic and political participation in American suburbs. The overall conclusions from this book underscore the need to better understand the implications of new multiracial dynamics and intergroup relations in American suburbs, as well as the responsiveness of local governments to the needs and concerns of newcomers as well as long-time residents. This book expands our understanding of the interplay among metropolitan governance, race/ethnicity, and politics in three ways: (1) by placing race/ethnicity, class, and suburbanization within the historical and social context of racial/ethnic exclusion and subsequent economic and place inequalities; (2) by moving beyond the outdated, insular characterization of suburban spatial location as a black/white dichotomy toward an examination of inter- and intragroup differences and similarities; and (3) by extending the lens of race, ethnicity, and politics research beyond the study of urban versus suburban localities toward the examination of the differences contained *within* suburban jurisdictions. This study of residential choice, constraint, and local government responsiveness helps us to better understand how immigrant and ethnic minority suburbanization has translated into social, economic, and political incorporation in American society.

I

Race, Ethnicity, Class, and the Suburban
Political Economy Dilemma

Contemporary suburban governments face fiscal and political constraints that traditional public choice and urban regime models fail to account for. I argue that demographic change has altered local politics in significant ways since these models were proposed. The decline of federally funded redistributive programs since the 1980s, coupled with increasing racial/ethnic diversity, influences how local institutional actors respond to the needs and concerns of their suburban constituents. The public choice framework emerged during the post–World War II white exodus to American suburbs. The urban regime framework emerged in the late 1980s during an ongoing debate about biracial and multiracial coalition politics in urban centers (Browning, Marshall, & Tabb, 1984). Within the latter framework, Stone's classic 1989 study of Atlanta, dubbed by its leaders as "a city too busy to hate," found that partnerships between unlikely collaborators did not necessarily grow out of a shared ideology. Instead, governmental and nongovernmental actors joined together based on specific common goals, purposes, and selective incentives to cooperate (Stone, 1989, 1993, 1998, 2005). Urban regime theories emerged as minorities in cities were gaining political power while some immigrant and racial/ethnic groups were beginning to gain greater spatial mobility amid increasing diversity in metropolitan areas.

Political realities began to change as the late 1980s ushered in retrenchment of federal aid to metropolitan areas, leading to greater fiscal austerity in many states and localities. The political economy dilemma facing contemporary suburban institutions refers to the intersection of institutional responsiveness and increasing demographic heterogeneity (social, cultural, racial/ethnic, economic, and political) in contemporary suburban jurisdictions. The proper role of local governments in addressing the needs and concerns of these new populations is hotly debated, particularly when the beneficiaries are immigrants who may or may not be undocumented.

For decades public choice theorists have predicted that the proper role of municipalities is the provision of local public goods and services that meet economic development interests and the interests of the upper-income populations who are their principal electoral constituents. Yet in certain suburban jurisdictions institutional actors act counter to these predictions (Frasure, 2005; Frasure & Jones-Correa, 2010). When private market mechanisms fail to provide goods and services to immigrants and ethnic minorities, some suburban municipalities have implemented policies and programs to foster these individuals' social, political, and economic incorporation, whereas others have not. Scholars in neither the urban regime nor public choice camps have attempted to explain how these different responses occur and what mechanisms drive them. Combining aspects of both public choice and urban regime approaches can offer a more comprehensive analysis of contemporary suburbia. Both frameworks offer great insights. As public choice theory suggests, for collective action to take place, selective incentives are needed to motivate actors. Urban regime scholars endorse this principle, but also remind us that suburban actors are conscious of both political and economic constraints. Synthesizing these ideas suggests that government officials and community-based organization leaders will cooperate and form public-private coalitions based, in part, on mutual self-interest (Stone, 1989).

The framework I call suburban institutional interdependency (SII) achieves exactly that melding, drawing insights from both approaches. Using it, I examine the formation of coalitions of local actors – specifically elected officials, bureaucratic service and regulatory employees, and community-based organization leaders – who implement policies and programs to address the needs of immigrant and ethnic minority newcomers in suburban jurisdictions. The next section will explain why suburban demographic changes require a different approach to the study of local governance.

The Decline of Urban Machine Politics and the Rise of Metropolitan Fragmentation

From the late nineteenth to the mid-twentieth centuries, political machines imposed an unofficial system of political organization in larger American cities.[1] By centralizing power, these machines facilitated the cities' growth. Machine politics operated on an exchange system: to win elections the political machines traded favors and benefits for votes, giving their supporters material as well as nontangible benefits (Brown & Halaby, 1987; Cornwell, 1964; Erie, 1988; Katznelson, 1973; Pinderhughes, 1987; Shefter, 1978; Trounstine 2008). Under the patronage system of the political machines, the winning parties in elections distributed government jobs, contracts, and other

---

[1] Some (in)famous machines include those of William Tweed (New York), James Michael Curley (Boston), Thomas Pendergast (Kansas City, MO), and Richard J. Daley (Chicago).

benefits to their supporters. The backers of the losing parties, in contrast, risked losing municipal jobs and political favors (Erie, 1988; Lowi, 1964). Ward and precinct leaders waived fines and posted bail for machine supporters. Machine captains aided business owners seeking building permits, zoning variances, city licenses, franchises, or construction contracts. In return local businesses were expected to provide the political machines cash kickbacks (such as campaign contributions) or to create jobs that the machines could dispense in exchange for votes. The machine apparatus also provided newly arrived immigrants, largely from European countries, with food, shelter, employment opportunities, and help with immigration paperwork and naturalization exams (Ross and Levine, 2005). The political machines thus offered many European (particularly Irish) immigrants a highly symbolic channel of social mobility, while retarding the social and economic growth of African Americans and other racial/ethnic emigrants to urban centers (Erie, 1988; Grimshaw, 1992; Hoyman & Faricy, 2009; Judd & Swanstrom, 1994; Katznelson, 1973; Pinderhughes, 1987; Shefter, 1978; Wong, 2006).

After decades of the parochialism and corruption of machine politics, reform movement advocates sought to replace that system with "good government." Reform measures – such as nonpartisan and at-large elections, as well as merit-based municipal hiring systems (civil service systems) regulating the hiring, promotion, and dismissal of municipal employees – became common practice in municipal governments (Trounstine, 2010). Several other factors helped to diminish the power of political machines, including restrictions on immigration (beginning in the 1920s), which ostensibly cut off the flow of potential future voting constituents in urban centers, along with racial tensions and rising polarization between blacks and whites (Ross and Levine, 2005). The growth of the welfare state and the rise of social welfare programs hastened the fall of the political machines as increasing numbers of immigrant and ethnic minorities received aid from the federal government through programs enacted beginning during the New Deal of the 1930s and especially in the Great Society and War on Poverty programs in the 1960s, making them less dependent on local political bosses.

Arguably one of the most important factors contributing to the fall of urban machine politics, however, was the acceleration of American suburbanization as a result of widespread metropolitan fragmentation following World War II, which produced a more mobile population with fewer ties to city neighborhoods. Metropolitan fragmentation, also referred to as political fragmentation, creates distinct political jurisdictions. In the *Politics of Exclusion*, Danielson (1976) argues that American suburbs are principally a political phenomenon. Expanding on this characterization nearly three decades later, Oliver writes:

Suburbanization is the process of populations moving from cities to outlying places (suburbs) that are part of the greater metropolis yet also politically distinct ... what separates cities and suburbs is not simply their street signs or types of buildings, but their differing political jurisdictions. Through borders, tax rates, zoning policies, and so forth, political institutions define the size, density, social composition and land use of suburban places. (2003, p. 1352)

Such distinct political jurisdictions and local (government) autonomy is, in many ways, the essence of suburbanization and the basis of local suburban politics. During the nineteenth century, reluctant to lose population, central cities used their annexation powers to incorporate neighboring areas into the city. By the late nineteenth century, however, upper-income white residents increasingly fled from central cities as lower-income international and domestic migrants moved into industrial centers. At the turn of the twentieth century, residential decentralization took hold as both upper- and middle-class white residents and business owners began to prefer the autonomy of small, suburban government structures. Residential decentralization and the resulting political fragmentation of metropolitan areas accelerated during the post–World War II era with the rapid expansion of American suburbs.

Suburban governments assumed local control over the physical and social environment. As Mark Schneider describes it: "Municipalities are political systems in which problems of aggregation and representation must be factored into the process by which local bundles of goods and services are set" (1989a, p. 15). The desire of suburban municipalities "to maximize the local tax base is a key ingredient of this political economy" (p. 24). The local market for public goods in suburbia is, to some degree, driven by a political economy that links the structure of local government to decisions about service and tax packages.

During the 1950s, amid rapid post–World War II suburbanization, a burgeoning group of public choice scholars, largely in political science and economics, argued that if government intervention occurred at all at the local level, it should be restricted to ensuring efficient allocation of local public goods (e.g., police and fire protection) rather than income redistribution. A public good is one "which should be produced, but for which there is not a feasible method of charging the consumers" (Tiebout, 1956, p. 416).[2] In theory, the efficient provision of a public good requires that the sum of all individuals' marginal benefits equals the marginal cost of producing the public good. Importantly, however, the provision of public goods and services has a fundamental problem that does not exist in the private market: the revelation problem. That is, in a public goods market it is difficult to gauge one's reservation price, meaning the maximum one is willing to pay for a particular good. For example, public goods are often financed through taxes, so people have an incentive to misrepresent

---

[2] Public goods may be pure or impure. Pure public goods have three main characteristics: (1) nonprovision: if left to their own free will, individuals may not provide a good even though the total benefits of the good exceed the total cost of providing it; (2) nonrivalry: one person's use does not reduce another's consumption, and it is inefficient to exclude those who do not contribute; and (3) nonexcludability (nonpurchasers): one cannot exclude noncontributing individuals from receiving the good (shared indivisibility). See Varian (1993) or any standard microeconomics text for a further delineation of public goods.

their preferences for those public goods in order to minimize their tax burden (Stiglitz, 1982).

The early works of Musgrave (1939) and Samuelson (1954) suggested that an individual would not voluntarily reveal their preference for a pure public good if it was nonexcludable (i.e., they would receive the benefit even if they did not directly contribute to paying for it). Advancing this logic, Olson (1965) argued that public goods cannot be provided efficiently because of the free rider problem of people seeking benefits without paying for them. That is, in order to establish the collective benefits of a public good, institutional organizations must force individuals to abandon their individual benefit-maximizing behavior by preventing them from pushing the cost of that good onto others. Without such external forces, individuals will free ride to obtain the benefits provided to all without bearing their share of the cost. According to these scholars, two hallmarks of public goods provision are that the "invisible hand" of the free market is insufficient to cover their cost, and therefore a coercive organization (government) is necessary to ensure the sharing of marginal costs.[3]

In contrast to pure goods, so-called *impure* public goods are characterized by either partial rivalry over or some excludability of benefits to some parties.[4] Public choice scholar Charles Tiebout (1956) set forth an early insight into impure public goods in his seminal article "A Pure Theory of Local Expenditures." In it he proposed a solution to the revelation problem in the provision of so-called *local* public goods. He observed that many types of public goods are actually local rather than pure and suggested that competition among local jurisdictions for members would lead us back to a market-like outcome. In the Tiebout model, consumer-voters will find it optimal to reveal their preferences through their choice of residential location within competing jurisdictions. Each jurisdiction represents a distinct bundle of amenities and services at a distinct price of taxation. The Tiebout model makes several important assumptions: consumer-voters are assumed to be rational, utility-maximizing actors who are fully mobile, they exercise their mobility until their preferences are fulfilled, and they have perfect

[3] Cost-sharing ratios are important to public goods provision. *Marginal cost* is the cost of a one-unit change in the level of purchase of a good. *Marginal benefit* is the benefit associated with a one-unit change in the level of purchase of a good. The *maximum benefit* point occurs where the marginal benefit equals the marginal cost. According to this logic, rational individuals will reach equilibrium by purchasing to that level. Choosing that level is choosing the "best alternative," or the optimal choice. However, without any ex-ante arrangements to share the costs of additional purchases, the net result of individual rational behavior in this situation will be suboptimal for the group, although each party might conceivably be made better off (Varian, 1993).

[4] For impure public goods, additional members lower the average cost of the good to all members (i.e., there are economies of scale). But if the average cost falls indefinitely, then the good is made available to all, returning its characteristic of "publicness." An example of an impure public good is a "club good" (Buchanan, 1965), whereby a voluntary group derives mutual benefit from sharing one or more of the following: production cost, members' characteristics, or a good characterized by excludable benefits (Sandler & Tschirhart, 1980, p. 1482).

information regarding their options. Employment for consumer-voters is unrestricted, and public services have no external economies or diseconomies of scale between communities. The model then assumes that jurisdictional competition between local governments ensues, forcing the hand of government to behave more efficiently (see Parks & Ostrom, 1981; M. Schneider, 1989a, 1989b).

The Tiebout model is attractive to public choice scholars because it predicts that ideally people will move to the communities with tax and expenditure policies that match their preferences, so that their location/mobility decisions convey information about their preferences, the free-rider problem "disappears," and the outcome is the efficient provision of goods and services (Conley & Wooders, 1997, p. 421). Local public goods have an element of privateness because the benefits accrue only to those who belong to that particular group or community and not to society at large: within the member community the good is a pure public good; between communities, however, it acts like a private good because those outside of the community receive no benefit (Stiglitz, 1982). In short, spatial mobility is the local public goods complement to the private market's shopping trip.

According to public choice scholars, income redistribution was most appropriately the responsibility of a federal (centralized) government that could bear the necessary costs. Nevertheless, redistribution was never a primary concern of public choice scholars, who instead focused on the question: "What are the necessary conditions for the allocative efficiency in the provision of collective goods?" (Olson, 1969). Olson discussed the division of responsibilities among different levels of government and asked what principles ought to guide the development of a rational pattern of jurisdictional responsibility: large-scale centralized government or a systematic reliance on small local governments with rational boundaries?

In answer to Olson's question, Ostrom, Tiebout, and Warren (1961) envisioned the "business" of governments in metro areas as providing public goods and services (also see Parks & Ostrom, 1981). Many public choice scholars would contend that metropolitan areas are driven by an economic logic that is biased toward allocative concerns and in favor of the upper class. Because jurisdictions need upper-income groups in order to maximize their resource potential, if they do not bias their public goods packages in favor of the upper class they fail in the competition for those residents (Buchanan, 1971; Peterson, 1981; but see Miller, 1981, for a critique). In fact, not to show such a bias is equivalent to economic irrationality, given that the only rational objective of urban governments is the "maximization of per capita fiscal dividend" (Buchanan, 1971; Miller, 1981). Bish (1971) further argues that local governments are prevented from engaging in redistributive programs that favor low-income groups because doing so would attract many low-income individuals to their jurisdictions. Furthermore, high-income groups rationally seeking their best interest will engage in redistribution only if they derive some benefit thereby (e.g., selective incentives) or to the limited extent that they are altruistic.

The economic sorting (vote-with-your-feet) models that public choice theorists proposed during the 1950s and 1960s suffer from severe selective historicism that glosses over historical, structural, and institutional practices that have profoundly shaped and reshaped the metropolitan political economy in ways that facilitated the growth of white middle- and working-class suburbanization, while retarding suburbanization for everyone else.

Arguably, one of the reasons public choice theorists pay little attention to issues of race stems from the model's origin in free-market philosophy. Capitalists must maximize profits, and to do so they must hire the most productive workers. Because race is an ascriptive characteristic, it is assumed to have nothing to do with "rational" capitalism. Rational actors (be they individuals, organizations, or states) are purposive and goal seeking, based on their own preferences. They rank their alternatives from best to worst, and then choose what is best for them based on their own preferences and tastes. According to this logic, rational actors might wish to indulge in their racial prejudices, but the pressure of economic competition will not afford them that luxury. Thus, racism is seemingly exogenous to the economic system of public choice modeling, stemming instead from irrational psychological prejudices. When this logic moves from the private sector to the public realm, historical legacies of de jure and de facto racial segregation and exclusionary housing policies become unnecessary in explaining spatial location patterns, even though these factors profoundly shaped individual residents' opportunities and constraints, as well as their sense of preferences/tastes, trust, reciprocity, and affection toward others.

Federally Funded Racial/Ethnic and Class Exclusion

Until recent decades, U.S. suburbs were characterized by the absence of significant racial/ethnic and class heterogeneity. In fact as late as 1993, "86 percent of suburban whites still lived in places with a black population below 1 percent" (Lipsitz, 1998, p. 7). Historically, these suburban residential patterns were preserved and shaped by government-sponsored discriminatory housing loan programs and exclusionary fiscal zoning policies. These federally backed programs were coupled with private-market practices that promoted widespread preferences in the rental, sale, and financing of suburban properties to non-Hispanic whites (Danielson, 1976; Dreier et al., 2004; Haynes, 2001; Jackson, 1985; Massey & Denton, 1993). Government action and private-sector power have been important influences in accelerating U.S. suburbanization (Danielson, 1976; Fishman, 1987; Freund, 2007; Jackson, 1985; Kleinberg, 1995; Lassiter, 2007; McGirr, 2001). Yet, ironically, many of the federal policies that have had the greatest impact on metropolitan America were neither explicitly urban nor suburban in their origin.

In an effort to lift the U.S. economy from the Great Depression, Franklin Roosevelt's administration ushered in a series of New Deal programs that dramatically changed the nature of federal government responses and redistributive policies toward individual citizens. New Deal programs were broad ranging, from those that sought to regulate the stock market to banking controls.[5] However, no program proved more influential in positioning the federal government in the private housing market than President Roosevelt's New Deal housing programs of the 1930s.

The Home Owner Loan Corporation (HOLC), established in 1933, provided low-interest loans to homeowners nearing foreclosure on their properties. These loans were based on a neighborhood rating system. Metropolitan areas largely populated by poor, predominantly black, Latino, or in many cases Jewish residents received the lowest HOLC ratings, and such groups were largely excluded from participation in the program. The Housing Act of 1937 was the first federally funded program to give direct aid to cities through a low-rent housing program. Unfortunately, this program facilitated the selection of tenants by race/ethnicity, subsequently locating new housing projects in racially segregated neighborhoods and thereby advancing the cycle of minority concentration in urban ghettos and barrios (Williams, 2003).

Several federally backed homeownership programs further positioned the federal government firmly in the private housing market. The Federal Housing Administration (FHA), established by Congress in 1934, provided federal assistance to middle- and working-class families seeking the means to buy a home by providing loan insurance for up to 80 percent of the value of an approved property. Subsequently, the risk of making a home loan was reduced, and banks became more willing to finance homes for millions of Americans, lowering down-payment requirements and interest rates. The federal government also provided similar assistance to millions of veterans returning home following World War II. Under the GI Bill of 1944, the Veterans Administration (VA) was authorized to insure home mortgages for veterans.

Arguably, the FHA and VA programs subsidized the growth of suburbs and largely ignored the deteriorating housing market in central cities. These programs did little to promote the purchase of apartments or the renovation of older housing units in central cities. Moreover, they enabled young, white middle- and working-class families to flee central cities and purchase suburban homes. As Thomas points out, "at least 40 percent of all homes sold each year from 1947 to 1957 were financed through FHA and VA mortgages" (1998, p. 37). In contrast, racial/ethnic minority groups had little access to suburban housing markets. Dreier, Mollenkopf, and Swanstrom observe that "between

---

[5] For example, the Securities Act of 1933 and the Securities and Exchange Act of 1934, establishing the Securities and Exchange Commission, addressed the stock market, while the Glass-Steagall Banking Act of 1933 separated commercial from investment banking and created the Federal Deposit Insurance Corporation.

1946 and 1959, blacks purchased less than 2 percent of all housing financed with VA and FHA help" (2004, p. 122; also see Williams, 2003). Housing built in all-minority subdivisions accounted for half of that percentage.

Real estate agents and other private-sector actors used a variety of unscrupulous tactics such as "blockbusting," often referred to as "panic-peddling," to trigger the turnover of white-owned property by effectively scaring white homeowners into a frenzy of selling. In one example of blockbusting, agents would conspicuously introduce a black family into the neighborhood then pressure whites to sell their homes promptly, and usually at a loss, in advance of a purported drop in property values once minority groups moved into the neighborhood. Realtors and real estate speculators also appealed to whites' fears. The property was then resold at inflated prices to African Americans who faced severely limited choices in the discriminatory housing market (A. Hirsch, 1983, 2013).

Redlining (which designated black and immigrant urban areas unsuitable for real estate lending), as well as restrictive, legally binding covenants that prohibited a buyer from reselling a home to someone of a different race, helped to fulfill the promise of economic and racial sorting while exacerbating the detrimental effects of racial, economic, and place inequalities (Baldassare, 1986; Massey & Denton, 1993; Thomas, 1998; Williams, 2003). As Thomas points out, "The contract signed by every Levittown homeowner included a standard clause that read, 'No dwelling shall be used or occupied by members of other than Caucasian race'" (1998, p. 40). Baxandall and Ewen highlight the language of the 1947 FHA guidebook for suburban development that explicitly endorsed such practices: "Protective covenants are essential to the sound development of proposed residential areas, since they regulate the use of land and provide a basis for the development of harmonious, attractive neighborhoods" (2000, p. 175). Other interventionist government policies sought to "renew" urban America by constructing an interstate highway system and subsidizing the construction of public facilities including hospitals and sewage plants (Ross & Levine, 2005; Williams, 2003). Such "helping hand" programs also played a crucial role in producing metropolitan inequalities through establishing preferences for investment in suburbs and disinvestments from central cities (Dreier et al., 2004; Ross & Levine, 2005).

In 1948, following U.S. Supreme Court rulings, the FHA dropped its overt language of racial group preferences, but, Baxandall and Ewen contend, "(u)nofficially the FHA accepted unwritten agreements and traditions of segregation as late as 1968, long after the boom was over" (2000, p. 175). By the time the FHA amended its discriminatory practices in the late 1960s, the federal government had underwritten the decline of central cities and the racial homogeneity of thousands of suburbs. The FHA had underwritten 7 million new homes, most of them in the suburbs and about 98 percent of them limited to whites only. The homeownership rate rose from 44 percent in 1934 to 63 percent by 1969. Home equity soon became the single most important source of wealth for middle-class families (Massey, 2007, p. 61). As Williams summarizes, "The FHA played a crucial role not only in cementing racial segregation but simultaneously in guaranteeing that middle-class whites would be dramatically privileged in homeownership, always the most successful generator of wealth for average Americans" (2003, p. 79). Freund (2007) argues that most white Americans would not own their homes today if not for the massive state interventions in the national mortgage market begun in the 1930s.

Simultaneously, government interventions combined with evolutions in Americans' ethnic prejudices to exacerbate the racial and economic imbalance between inner cities and suburbs. Certain white ethnic groups, such as Jews and Italians, historically considered "inferior races" and thus segregated in their own neighborhoods, became a part of the "melting pot" after World War II. Loss of ethnic distinctiveness was seemingly a small price to pay for a piece of the American dream, and these groups invested in a racial identity as "white" Americans and made their way to the suburbs, depopulating historically European American ethnic enclaves in the inner city. In the newly developing suburban neighborhoods beyond the urban fringe, ethnic divisions among whites became less salient, while racial divisions became increasingly marked. Meanwhile, federal "urban renewal" programs initiated after World War II cleared large parcels of land, razing homes and apartment buildings in working-class and poor areas of the inner city to make way for new upper-income apartment complexes, modern university campuses and hospitals, and expanded central business districts (Ross & Levine, 2005).

Certain urban communities, facing an exodus of businesses and middle-class residents, were deemed blighted and unfit for habitation and investment. The African American and largely non-European immigrants living there were unable to sell their properties and relocate, impeding the growth of suburbanization among people of color while advancing the housing opportunities, and consequently the wealth, of white suburbanites. As Lipsitz writes, "During the 1950s and 1960s federally assisted urban renewal projects destroyed 20 percent of the central city housing units occupied by blacks, as opposed to only 10 percent of those inhabited by whites.... Even after most urban renewal programs were complete by the 1970s, black central-city residents continued to lose housing units at a rate equal to 80 percent of what had been lost in the 1960s. Yet white displacement declined back to the relatively low levels in the 1950s" (1998, pp. 6–7).

Following a series of riots in urban centers around the country in the 1960s, along with passage of the landmark Civil Rights Act (1964) and Voting Rights Act (1965), the federal government faced new pressures to revise its pro-suburban bias, particularly in FHA and VA loan guarantees. Yet the privileging of white homeownership continued. The legacy of decades of discrimination and inequality in the housing market meant that not all eligible families could benefit from federal-government-sponsored housing programs. "From 1960 to 1977 four million whites moved out of central cities, while the number of whites living in suburbs increased by twenty-two million. During the same years, the inner-city black population grew by six million but the number of blacks residing in suburbs increased by only 500,000" (Lipsitz, 1998, p. 72).

The passage of the Fair Housing Act (Title VIII of the Civil Rights Act of 1968) and other programs such as the Community Reinvestment Act of 1977 have helped to relieve, but have not eliminated the constraints placed on minorities (Ross & Levine, 2005; Williams, 2003). The tactics of redlining, racial steering, and blockbusting are no longer legal, but arguably still exist in some de facto forms (Yinger, 1995). According to the U.S. Department of Housing and Urban Development, the Fair Housing Act "prohibits discrimination in the sale, rental, and financing of dwellings, and in other housing-related transactions, based on race, color, national origin, religion, sex, familial status (including children under the age of 18 living with parents or legal custodians, pregnant women, and people securing custody of children under the age of 18), and handicap (disability)" (U.S. Dept. of Housing and Urban Development, 2013). The Community Reinvestment Act of 1977 was designed to reduce discriminatory credit practices against low-income neighborhoods (i.e., redlining) by encouraging private lenders to meet the needs of borrowers in all segments of their communities, including low- and moderate-income neighborhoods. The act mandated that any banking institution that receives FDIC insurance be evaluated by federal banking agencies to determine that it offers credit opportunities in all communities from which the bank takes deposits.

These "corrective" housing policy measures helped to crack open the closed system of suburban life for immigrant and racial/ethnic minority groups. As a result, post-1980 immigrants do not face the same institutional and structural barriers to suburban entry as their predecessors did, making suburbanization an attainable dream for some newcomers to America. Like those early twentieth-century immigrants and ethnic minorities who relocated to urban enclaves in search of greater social and economic opportunity, more recent immigrant groups seek the historical benefits of suburban life – individualism, upward mobility, opportunity, and privilege. Although these benefits may not hold the same meaning for new immigrants as they historically did for whites, such opportunities are more widely available for immigrant and racial/ethnic minority groups with relatively high incomes and levels of educational attainment, such as Asians, the most suburbanized minority group in the United States (Logan, 2003).

The increasingly heterogeneous context of many suburban jurisdictions, leading to greater likelihood of redistribution, appears to be the kryptonite that has destroyed the economic efficiency of pioneering public choice frameworks like Tiebout's (1956) model of metropolitan fragmentation. Such models were developed during the postwar period, when much greater flows of federal dollars served to develop and maintain the economic and racial/ethnic homogeny of suburban neighborhoods and concentrate minorities in the inner cities. During that era, the practice of economic sorting across politically fragmented suburban areas was aided by exclusionary zoning, racial covenants, and other de jure and de facto policies that largely exempted suburban jurisdictions from dealing with the redistributive concerns their urban counterparts were facing.

The 1980s served as a critical juncture for U.S. metropolitan areas. The exodus of large numbers of racial/ethnic minority migrants from central cities to suburbia coincided with the era of conservative "new federalism," which ushered in a dramatic retrenchment of federal aid to metropolitan areas. Severe cuts in federal aid to address local redistributive pressures removed the resources that had enabled local jurisdictions to hold the national government responsible for redistributive policies. Localities were asked to do more with fewer resources and in the face of emerging demographic shifts.

Tangential to these developments in the 1980s, scholars of urban politics dubbed the governing challenges facing metropolitan areas in this new fiscal climate as the "imperatives of growth versus the logic of governance" debate. In his book *City Limits*, Paul Peterson is credited with merging tenets of several disparate approaches to the study of urban political economy. In this synthesis, Peterson argued that it is in the interest of urban regimes to adhere to the imperatives of economic development and leave redistributive concerns to the federal government: "The pursuit of a city's economic interests, which requires an efficient provision of local services, makes no allowance for the care of the needy and unfortunate members of the society. Indeed, the competition among local communities all but precludes a concern for redistribution" (1981, pp. 37–38).

Although public choice theorists had promulgated this logic decades earlier, Peterson's exposition of it stated that the unitary interest of the city should be economic development. Although one can never know definitively the reasons a particular business or individual enters or exits a jurisdiction, public choice reasoning predicts that municipal governments that act to redistribute local resources risk the flight of the upper-income and business communities. Under this logic, suburban governments should stick to promoting allocative policies such as libraries or police and fire protection.[6] Of course, it was easy to promote redistribution as a concern of the federal government rather than local governments because it was the federal government that underwrote the development of suburbia, while facilitating the decline of urban areas and turning a blind eye to racial discrimination against minority and poor residents in inner-city neighborhoods.

One of the primary alternatives to public choice models of local spending and government action has come from urban regime scholars. Developed inductively through prototypical case studies (Sanders & Stone, 1987b; Stone, 1989), "(r)egime analysis views power as fragmented and regimes as the collaborative arrangements through which local governments and private

---

[6] Also see *The Price of Federalism*, where Peterson documents his fears concerning the devolution of social welfare programs to the states.

actors assemble the capacity to govern" (Mossberger & Stoker, 2001, p. 812). Regime theory rejects both pluralist assumptions that governmental authority is adequate to make and carry out policies, and structuralist assumptions that economic forces determine policy. Urban regime analysis concerns how local actors mediate external pressures such as economic change as well as the role of "civic cooperation," or the internal dynamics of coalition building and the informal modes of coordination across institutional boundaries (Sanders & Stone, 1987a; Stone, 1989, 1993; also see Dowding et al., 1999; Mossberger & Stoker, 2001).

Regime theorists argue against the notions that a city has a "unitary interest" or that an economic development imperative is emblematic of that unitary interest. Instead, they suggest that local governments are simultaneously constrained by a political logic whereby public officials need to build and maintain electoral coalitions sufficient both to win office and to govern (Sanders & Stone, 1987a, 1987b; Stone, 1989; Swanstrom, 1988). These theorists argue that given the dynamic nature of urban regime structures, the economic reductionism of the political economist camp is unrealistic and apolitical. In the view of regime theorists, electoral politics matters and economic imperatives must be weighed against the necessity for elected officials to build and sustain broad electoral coalitions. To maintain the support of constituents, local politicians must negotiate a delicate balance between efficiency (economic growth) and equity (redistribution) (Ross & Levine, 2005; Swanstrom, 1988). Mossberger and Stoker (2001) aptly summarize Stone's description of political power and cooperative behavior:

Stone (1989, 229) described the political power sought by regimes as the "power to" or the capacity to act, rather than "power over" others or social control. Achieving the capacity to act is by no means certain; cooperation needs to be created and maintained (Stone, 1993). Regimes overcome problems of collective action and secure participation in the governing coalition through the distribution of selective incentives such as contracts, jobs, facilities for a particular neighborhood, and so on. As Stone pointed out, the benefits realized by participants may be purposive as well as material – for example, the opportunity to achieve an organization's particular goal, such as civil rights.

Combining contentions of the public choice and the urban regime approaches, one might reasonably conclude that (1) redistributive programs/policies are less likely in the fragmented, competitive contexts of U.S. metropolitan areas, particularly following the 1980s cuts to intergovernmental transfers from the federal government to states and localities; and (2) any redistribution that did occur would result from electoral pressures as elected officials sought to maintain their governing coalitions. In fact, however, some contemporary suburban jurisdictions are working with community-based nonprofit organizations to provide goods and services to foreign-born residents in the absence of either federal or state government aid for redistributive spending (as public choice theorists would expect), or electoral pressures from voters acting as part of electoral coalitions (as urban regime theorists would predict). Neither approach can adequately explain the mechanisms that drive these collaborations.

By implementing programs to address the needs of struggling segments of their demographically diverse populations, institutional actors in these suburban jurisdictions are seemingly acting counter to their localities' economic development interests and the interests of the upper-income residents who are still their principal electoral constituents. The implication is that both public choice and urban regime models require some reexamination, particularly in light of the political economy dilemma facing many suburban jurisdictions experiencing unprecedented flight of the non-Hispanic white population (either back to gentrified central cities or farther into exurbia) and a subsequent influx of lower-income immigrant and racial/ethnic minorities, many of whom are noncitizens, ineligible to vote or disinterested in voting, and in need of redistributive goods and services.

As Schneider points out, contrary to the original Tiebout model, "in a democratic society, the market force of citizen/consumer sovereignty is reinforced by the norms of government responsiveness to the interests and demands of its citizens and by the various electoral processes that enforce these norms" (1989a, p. 23). While this extension of Tiebout's original formulation is merited, Schneider's analysis still fails to explain what happens when a large number of suburban newcomers are low-income noncitizens (therefore ineligible to vote), yet nevertheless need local public goods and services.

Many of the suburban public-nonprofit partnerships examined in this book developed within a political environment but outside of traditional mainstream electoral politics: the most direct beneficiaries are nonvoters, often even noncitizens. As this analysis explains, the enfranchisement factor has important implications for the incorporation of recent suburban immigrants. Historically, the political incorporation of immigrant "consumer-voters" in urban centers was inextricably tied to their electoral incorporation.

In the post-1980s wave of immigrant suburbanization, institutional responsiveness to newcomers' needs often precedes their political incorporation, at least in terms of their likely electoral mobilization (Frasure & Jones-Correa, 2010; Jones-Correa, 2008). Again, what makes this wave of immigration and racial/ethnic spatial mobility to American suburbs unique is the lack of federally funded redistributive programs to address the needs of newcomers. Regardless of the merits or failures of past federal programs and policies directed at urban centers, today no similar widespread programs are available to help confront the redistributive concerns facing local governments.

The origins of community-based initiatives can be traced back to the interventions of the settlement house movement, in the late nineteenth and early twentieth centuries. Yet, the most notable initiatives supported by the federal government were the Community Action Program (CAP) and the Model Cities programs, enacted during the 1960s War on Poverty. "CAP established community action agencies (CAA) at the local level to combine and redirect a wide range of federal, state, local, and private resources to make a comprehensive attack on poverty" (GAO, 1995, p. 13). Model Cites is a common name for the Demonstration Cities and Metropolitan Development Act. This program "sought to rebuild deteriorated neighborhoods in selected cities by coordinating the array of resources from assistance programs at all levels of government, particularly in housing, education, health, and transportation" (GAO, 1995, pp. 13–14). However, funding for these programs was spread so thin that there was no critical mass of resources for a sustained, multipronged "war on poverty" in any targeted city. At the federal level significant congressional infighting ensued, as the federal government sought to implement programs at the local level.

Historically urban conservatism has its roots in business-backed reform movements of the late nineteenth and early twentieth centuries that aimed to weaken political machines, labor unions, and racial and progressive urban reforms. The goals were to keep taxes low and to deliver public services as efficiently as possible. Leaders called for good governance strategies and pushed for at-large elections and elimination of partisanship from local elections, while drawing strength from white backlash against urban liberalism and progressive policies of the 1960s (Williams, 2003).

Devolution to the states was not a unilaterally conservative political undertaking. All presidents since Richard Nixon have followed the theme of "New Federalism," yielding program autonomy to the states. Since the 1980s, under both Republican and Democratic administrations, repeated cuts in federal aid to address local redistributive pressures have removed the resources that had enabled local jurisdictions to make the national government responsible for redistributive policies. President Ronald Reagan went a step further in terms of program devolutions and terminations. His administration was not interested in using federal government resources to stimulate urban economic development but instead pursued national economic growth policies. It emphasized reducing government regulation, limiting the scope of government, promoting business growth, and "freeing" the marketplace to create "trickle-down" benefits to the poor. Cities and suburbs were left to largely fend for themselves financially.

The New Democrat, President Bill Clinton, was pragmatic and took a limited approach to urban affairs. His goals were shaped by the political events that took place early in his presidency – the battle over the crime bill, the defeat of his health care plan, and the 1994 Republican takeover of Congress. Clinton's urban policy initiatives were all implemented by any "nonurban means necessary." Such stealth urban policies pursued urban goals through nonurban program initiatives that were not perceived as focused on metropolitan areas such as Head Start, expansion of earned income tax credits, and the crime bill (Williams, 1998, 2003). Instead, Congress and the Clinton administration established the Empowerment Zone (EZ), Enterprise Community (EC), and Renewal Community (RC) programs "to reduce unemployment and generate economic growth in selected Census tracts" (GAO, 2010). These programs were administered by the U.S. Department of Housing and Urban Development (HUD) from 1994 until 2011.[7] These programs took a broader approach rooted in the George H. W. Bush years. However, Clinton focused on government subsidies and promoting civic engagement. Clinton's New Democrat strategy involved countering the distrust of government with an image of reinvented government focused on individual responsibility and on sanctions for bad behavior, as well as on highlighting the long-term benefits of investing in people so that they could be productive workers and citizens. Clinton's New Democrat image helped him to win reelection but did little for sustained coalition building toward policy making in cities and suburbs (Imbroscio, 2006). Weir argues that Clinton positioned himself as a New Democrat with the goal of repositioning the Democratic Party so that it was no longer vulnerable to the wedge issues of race, poverty, and "values" (1998, p. 506). Yet, in doing so, Clinton "moved to the center of the political spectrum that had itself been pushed sharply to the right by the congressional Republican majority. As the president moved right, he pulled a substantial bloc of congressional Democrats with him on most major issues."

In 1996 with bipartisan support the Clinton administration completely overhauled welfare through the Personal Responsibility and Work Opportunity Reconciliation Act, which replaced Aid to Families with Dependent Children with block grants to states entitled Temporary Assistance to Needy Families. These reforms resulted in major cuts in the food stamp program and reduced or eliminated federal eligibility for legal immigrants for their first five years of U.S. residence (Fix & Passel, 2002; Singer, 2004). State governments subsequently enacted welfare policy reforms, often without a clear sense of their implications at the municipal level. Arguably, state-level political leaders, not wanting to be seen as "soft" on welfare, erred on the side of withholding benefits from needy constituents (Williams, 1998, 2003).

The era of the Great Society and big-government solutions targeted toward metropolitan areas is seemingly over. Despite the controversial 2010 Patient Protection and Affordable Care Act (also known as ACA or "Obamacare"), a great resurgence of federally funded redistributive programs to address affordable housing or greater employment and educational opportunities for immigrants, minorities, and low-income residents seems unlikely. The central tenets of institutional interdependency described later to address these concerns may prove generalizable in a variety of local settings. However, as described in the introduction and expanded on in this chapter, there are many factors related to the development of centralized (city) versus fragmented/decentralized (suburban) government structures, and the politics of post-1980s immigration and

---

[7] However, on February 1, 2013, the U.S. Congress Joint Committee on Taxation extended the program for another two years, to end December 31, 2013.

ethnic minority migration to suburbs, which make SII particularly applicable
to an American suburban context.

Suburban Institutional Interdependency (SII)

The Actors and Their Interests

The racial/ethnic and economic changes in suburbia outlined earlier have introduced a host of new actors and issues into suburban politics, leading me to
propose a new approach to the study of post-1980 suburbia, called suburban
institutional interdependency (SII). The interdependent actors involved include
elected officials, bureaucratic and regulatory agencies, community-based nonprofit organizations, and other institutions such as ethnic media outlets, religious institutions, and businesses. Although a multiplicity of actors could be
involved in the suburban political economy, for simplicity this analysis focuses
on a select group of institutional actors and suburban residents who potentially play important roles in the provision of local goods and services to an
increasing diverse constituency.

In a suburban jurisdiction, each actor examined in this study – elected,
bureaucratic, and nonprofit – holds certain tangible and intangible resources
at its disposal. For example, when it comes to allocating local public goods
and services, elected officials in the county government hold the purse strings.
Through a budgetary line item, they have the power to shift suburban school
funding from magnet or talented and gifted programs to English as a second
language programs, to provide more funding for translation services at government agencies, or to direct financial support to some community-based organizations over others.

Yet the fact that the voting-eligible population has not kept pace with the
rapid changes in suburban demographics can hinder the political will of some
political leaders to act. In his study of Congress, David Mayhew (1974) contends that elected officials, rather than being policy makers, are single-minded
seekers of reelection, which they achieve in large part via (1) "position-taking"
on select issues (also see Fiorina, 1977); (2) taking advantage of credit-claiming
opportunities, often through pork barreling and other distributive programs
(also see Fenno, 1973); and (3) advertising. Political leaders are also believed to
develop different styles that match the nature of their constituent groups, and
thereby to develop a strong link with their constituents (Fenno, 1978). Through
interviews and participant observation, Fenno observed that House members,
for example, see their constituent groups as distinct sets of networks. The key
to gaining support within these networks is increasing and enhancing constituent trust. Feiock and colleagues suggest, "Elected officials' aversion to risk and
short time horizons make them sensitive to the possibilities of being misled
by wrong or irrelevant information. Maintaining multiple information sources
can control this risk. Even if creating the additional links involves additional
time and resources, it provides information verification and self-constraint

mechanisms. Network actors tend to look for reliable and valuable information" (Feiock et al., 2010, pp. 246–247) (also see McGovern, 2009).

Bureaucratic entrepreneurs, on the other hand, are viewed as agency budget-maximizers (Downs, 1957; Niskanen, 1971).[8] When their sponsors – in this case state and local governments represented by local elected officials – lack political will to act on concerns facing immigrant newcomers, bureaucratic agencies are often left without the budgets to address this population's needs. This is unfortunate because from housing to education, zoning to law enforcement, bureaucratic service and regulatory agencies are the premier institutional arm of suburban municipal government for newcomers. Such agencies are responsible for providing local public goods and implementing programs or services that directly affect the day-to-day lives of suburban newcomers. According to Feiock, "the career ambitions of managers lead them to seek to capture a portion of the benefits of local government activity, particularly when those activities produce efficiency gains" (2009, p. 370).

Given these constraints, both political and bureaucratic entrepreneurs often turn to nonprofit community-based organizations (CBOs) for support. Public-nonprofit efforts to respond, or at least appear to respond, to local policy concerns are not new. CBOs have historically been a vital avenue of immigrant and ethnic minority incorporation, particularly in urban areas, and often have had an intimate relationship with this community. According to LeRoux, "Nonprofits represent alternative institutional forms to those born of the market and the state. As such, they are characterized by a distinct set of properties that suggest they are uniquely equipped to function as civic intermediaries" (2007, p. 412). Nonprofits take a variety of forms, such as voluntary organizations, social service agencies, interest groups, legislative advocacy, and lobbying organizations promoting civic engagement and participation among their constituents, or a combination thereof. However, the role of suburban nonprofit organizations is increasingly important in this current era of devolution, placing a greater burden on CBOs to deliver direct services to their constituents through competitive, government service contracts (Frasure & Jones-Correa, 2010; Graauw, 2008; Graauw, Gleeson, & Bloemraad, 2013; Marwell, 2004; Salamon, 1995).

CBOs often act to lower the transaction costs associated with overcoming language and cultural barriers between newcomers and existing residents (Frasure & Jones-Correa, 2010). Local elected officials and bureaucratic service and regulatory agency employees also depend on CBOs to facilitate their access to and level of trust with immigrant and ethnic minority populations, and to formally and informally disseminate information concerning public

---

[8] Also see Frohlich and Oppenheimer, who define a political entrepreneur as "an individual who invests his own time or other resources to coordinate and combine other factors of production to supply collective goods" (1978, p. 68). Such individuals take a political interest in performing a collective goal for self-interested reasons or to advance themselves and their private interests.

policies and programs. Communication is often achieved via ethnic print and electronic media outlets or ethnic church groups.

In a 2009 Urban Institute study of immigrant-serving nonprofits in the Washington, DC, metropolitan area, researchers found that more than half of these 221 organizations have religious affiliations. They also found that "Seventy-six percent of these religion-related nonprofits (212) are congregations that have registered with the IRS, perhaps because churches, mosques, and synagogues perform multiple functions for the immigrant community" (de Leon et al., 2009, p. 9). They further contend, "Congregations are often the first and main points of contact for newcomers. They provide a ready-made community with shared religion, language, culture, and norms. Religious community leaders are often keenly aware of newcomers' needs. They often provide direct services or educate individuals and families about how and where to find help" (de Leon et al., 2009, p. 9). The study finds that in addition to helping to integrate immigrants through programs and services, metro DC immigrant-serving nonprofits fill the gaps in government service provision (particularly in areas with shrinking budgets) and act as liaisons, helping government agencies reach immigrant populations with culturally and linguistically appropriate services. They are channels through which funders, elected officials, and government agencies can reach immigrants. Nonprofits also serve as "advocates and civic and political representatives of immigrants and racial/ethnic minorities. They promote civic engagement and train individuals to be advocates and leaders of their own communities. They provide immigrants with board and volunteer opportunities" (de Leon et al., 2009, pp. 32–33).

LeRoux states, "Government funding provides the resources for nonprofits to expand their capacity, while government is able to capitalize on the resources of nonprofits, including voluntary labor, flexibility, and creative programs that are often difficult to implement in rule-bound public bureaucracies. On the other hand, government funding may complicate nonprofits' political-empowerment activities. Organizational leaders may be reluctant to mobilize clients and members, fearing unfavorable consequences related to political support and funding levels" (2007, p. 412; also see Graauw, 2008; Salamon, 1999). Yet Marwell argues that the potential process of local elected officials providing immigrant-serving organizations with resources (e.g., government contracts) in exchange for votes can potentially produce a "triadic exchange among CBO, client/voters, and elected officials … in essence a new version of machine politics" (2004, p. 23) (also see Owens & Yuen, 2011). These factors will be addressed in the case studies to follow, specifically the case of suburban day labor.

The Strategies
Although the power relationship remains unbalanced between the local government and nonprofit organization, the changing demographics in suburbia

necessitate the cooperation of otherwise unlikely actors at the decision-making table. Neither bureaucrats nor elected officials are expected to act alone, but instead turn to nonprofit CBOs as allies. Meanwhile, CBOs receive benefits from bureaucratic agencies that hold institutional resources (e.g., government contracts, formal meeting space) and can reduce the former's overhead costs (e.g., by printing materials for dissemination).

Building on theories of agency and social networks to identify the benefits and transaction costs of collaboration, Feiock and collaborators examined the role of institutional collective action (ICA) problems that "arise from fragmentation of service responsibilities among a multitude of governments and authorities in metropolitan areas.... The ICA framework extends theories of contracting and individual-level collective action to institutional actors such as cities, counties, and government agencies" (Feiock et al., 2010, p. 241). As Feiock explains:

Collaborative groups are informal associations or multilateral agreements among local actors that provide mechanisms for information exchange, program coordination, and joint action. Informal group decisions can take the form of collectively reinforced shared understandings and expectations that, although only socially enforced, are binding. Alternatively, where local actors confront high-risk cooperation dilemmas with the potential for other governments to act opportunistically, they may seek the mechanism based on external authority or seek clustered reciprocal or strong-tie network relationships. (2009, p. 365)

Generalized reciprocity helps to stabilize these interdependent relationships, at least in the short run. As Putnam states, "an effective norm of generalized reciprocity is bolstered by dense social networks of social exchange. If two would-be collaborators are members of a tightly knit community, they are likely to encounter one another in the future – or to hear about one another through the grapevine. Thus, they have reputations at stake that are almost surely worth more than gains from momentary treachery. In that sense, honesty is encouraged by dense social networks" (2000, p. 136). Feiock and colleagues argue: "(c)onfronted with uncertainty of cooperation with potential competitors, local actors attempt to overcome the credible commitment problem by exercising 'the norm of reciprocity.' Even informal relationships for discussion and advice are governed by reciprocity to deter opportunism and the free-rider problem" (2010, p. 249).

Furthermore, as Mancur Olson contends, selective incentives are another key organizing factor. In *The Logic of Collective Action* (1965), Olson observes that in many instances what individuals can achieve as a group often falls short of what each party ideally wants. Olson's position is counter to those scholars who suggest that group or individual engagement in collective action to achieve a public good arises naturally from acting on a common interest. Olson maintains that "unless the number of individuals in a group is quite small, or unless there is coercion or some other special device to make individuals act in their common interest, rational, self-interested individuals will not act to achieve their common or group interest" (1965, p. 2). If collective action is undertaken to obtain a public good, the product of this action incurs the additional cost of compromise and accommodation on the specific issue (Olson, 1965, p. 31). At the heart of Olson's argument is the free-rider problem. Thus, "each person is motivated not to contribute to the joint efforts, but to free-ride on the efforts of others. If participants choose to free-ride, the collective benefit will not be produced" (E. Ostrom, 1990, p. 6; also see Frohlich and Oppenheimer, 1978, chap. 2). In short, free riding leads to a suboptimal outcome or "less than the optimal level of the provision of the collective benefit" (E. Ostrom, 1990, p. 6). According to Olson's reasoning, in order to overcome free riding, collective action must be accompanied by selective incentives to reward those actors who contribute and punish those who fail to adhere. Selective incentives for collaboration often manifest in the form of government interventionist strategies (e.g., government regulations, civil rights legislation), which are often justified based on the failures of private markets to effectively provide goods and services to those who cannot provide for themselves. Notably, the more socially heterogeneous a group, the less the power of potential selective incentives. Socially heterogeneous groups are less likely than homogenous groups to agree on the exact nature of the collective good, or on how much it is worth (Olson, 1965, p. 24). Because homogenous groups are more likely to achieve consensus, selective incentives are more likely to motivate them.

Unfortunately, the static nature of Olson's group theory analysis weakens the strength of his logic (Chong, 1991; Hardin, 1982; E. Ostrom, 1990; Stevens, 1993). Because many group interactions are face to face and are repeated on a regular basis, these groups have opportunities to build consensus on the nature of selective incentives and to strengthen norms of trust and reciprocity necessary to form cooperative agreements (Axelrod, 1984). As Hardin argues, Olson's thesis about the weakness of selective incentives may be applicable in a "one-shot effort but not in an ongoing effort ... even in one-shot efforts Olson's conclusion may not apply if the group itself is ongoing, since it may assimilate the present one-shot effort to a series of group related efforts" (1982, p. 173). Likewise, Ostrom agrees that Olson's model of collective action "can successfully predict strategies and outcomes in fixed situations" (1990, p. 183), but she asserts that "individuals are perceived as being trapped in a static situation, unable to change the rules affecting their incentives" (p. 182). Regarding the static nature of Olson's model of collective action, which she applies to common-pool resources (CPRs), E. Ostrom writes:

They are useful for predicting behavior in large-scale CPRs in which no one communicates, everyone acts independently, no attention is paid to the effects of one's actions, and the costs of trying to change the structure of the situation are high. They are far less useful for characterizing the behavior of appropriators in the smaller-scale CPRs.... In such situations, individuals repeatedly communicate and interact with one another in a localized physical setting. Thus, it is possible that they can learn whom to trust, what effects their actions will have on the other and on the CPR, and how to organize themselves to gain benefits and avoid harm. When individuals have lived in such situations for a substantial time and have developed shared norms and patterns of reciprocity, they possess social capital with which they can build institutional arrangements for resolving the CPR dilemma. (1990, p. 184)

Thus, Ostrom goes beyond Olson's conception of selective benefits by adding a dimension of trust and reciprocity that could develop through repeated interactions. Similarly, Stevens asserts that "the efficacy of large groups in voluntarily providing public goods is a complex issue, not the simple matter that Olson described in 1965.... Olson's analysis was static and timeless, but many collective action problems are dynamic" (1993, p. 103).

Many organizational dilemmas, like those suburban jurisdictions confront, involve repeated interactions, and to defect repeatedly is not necessarily the dominant strategy. In this context, then, it is useful to extend Olson's model to include political entrepreneurs as well as purposive benefits – or what I refer to as quasi-selective incentives or benefits – that might motivate individual actors to join or cooperate with a collaborative effort. Whereas Olson largely limits his analysis to the tangible material benefits of participation, Salisbury (1969) (as described by Stevens, 1993) emphasizes that there may also be intangible "purposive benefits, an intangible reward associated with an ideological or value-oriented goal" (Stevens, 1993, p. 193). Salisbury also suggests a possible "solidary benefit" relating to the "social rewards for being part of the process of working toward goals and outcomes" (Stevens, 1993, p. 193).

These types of nontangible benefits may also have an element of "altruism or gaining of utility when another person gains utility from an improved outcome" (Hardin, 1982, p. 103). Hardin refers to these as "extra-rational" incentives that move beyond the rational model toward levels of morality and a "desire to participate for the sake of participation." In fact, Hardin suggests that "if correct calculation of self-interest was all that motivated action, there would be no environmental groups, nor any consumer, women's liberation, pro-life, or other such public groups" (p. 118).

In Chapters 3–5, I also consider the relationship between suburban institutional interdependency (SII) and public officials' ethos and partisan ideology, specifically how these factors might influence public-nonprofit partnerships and the ability to "get things done" concerning the three policy issues examined. Recent studies of local government response to immigration and immigrant policy concerns in American cities suggest that partisan ideologies and electoral politics are important considerations for local officials (Ramakrishnan & Bloemraad, 2008, 2011; Ramakrishnan & Wong, 2007, 2010; Singer, Wilson, & DeRennzis, 2009), and often to the benefit of their political supporters (Mladenka, 1980). Some scholars also argue that bureaucratic norms and professional missions play a role (de Leon et al., 2009; Jones-Correa, 2008; P. G. Lewis & Ramakrishnan, 2007;

Marrow, 2009; Marschall, Rigby, & Jenkins, 2011; Meier & O'Toole, 2006; Meier, Stewart, & England, 1991; Mladenka, 1981). For example, Jones-Correa finds that bureaucratic norms and administrators' own ethos were the key factors behind a push for redistributive policy change, and further that the language actors used to describe their own positions in favor of redistribution are purely normative (2008, p. 318).

Suburban political ethos refers to the culture of the political environment in a suburb. Montgomery County, Maryland, has traditionally been viewed as liberal, with a long-standing progressive tradition, whereas Fairfax County, Virginia, has traditionally been viewed as more conservative (Cantor, 2010). Montgomery County is a Democratic Party stronghold. The county functions under a council/executive form of government, with executive and legislative branches. Democrat Doug Duncan served as county executive from 1994 to 2006. Ike Leggett, also a Democrat, has served as county executive since 2006. He was the first African American county executive elected in Montgomery County, capturing 67 percent of the ballots cast in a three-way race. He was reelected for a second term in 2010 after running unopposed in the Democratic primary (Office of the County Executive, 2013).

All nine members of the county council are Democrats.[9] The face of state and local leadership has changed significantly over the past decade. Minorities have been elected to state and local offices, including the House of Delegates, the County Council, and the local school board. In 2013 the Montgomery County Council included two African Americans (Valarie Ervin and Craig Rice) and one Latina (Nancy Navarro). In 2004 Navarro was the first Latina elected president of the Montgomery County School Board, a title she held for two consecutive terms (Navarro, 2013). She was elected to represent District 4 on the County Council in a special election in 2009 and reelected in the general election of 2010. Navarro served as council vice president for the 2011–2012 session and council president for the 2012–2013 session.[10]

Virginia is traditionally viewed as conservative and Republican. However, there are signs of an increasing split between the views and political behaviors of northern Virginia voters compared to the rest of Virginia. Northern Virginia is divided between the inner suburbs close to the District of Columbia; namely Arlington, Alexandria, and Fairfax Counties – and the "exurbs" of Prince William, Loudon, and nine other counties. In voting record and issue preference the three inner suburban counties tend to be more liberal than the exurbs (Virginia Politics Northern Virginia Style, 2011). The liberal shift in northern

---

[9] Elected to four-year terms, five members of the council are elected by the voters in their respective districts and the remaining four members are elected at-large by all voters in the county.

[10] Born in Caracas, Venezuela, in 1998 she cofounded and for six years served as codirector of a nonprofit called Centro Familia in Montgomery County, aimed at improving economic and educational conditions for Latino and other immigrant communities. In October 2011, President Barack Obama appointed her as a member of the President's Commission on Educational Excellence for Hispanics, where she serves on the Early Childhood Education Committee.

Virginia has been attributed to Fairfax County's increased political leverage in the state as its population has increased. Six of the 100 fastest growing counties from 2000 to 2007 lie in northern Virginia (B. Lewis, 2008). In 2012 Fairfax County was the most populous jurisdiction in the Washington metro area, accounting for 19.8 percent of its population (U.S. Census Bureau, 2013).

Fairfax County is governed under the urban county executive form of government. By 2013, the nine seats on the Board of Supervisors were divided between six Democrats and three Republicans (Fairfax Democrats, 2013).[11] Since 1995 a Democrat has served as chairman of the board.[12] Despite the economic downturn, Fairfax County still holds the second highest median income of any local jurisdiction in the United States, at $105,797 (Fairfax County, 2011). In parts of the county voters remain affluent and very concerned about potential tax increases. Republican leaders have expressed concern about the political and social consequences of recent demographic shifts eroding support for the GOP (Khoury, 2012). However, immigration, public education, language access, and more recently voting rights have become highly contentious issues as demographics have changed. Facing a downturn in property tax revenue and state funding, Fairfax County supervisors struggle to balance devastating budget cuts to the county's awarding-winning school district against demands for English as a second language (ESL) services coming from an increasingly diverse, lower-income immigrant population. In recent years Fairfax schools have increased class size. For example, in 2010, 4,000 new students were added without any increase in school funding. Thus, moving forward rising enrollment is predicted to be the primary driver of increased education spending, which sparks divisions between county officials (Chandler & Kravitz, 2010).

So, is suburban government responsiveness really all about local government leaders' partisanship, ethos, or their ideological sense of right and wrong? These factors certainly mattered to the actors interviewed for this study. However, the case studies in Chapters 3–5 suggest that suburban institutional interdependency changes the way we should think about government actors' partisan and ideological decision making around redistribution in American suburbs. In the face of rapidly changing demographics and scarce fiscal resources to address new public policy concerns from the unyielding influx of immigrants and ethnic

---

[11] The county is divided into nine supervisor districts. One supervisor is elected from each district to the Fairfax County Board of Supervisors every four years (without term limits). The chairman of the board is elected by the county at large. The county executive – the administrative head of the county government – is appointed by the Board of Supervisors.

[12] Republican chair Tom Davis was succeeded by Katherine Hanley, a Democrat from the Providence District (1995–2003). Gerry Connolly served as chairman from 2003 to 2007, then in 2008 was elected to serve in the U.S. House of Representatives from Virginia's 11th District. In 2009, current chairwoman Sharon Bulova, also a Democrat, was elected in a special election and in 2011 was reelected (Conroy, 2012), after representing the Braddock District on the Board of Supervisors for twenty-one years (Fairfax County, 2013).

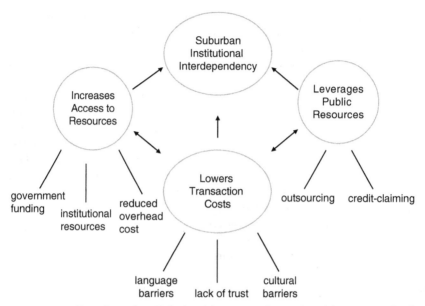

FIGURE 1.1. Interdependent Relationships among Institutional Actors in Suburbia.

minorities to suburban jurisdictions, such explanations alone do less to explain how public-nonprofit partnerships are developed, maintained, or dismantled during the development and implementation of policies/programs.

Scholars will continue to debate the motivations of local government actors who seek to offer services to immigrant and ethnic minorities and the extent to which ideology matters. An age-old debate will also continue regarding the extent to which economic development versus redistributive policy making (or some combination of the two) served as government actors' true motivations (Peterson, 1981; Swanstrom, 1988). However, in the new suburban context, we can no longer afford to ignore the role of interdependent relationships or how policies/programs actually get implemented or dismantled. By building on reciprocity, selective incentives, and repeated interactions, I argue that alliances between elected officials, bureaucrats, and nonprofits lower transaction costs and bolster additional leverage to overcome a host of problems associated with addressing newcomer concerns in a changing suburban landscape. As Figure 1.1 illustrates, this interdependent relationship forms for at least three reasons:

1. **SII increases access to resources:** Collaboration gives CBOs access to programmatic funding and resources available in the public sector.
2. **SII increases legitimacy and lowers transaction costs:** For public agencies, alliances with CBOs lower the transaction costs associated with overcoming language and cultural barriers between newcomers and existing residents.

3. **SII leverages public resources:** Partnerships allow local bureaucrats to minimize outlays of their scarce resources to deal with the problems associated with suburban demographic shifts by essentially outsourcing much of the effort to nonprofit agencies, while still taking credit for the programs these CBOs initiate, maintain, and staff.

To better explain how local institutional actors respond to the rapidly changing demographic shifts taking place in American suburbs, in Chapter 2, I use national census data and the results of five separate native-language focus groups among settlers in suburban Washington, DC, to understand which factors influence immigrant and native-born racial/ethnic minorities to move to or within a multiethnic suburb, and which factors promote or deter neighborhood interactions among racial and ethnic groups. Then, in Chapters 3, 4, and 5, I examine the other side of the coin, applying the SII framework to explain the logical and practical reasons local institutional actors form alliances to respond to policy issues of day labor, public education, and language access in suburbia.

2

New Neighbors in Suburban Washington, DC

*Immigrant and Ethnic Minority Settlement
Surrounding the Nation's Capital*

This chapter provides the contemporary social, demographic, and political overview of multiethnic suburban Washington, DC. This background sets the stage and helps to frame the development of the suburban institutional interdependency (SII) framework used in the case study presented in Chapters 3–5, whose goal is to explain how suburban institutional actors respond to and implement often controversial policies/programs for immigrant and racial/ethnic minorities. To explain how suburban institutional actors respond to the needs and concerns of immigrant and ethnic groups, it is first important to understand which factors influenced their residential choices or constraints.

Recent immigrant and racial/ethnic minority settlement has often occurred in multiethnic metropolitan areas like suburban DC, or in what Frey (2011) calls *melting pot metros*. These are metropolitan statistical areas (urban or suburban) where at least 35 percent of residents are nonwhite. I use *multiethnic* and *melting pot* interchangeably to describe such areas. In 2010, 36 of the 100 most populous metropolitan areas nationwide (i.e., with populations exceeding 500,000) fit this demographic classification.[1]

The residential choices and settlement patterns of immigrant and racial/ethnic minority groups to and within multiethnic metros are important for several reasons. First, existing research concerning their residential patterns is limited in several ways. Their residential patterns and the implications

---

[1] Thirty-six multiethnic metropolitan statistical areas (urban or suburban) where at least 35 percent of residents are nonwhite in 2010: Albuquerque, NM; Atlanta, GA; Austin, TX; Bakersfield, CA; Charleston, SC; Chicago, IL; Columbia, SC; Dallas, TX; El Paso, TX; Fresno, CA; Honolulu, HI; Houston, TX; Jackson, MS; Lakeland, FL; Las Vegas, NV; Los Angeles, CA; McAllen, TX; Memphis, TN; Miami, FL; Modesto, CA; New Orleans, LA; New York, NY; Virginia Beach, VA; Orlando, FL; Oxnard, CA; Phoenix, AZ; Richmond, VA; Riverside, CA; Sacramento, CA; San Antonio, TX; San Diego, CA; San Francisco, CA; San Jose, CA; Stockton, CA; Tucson, AZ; Washington, DC/MD/VA.

thereof are often studied from a large urban or central city perspective, and therefore fail to account for the suburban experience. Moreover, past studies are largely limited to a demographically narrow black/white or Latino/white dichotomy, thus overlooking the emergence of multiethnic communities (but see Alba & Logan, 1991; Alba et al., 1999; Iceland, 2004; Logan, Zhang, & Alba, 2002).

Second, very little research has examined the emergence of multiethnic areas or what factors influence whether immigrants and racial/ethnic minorities choose to reside in a suburb rather than the central city of a multiethnic metro. One possible explanation is that multiethnic suburbs are simply the outgrowth or spillover of their urban counterparts. For example, multiethnic metros are found primarily in high-immigration zones of the United States, such as New York, Los Angeles, San Francisco, Miami, and Chicago (Frey, 2003a, p. 160). However, this explanation has several limitations. It fails to explain the specific factors driving various racial/ethnic minorities to settle in a suburb versus another location type. For the suburbanization of whites during the postwar emergence of so-called chocolate cities and vanilla suburbs (Farley, 1978), spatial assimilation factors (e.g., income and educational attainment) and place stratification factors (e.g., racial/ethnic background) strongly influenced settlement patterns. Do these factors hold the same explanatory power for minority suburbanization? How do these explanatory factors vary for immigrant versus native-born suburbanites, as well as for longtime immigrants who reside for a period in the urban core before moving outward versus recent immigrants who settle directly in a multiethnic suburb? As Charles contends:

The emergence of ethnic suburban enclaves may account for this apparent weakening of the traditional spatial assimilation process by making residence in high-status, suburban communities an option for recently arrived non-English speakers with at- or above-average social class characteristics. (2003, p. 179) (also see Alba, Logan, & Stults, 2000; Alba et al., 1999; Logan et al., 2002)

Third, according to Frey (2003a), the suburbs of multiethnic metropolitan areas also experienced the greatest outmigration of non-Hispanic whites; yet existing spatial assimilation and place stratification models have largely assumed that suburban settlement would result in closer proximity of minorities to non-Hispanic whites. To what extent, if any, are multiethnic suburbs creating new patterns of residential sorting by race/ethnicity?

Although Frey's demographic typology provides an opportunity to examine metropolitan areas as the unit of analysis, a limitation of this typology is that it fails to account for the intra-metropolitan differences *within* specific multiethnic metropolitan areas. It is precisely these differences that can enable researchers to examine the extent to which residential mobility is influenced by sorting out by race/ethnicity, class, or other factors. The exclusive use of statistical indicators could "mask variations across metropolitan areas and variations in residential patterns across different racial and ethnic groups" (Frey, 2003a, p. 155). Arguably, a mixed-methods approach, using both qualitative and quantitative data, is more likely to yield a nuanced picture of recent immigrant and racial/ethnic minority suburbanization.

Qualitative analyses – whether from elaborations to closed-ended questions or in-depth interviews – represent another direction for future research. The next logical step in this case is to explore the attitudes, perceptions, and justifications of Hispanics and Asians for their neighborhood racial composition preferences; this is particularly important for capturing the importance of immigration-related characteristics. (Charles, 2003, p. 200)

I focus this analysis at the county level, and the intra-metropolitan differences therein, for several reasons. First, for decades the U.S. Census Bureau has conducted geographical mobility/migration surveys in which movers are classified by "type of move" and "characteristics of movers" (J. Schachter, 2001a, 2001b). The bureau's long-standing "type of move" categories identify whether moves occurred intra-county (same county), inter-county (different county but same state), state-to-state, or from abroad. Second, from a public policy perspective, the county government is often responsible for allocating state funding to localities. For example, Prince George's and Montgomery Counties border each other, but the allocation of funding and resources for public education and other goods and services is vastly different. For many residents, the quality of public education, police and fire protection, shopping, and recreational opportunities in the two jurisdictions are worlds apart. Moreover, there are certain widespread assumptions, whether fact or stereotype, regarding the two counties' delivery and quality of local goods and services. Third, whether due to individual preferences or constraints, in both jurisdictions the majority of moves each year are intra-county; why people decide to sort themselves into a particular suburban county or elect to exit a county is, therefore, important to examine.

In this chapter, I first review the various explanatory factors that the spatial assimilation, place stratification, and economic sorting theories focus on. Then to create a context for this examination, the next section provides a snapshot of suburban Washington's contemporary socioeconomic and household characteristics by racial/ethnic composition. Next, I employ a mixed-method approach, balancing census figures for metropolitan Washington, DC, with case study research focused on the so-called national capital suburbs, closest to the District of Columbia. The data for the case study come from five separate focus groups conducted in five different native languages with black (English), Latino (Spanish), Chinese (Mandarin), Korean (Korean), and Iranian (Farsi) residents of inner-ring suburbs. I use these data to examine (1) what factors influence minority spatial location patterns *within* the metro Washington suburbs; and (2) what factors promote or deter neighborhood interactions between racial/ethnic groups settled there.

Both descriptive statistics and some of the focus group results reveal a persistent social hierarchy by race. Racial/ethnic disparities were especially marked in socioeconomic status (SES) and household demographic characteristics. The overall focus group findings suggest three distinct takeaways as driving suburban residential selection or constraints. First, corroborating economic sorting theory, the perception of a county's delivery of goods and services (e.g., public safety, school quality), was an influential factor driving residential location decisions for many, but not all respondents. Second, in line with spatial assimilation theory, individual income and affordable housing constrained suburban residential selection for some discussants, particularly among blacks. Third, confirming the place stratification theory, racial preferences and avoidance of certain racial groups, which emanated from negative stereotypes and reported experiences of living in particular areas, also influenced residential decision making. Most striking are the intersections of identity and how the interlocking systems of persistent racial hierarchies, immigration, reported discrimination, and social class continue to structure multiethnic spaces beyond the urban core.

Regarding neighborhood interactions, respondents reported that lack of time and desire impedes their neighborhood interactions and engagement in activities outside of their immediate families. For many Chinese, Korean, and Iranian (but less so Latino) discussants, language and cultural barriers also curtailed their desire to participate in community activities (language access for limited English proficient adults will be discussed in greater detail in Chapter 5). Given cultural and language barriers, many discussants reported that they did not know how to begin getting involved in community activities.

Residential Location Choice: Spatial Assimilation, Place Stratification, and Economic Sorting

An interdisciplinary group of researchers has long examined the determinants of residential selection and mobility in the United States, particularly among blacks and whites. Next I examine what the sociological and political economy approaches, both theoretical and empirical, have to say regarding spatial location.

Spatial Assimilation

Urban ecologists, adhering largely to the Chicago School of urban sociology, examined how immigration and rises in individuals' socioeconomic status (particularly income levels) influenced early suburbanization patterns (Burgess, 1925; Park, 1926). The traditional, sociologically oriented spatial assimilation theory predicts that immigrant groups typically spend a generation or more in central city enclaves. With rises in income and educational attainment, the second- or third-generation descendants tend to exit urban ethnic enclaves for (ideally) more heterogeneous suburban neighborhoods. Baldassare summarizes the logic of this model:

An "invasion and succession" process in older, inner-city neighborhoods drove sub-urban growth. City areas became the destination points for recent, poor, immigrant workers. New residents moved to these areas because of their inexpensive housing and proximity to work. As a result of the "invasion," many of the long-term residents of these inner-city areas moved to suburban areas further away from the central business district ... all of this occurs because long-term residents can afford the higher costs of housing and city-to-suburb commutes. Thus suburbs developed in an urban context of population growth and rising incomes. (1992, pp. 479–480)

The measures used to test the spatial assimilation model remain important in examining residential location attainment for both immigrant and native-born racial/ethnic groups. Alba and Logan find that socioeconomic factors like income and education are greater determinants of suburbanization for certain racial/ethnic minority groups than for non-Hispanic whites (1991, 434). Given that minority populations (particularly blacks and Latinos) have disproportionately lower levels of income and educational attainment, it is generally expected that as income and educational levels increase for these groups, the likelihood of their suburban settlement also increases. However, rises in income and educational attainment are traditionally thought to *deter* settlement in ethnic or multiethnic neighborhoods (Logan et al., 2002, p. 307).

The rapid emergence of multiethnic suburbs around large metro areas since the 1980s requires us to reevaluate these sociological expectations regarding the residential patterns of recent immigrants. As Alba and his colleagues contend, "recent immigrants seem much more inclined to settle outside of urban enclaves than were immigrants in previous eras, whose experience is recorded in the spatial assimilation model" (1999, p. 458). They further note, "the pattern of rapid or immediate suburban entry, combined with the large concentration of recent immigrants in a few metropolitan areas, raises the question of whether suburbanization holds the same meaning for recent immigrants that it held for previous groups" (p. 446).

Unlike the distinct connotations of achieving the American dream – individualism, upward mobility, and prosperity – inherent in post–World War II suburban relocation patterns, migration directly to "suburbia" may have little meaning of "upward mobility" or "greater opportunity" for recent immigrant and ethnic minority migrants. In fact, the recent phenomenon of immigrant groups forgoing the traditional passage through the urban core may undermine the individual-level processes inherent in spatial assimilation theory; namely, achieving socioeconomic mobility and capital for "purchase of entry" into suburbia (Alba et al., 1999). Thus, further examination of spatial assimilation theory is warranted, particularly for recently suburbanized immigrant and racial/ethnic minority newcomers.

Place Stratification

While there is strong evidence to support the spatial assimilation model, the explanatory power of the model often varies by race and ethnicity (Alba & Logan, 1992, 1993; Massey & Denton, 1988a; South & Crowder, 1997). African-origin racial/ethnic groups (and perhaps other less-studied ethnic groups) have long been anomalies to the spatial assimilation model in terms of their lack of mobility to the suburbs, leading to development of the place stratification model as a more likely factor of their spatial location patterns (Massey, 1985; Massey & Denton, 1988a).

As Woldoff and Ovadia note, "Where the spatial assimilation model has been disappointing is in accounting for the residential outcomes of African-Americans and African-origin Hispanics" (2009, p. 68). Place stratification theory was developed to address the limitations of the spatial assimilation model. According to this model, race/ethnicity continues to play a role in determining where an individual resides, whereas residential mobility is a reflection of status in the social hierarchy (Alba & Logan, 1993; Logan & Alba, 1993; Logan & Molotch, 1987). Increases in socioeconomic status are *less* likely to translate into residential proximity to non-Hispanic whites for blacks and other groups with African phenotype than for other racial/ethnic minorities (Iceland & Wilkes, 2006; Massey & Denton, 1988a; Massey & Fischer, 1999). According to this model, structural and institutional discrimination constrains mobility opportunities for groups with a distinct African phenotype (Alba & Logan, 1993; Logan & Molotch, 1987), and this discrimination limits their residential choices, regardless of their income and educational attainment. Strong evidence indicates that differential patterns of spatial location occur based, at least in part, on racial preferences or prejudices, lending support for the place stratification model (Alba & Logan, 1991; Charles, 2000, 2001; Zubrinsky & Bobo, 1996; also see Clark, 1992; Clark & Blue, 2004).

On the other hand, Harris finds limited support for a purely racially based hypothesis (1999b, 2001). Instead Harris proposes a "racial proxy hypothesis" focusing on class factors rather than racial factors. He notes that "respondents' higher satisfaction with neighborhoods composed of fewer black residents was found to be largely a reflection of preferences for relatively affluent, safe, well-maintained neighborhoods with good schools" (2001, p. 113). Yet the fact remains that African Americans disproportionately continue to live in highly segregated communities, even in suburbia.

In their seminal work *American Apartheid* (1993), Massey and Denton found that middle-class blacks are more likely to live near poor blacks than middle-class whites are to live near poor whites. Iceland and Wilkes (2006) note that at all levels of socioeconomic status blacks continue to be more segregated from whites than Asians or Latinos are. Other communities of color, such as Asian Americans and to some extent Latinos, are somewhat more likely to live in ethnically and racially diverse neighborhoods (Logan, 2003).

As Charles clarifies, "At first glance, these perspectives may appear oppositional. Upon closer inspection, however, these seemingly oppositional explanations complement one another. Race still matters; however, its relative importance – and that of socioeconomic status – depends on group membership" (2003, p. 103). The long-standing debate in the social science literature concerning the impact of class versus racial factors on spatial location patterns is exacerbated by inconsistent findings regarding how well place stratification models explain Latino and Asian suburbanization, particularly when such groups sort themselves into multiethnic suburban areas. While only a limited number of studies have examined place stratification beyond a black/white dichotomy, class factors seem to play a larger role in explaining spatial location patterns for Latinos and Asians than for blacks (Logan, Stults, & Farley, 2004; Massey & Denton, 1988a).

Other theoretical models accounting for the role of racial preferences in contributing to residential sorting have also been limited to contrasts between blacks and whites. In "Dynamic Models of Segregation," Nobel laureate Thomas Schelling (1971) was among the first scholars to model the dynamics of residential sorting with attention to racial preferences. Schelling's theory explained how individual-level racial preferences, even if small or non-uniformly shared by all group members in a neighborhood, might give rise to aggregate-level patterns of racial sorting out, racial turnover in a neighborhood, and subsequently continued residential segregation. Twenty years later, William Clark reexamined and largely corroborated the central tenets of this model, concluding that "the patterns of separation are likely to be reinforced by preferences for living and socializing with neighbors of similar class and interests, and by mobility that emphasizes short-distance relocations" (1991, p. 17).

More recent extensions of Schelling's work examine the role of ethnic preferences and racial distancing on residential segregation, but also account for preferences in housing quality and neighborhood status (Clark, 2006a; Fossett, 2006, 2011). While these studies underscore that residential preferences matter and continue to have a profound influence of high levels on ethnic segregation, these studies largely use an outdated black-white binary, not representative of demographic shifts, particularly in American suburbs (Clark, 1991, 1992; Lewis, Emerson, & Klineberg, 2011).

Notably, a contentious debate remains between those who emphasize social distance and preference explanations (but see Clark, 2006a, 2006b; Fossett, 2006) and those who emphasize discrimination in, for example, the housing and lending markets (Bobo & Zubrinsky, 1996; Charles, 2003; Yinger, 1995) as primary culprits for persistent residential segregation. Historically, black migrants and some immigrant groups, particularly those from Latin America, have operated in a severely constrained housing market that offers them fewer residential choices than other groups, especially non-Hispanic whites (Logan et al., 2002). Once these groups gather the economic means to seek the "promised land" of suburbia, it remains unclear which type of suburban community they will choose, and why.

Economic Models of Spatial Sorting: "Voting with Your Feet"

Whereas sociologists usually look to spatial assimilation and place stratification theories to explain micro-level spatial location decisions, political economists, particularly some public choice theorists, examine macroeconomic determinants such as local tax rates and community services to deduce microeconomic motivations for residential choices. Economic sorting serves as a final theoretical predictor for choice of residence in this study. Vote-with-your-feet models (Tiebout, 1956) predict that individuals will sort out based on the areas offering those goods and services that meet their preferences (e.g., high-quality public education). Residential mobility is especially important to political economists interested in the efficiency of local municipal government, particularly the provision of local public goods and services.

Variants of the Tiebout model remain particularly interesting to an interdisciplinary group of scholars concerned with how spatial sorting models explain mobility patterns; as a group these scholars are popularly referred to as public choice theorists. As the original Tiebout hypothesis contends:

The consumer-voter may be viewed as picking that community which best satisfies his preference pattern for public goods. At the central level the preferences of the consumer-voter are given, and the government tries to adjust to the pattern of those preferences, whereas at the local level various governments have their revenue and expenditure more or less fixed. Given these revenue and expenditure patterns, the consumer-voter moves to that community whose local government best satisfies his set of preferences. (1956, p. 418)

Accordingly, local governments are viewed as operating based on free-market principles, similarly to the way a private corporation would work. Local governments seek to attract "high-value" residents who contribute tax dollars to the local economy while requiring relatively few returns in the forms of public services – particularly those services that require the redistribution of wealth at the local level. According to such logic, the metropolitan fragmentation of big governments into smaller, local government jurisdictions (i.e., suburbanization) and ease of mobility – or the ability of people to "vote with their feet" – create competition among local municipalities, resulting in more efficient provision of goods and services at the local level, universally benefiting consumer-voters (Conley & Wooders, 1997; Tiebout, 1956). In theory, individuals' location decisions convey information about their preferences, in terms of what tax rates they are willing to pay for the lifestyle they desire. Local taxation regimens will tend to sort out residents in local jurisdictions according to class (Bish, 1971; Buchanan, 1971; Peterson, 1981; M. Schneider, 1989a; Tiebout, 1956), producing suburbs that are socioeconomically homogenous and distinctly different from other competing jurisdictions.

Such theoretical models of spatial sorting assume that an individual has complete freedom to move to whatever community practices the tax and expenditure policies that match his or her preferences (Hirschman, 1970;

Tiebout, 1956), and these earlier models do not account for any other factors that might impose constraints on mobility, such as race or systemic
inequalities. Breaking apart the nuances of the original (Tiebout, 1956)
model reveals its problems for the study of minority suburbanization. To be
clear, economic sorting models can be useful for explaining the forces that
create and maintain economically homogenous suburban neighborhoods,
promote white flight to the suburbs, and drive government fragmentation.
Public choice theory, however, largely disregards the centrality of race, ethnicity, and class dynamics in American politics, treating local public goods
as if they were embedded in or operating within a perfect or near-perfect
competitive-market-like structure.

As Bruce Hamilton points out, if Adam Smith's "invisible hand" of the marketplace were truly the primary force at work, economic stratification would
disappear as individuals sought their greatest good. The "efficiency" of the
Tiebout model is in fact not a natural outcome of free-market forces, but is
achieved through the enforcement of exclusionary zoning and systemic restrictions on access to economic privilege, which function to restrict individual
choice and produce *income stratification*. Exclusionary mechanisms such as
fiscal zoning ensure that homeowners in a given jurisdiction are very homogenous economically; generally they pay the same rate of property tax, and there
is little to no income redistribution within that area.

Moreover, early public choice models largely ignore the negative
by-products of economic sorting: residential, income, and subsequently
racial segregation. In his pivotal contribution to the debate, Miller points
out what public choice models overlook: "Because the distribution of consumers is linked with the distribution of resources, low-income cities have
also been low-resource cities; the sorting out of metropolitan population by
income class has been detrimental to low-income individuals" (1981, p. 182).
Consequently, as Miller further explains, "while [metropolitan] fragmentation may promote multiple, responsive, small-scale demand-revealing mechanisms for homogenous neighborhoods, it may also result in increases in
income and economic segregation. And if income and racial segregation are
empirically associated with the concentration of resource-draining problems
like crime, then fragmentation may actually work against the welfare of individuals in the low-income and minority jurisdictions, contrary to the original
Tiebout expectation" (1981, p. 182).

These concerns raise questions regarding the extent to which the underlying tenets of vote-with-your-feet models are outdated and lack power
to explain the residential mobility of more recent immigrant and ethnic
minority suburbanites. Historically, the "burbs" were fashioned to accept
only a select group of individuals into the "club," but civil rights legislation has opened the door to many people previously denied entry. In
the American political economy, class dynamics are inextricably linked to

racial dynamics. The two cannot be viewed as mutually exclusive, particularly in suburbia.[2] Given demographic trends in recent decades, it is important to consider how racial and class dynamics are shifting or are continuing to be reinforced, and what implications these changes have for how political economy sorting models will fare in the future.

I argue that scholars in both the spatial assimilation and residential choice camps have failed to explain *why* some immigrant and ethnic minority groups are bypassing urban areas altogether for suburban life and why such groups would sort themselves into certain types of suburbs, specifically multiethnic areas. As noted in chapter 1, economic sorting (vote-with-your-feet) models put forth by some public choice theorists suffer from severe selective historicism that glosses over historical, structural, and institutional practices that have profoundly shaped and reshaped the metropolitan political economy in ways that facilitated the growth of white middle- and working-class suburbanization while impeding suburbanization for everyone else. Given their lack of historical and social context, it is impossible to use economic sorting models alone to explain where preferences emanate between different immigrant and ethnic minority groups.

Little research in the public choice paradigm has addressed these concerns, particularly in light of suburban demographic shifts. Some scholars examine patterns of suburbanization in light of both local public finances and race/ethnicity. M. Schneider and Phelan contend that "A strong tax base gives communities a wide range of policy options: it enables communities to choose either good services at a modest tax rate or low levels of services at a commensurately lower tax rate. In contrast, communities with a poor tax base are often confined to the worst of all worlds: they must tax themselves heavily to generate even the modest revenues" (1993, p. 275) (also see M. Schneider & Logan, 1982). Concomitantly, these scholars find that communities with poor tax bases are also areas where blacks are more likely to suburbanize. Moreover, as Charles points out, "Minority suburbs – although better off than poor minority neighborhoods – tend to be less affluent, have poorer quality public services and schools, and experience more crime and social disorganization compared to the suburbs that comparable whites reside in" (2003, p. 176) (also see Alba et al., 1999; Farley, 1970; Guest, 1978; Logan & Schneider, 1984; Logan & Stearns, 1980; Logan et al., 2002; Massey & Denton, 1993).

Economic sorting models can no longer afford to ignore the effects of racial and class-based preferences on spatial location choice or constraints. Models of minority suburbanization must incorporate racial and class factors as presented in the spatial assimilation and place stratification models. Yet the failure of these sociological models to account for features of the political economy

---

[2] Following publication of *The Declining Significance of Race* (Wilson, 1980), a great debate ensued in the sociology and political science arenas concerning the impact of race versus class on political and social behavior as well as public policy outcomes (see, e.g., Dawson, 1994).

similarly leads them to omit valuable information concerning the relationship of race, ethnicity, and class composition to metropolitan economic factors such as property taxes and housing values, which are considered important components of spatial location decision making (Harris, 1999a). Therefore, a more inclusive examination of minority suburbanization should account for racial and class preferences as well as economic contextual factors.

Demographic Profile of Suburban Washington, DC

Metropolitan Washington, DC, provides an excellent site to explore demographic change and local government responsiveness. By 2000, it ranked fourth, after Los Angeles, New York, and Chicago, among the nation's multiethnic metros, with more than 80 percent of its metro area located in suburbs (Frey, 2003a). The DC metro area is also particularly relevant because of the rapid growth of its immigrant population since 1980. With 22 percent of residents foreign born, it houses the seventh largest concentration of immigrants among all large U.S. metro areas (21.5 percent foreign-born), following New York, Los Angeles, Miami, Chicago, Houston, and San Francisco. Between 1980 and 2010 the area's foreign-born population grew rapidly, from 256,535 to 1,223,159, with more than 1 million of those new residents arriving between 1990 and 2010 alone, a similar scale of growth to that experienced in Houston, San Francisco, and Dallas–Fort Worth (Singer, 2012).

According to Singer (2012), immigrant settlement in metro DC was driven by economic, political, religious, and academic reasons as well as by refugee resettlement such as that carried out by Vietnamese following the Vietnam War in the 1970s; by Central Americans following civil conflict in the 1980s (particularly immigrants from El Salvador); and by Ethiopian and Somali refugees in the 1990s (also see Singer & Wilson, 2006).

Unlike Chicago, Los Angeles, or New York, the District of Columbia has not historically been an industrial/manufacturing or commerce-based metropolis. Instead, it is "historically exceptional" because its major employer is the federal government and government-related agencies (Gale, 1987; Manning, 1998). Like other large metro areas, however, its suburban jurisdictions were largely exclusionary bedroom communities until World War II. Postwar, the metropolitan area witnessed a great decentralization of people and industries to the suburbs.

This study focuses on the three largest counties in the DC metro region: Fairfax County, Virginia, and Prince George's and Montgomery Counties in Maryland (see Figure 2.1). These three inner-ring suburban areas, ranging along the edge of the nation's capital, house a majority of the region's foreign-born population. Since 1980 the total population of these suburbs has grown by 50 percent, and their immigrant population has more than quadrupled. By 2000, these areas accounted for 55 percent of the total metropolitan population and 71 percent of the foreign-born population (Price & Singer, 2008).

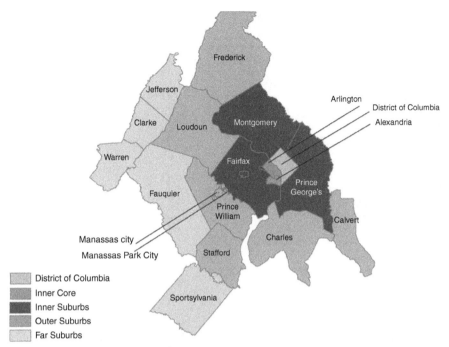

FIGURE 2.1. Metropolitan Washington, DC.
Source: Brookings Classification of the Washington Metropolitan Area as defined by the Office of Management and Budget Metropolitan Area, 2003.

By 2010, the Washington, DC, region dominated the latest list of highest-income U.S. counties. The median household income of the region was $84,523. The national median income for 2010 was only $50,046 (Bass & Homan, 2011). Fairfax and Montgomery Counties are two of the most populous counties in the metro region and among the wealthiest in the United States. Both counties rank among the top ten counties of 250,000 persons or more in terms of estimated median household income. By 2010, the population of Montgomery County had reached 971,777 (up from 873,341 in 2000), and it ranked tenth nationwide in median household income (Montgomery County Planning Department, 2012). In the same year, the population of Fairfax County totaled 1,081,726 residents (up from 969,749 in 2000). Fairfax ranked the second wealthiest county nationwide in median household income, following Loudoun County, also located in northern Virginia. The third study site, Prince George's County, is a majority-black suburb that holds the title of the wealthiest black county in the nation. Among the thirty-three U.S. counties with the largest number of black households earning more than $200,000 per year in 2008, Prince George's won handily with 8,397 households; Montgomery County ranked fifth, with 2,894 households

TABLE 2.1. *Racial/Ethnic and Immigrant Composition of the Three Study Counties, by Percentage*

Racial/Ethnic Origin	1980 (%)	1990 (%)	2000 (%)	2010 (%)
Montgomery County, MD				
Non-Hispanic white	81.6	69.2	59.5	49.3
Non-Hispanic black	8.8	12.2	14.8	16.6
Non-Hispanic Asian	3.9	7.4	11.3	13.9
Hispanic	3.9	8.2	11.5	17.0
Foreign-born	12.0	18.6	26.7	32.2
Fairfax County, VA				
Non-Hispanic white	86.2	77.5	65.3	53.4
Non-Hispanic black	5.8	7.6	8.6	9.7
Non-Hispanic Asian	3.3	8.3	13.1	18.4
Hispanic	3.8	6.3	11.0	16.1
Foreign-Born	9.1	15.6	24.5	30.3
Prince George's County, MD				
Non-Hispanic white	54.2	42.1	26.0	14.8
Non-Hispanic black	40.3	50.8	62.0	65.3
Non-Hispanic Asian	1.5	2.2	3.9	4.1
Hispanic	3.0	4.1	7.1	15.7
Foreign-Born	8.0	10.0	13.8	19.9

Sources: U.S. Census Bureau, 1980, 1990, 2000, 2010 censuses.

(Higley, 2010). However, it ranked sixty-ninth in nationwide median household income. Recently, the demographics of Prince George's are shifting as Latinos increasingly move in, totaling 15.7 percent of the population as of 2010. The 2010 total population was 863,420 (up from 796,763 or 7.72 percent since 2000).

Table 2.1 details the racial/ethnic and foreign-born percentage breakdowns of Montgomery, Fairfax, and Prince George's Counties from 1980 to 2010. The immigrant population in Montgomery County rose from 37,000 in 1970 to 233,000 by 2000, when it accounted for 26.7 percent of the total population (Singer, 2003, p. 4). By 2010 that percentage had risen to 32.2 percent. Further, while the non-Hispanic white population decreased from 82 percent in 1980 to 49 percent in 2010, both the Asian and Hispanic populations grew by some four times in the same time frame. By 2010, more than three-quarters of the Asian population and two-thirds of the Hispanic population were foreign born. Meanwhile the black population increased more modestly, roughly doubling.

Similar demographic patterns occurred in Fairfax County, the largest county in Virginia and among the largest in the nation (surpassing the population of the District of Columbia by 500,000 persons). The immigrant population of Fairfax County grew from 16,000 in 1970 to 250,000 in 2000 – comprising 24.5 percent of the total population (Singer, 2003).

Between 1980 and 2010, the non-Hispanic white population decreased from an overwhelming majority to a little more than half the total population, while the Asian and Hispanic populations soared, by roughly five and four times, respectively. Notably the black population remained low and relatively stable, increasing from only 6 percent to 10 percent in the same period. Mirroring the situation in Montgomery County, by 2010, nearly three-quarters of the Asian and Hispanic populations in Fairfax County were foreign born.

In Prince George's County, blacks became the majority racial/ethnic group by 1990, and made up 65 percent of the population in 2010, followed by Hispanics and whites (16 percent and 15 percent, respectively), and Asians at 4 percent. The Latino population doubled between 2000 and 2010. By 2010, 74 percent of the Asian population and 60 percent of the Hispanic population were foreign born.

The historic and hard-fought battles to integrate the once predominantly white Prince George's County, beginning largely in the 1970s, were a notable development. The enormous success of many black Prince Georgians – from lawyers and doctors to small business owners, policy makers, and college professors – helped solidify a new black middle class in the region (see Johnson, 2002). However, the oft-touted fact that Prince George's County is the most affluent black county in the country is packed full of ironies. For example, as Table 2.2 shows, the median household income in Prince George's County in 2010 was $70,019, substantially lower than in adjacent Montgomery County ($89,155) and much lower still compared with the six-figure median income in Fairfax County (Montgomery County Planning Department, 2012). Meanwhile, individual and family poverty rates in Prince George's County are nearly two points higher than in its neighbor, Montgomery County, and are almost twice the rates in Fairfax County. The federal poverty line varies with the size of a family, but, for example, it stood at $22,050 for a family of four in 2010. In 2010, 9.9 percent of Marylanders, 11.1 percent of Virginians, and 15.3 percent of the U.S. population had incomes below the poverty level (Bishaw, 2012).

In 2010, the homeownership rate in Prince George's County was 62.8 percent and the median value of owner-occupied housing units was $286,100, as compared to Montgomery County's median house value of $447,200 and 67.6 percent homeownership rate, which is on par with the homeownership rate for the state of Maryland (67.5 percent) (U.S. Census Bureau, 2010a). Homeownership rates and home values are, not surprisingly, highest of all in Fairfax County but not largely different from Montgomery County. Notably, in 2000, the median rent was highest in Montgomery County ($1,466), followed by Fairfax County ($1,383) and Prince George's County ($1,182).

Table 2.2 also shows that as of 2010 the foreign-born population is overall much less inclined to settle in Prince George's County (20 percent) than in Montgomery (32 percent) or Fairfax (30 percent) Counties. Correspondingly,

TABLE 2.2. *Select Summary Statistics for Targeted Counties, 2010*

	Fairfax	Montgomery	Prince George's
School-age child present	34.4%	33.2%	30.6%
Married	57.4%	53.4%	40.1%
Female-headed	9.2%	11.3%	20.4%
Foreign born	30.3%	32.2%	19.9%
Language other than English spoken at home	38.1%	39.3%	19.3%
Median household income	$103,010	$89,155	$70,019
Families below poverty level	3.6%	4.9%	6.3%
Individuals below poverty level	5.8%	7.7%	9.4%
Median home value	$462,00	$447,200	$286,100
Homeownership rate	69.9%	67.6%	67.5%
Median rent	$1,383	$1,466	$1,182

Source: 2010 American Community Survey, U.S. Census Bureau, 2010.

the percentages of the population speaking languages other than English in the home are higher in both Fairfax (38 percent) and Montgomery (39 percent) Counties than in Prince George's County (19 percent).

Family structures are similar in Fairfax and Montgomery Counties, with rather more than five in ten households headed by a married couple and only about one in ten headed by a woman. In contrast, in Prince George's County only four in ten householders are married and a woman heads two in ten households. The percentage of families with school-age children is similar, ranging from 31 percent in Prince George's County to 34 percent in Fairfax County (Department of Neighborhood and Community Services, 2011; Montgomery County Planning Department, 2012; U.S. Census Bureau, 2010c).

This study is among the first to examine the growing Iranian population in suburban Washington, DC. The U.S. Census Bureau collects data only on Iranian ancestry, opening the door for widely discrepant population estimates. For example, whereas the U.S. Census reported the number of U.S. residents of Iranian ancestry at 338,000, the Iranian Interest Section in Washington, DC, gave an estimate of 900,000 (Rafii & Soroya, 2003). Population estimates are complicated by the inclusion of multiracial categories in the 2000 census. Because there is no specific census designation for Middle Eastern heritage, respondents might choose to write in "Iranian," "Persian," "Persian American," "Iranian American," or some other ethnic designation. Others may simply check the "White" or some other box. According to "Strength in Numbers," a 2003 National Iranian American Council (NIAC) report, the Washington, DC, metro area houses the fourth largest concentration of Iranians in the United States, particularly in Maryland (12,935, or 0.24 percent of the state's population) and Virginia (14,970, or 0.21 percent of the state's population).[3] Although the figures should be viewed with caution, in the 2010 census 289,465 respondents marked "Iranian alone or in combination," and 215,640 Iranians marked "Iranian alone." A little more than 10,000 Iranians reported living in Maryland, and 11,835 live in Virginia (U.S. Census Bureau, 2010b).

Since the Iranian political revolution of 1979, many Iranians have emigrated to the United States, Europe, and Asia (Ghaffarian, 1998). Many of these émigrés were among the highly educated class in Iran. "The developed countries and especially the US have greatly benefited from the pool of the highly educated and experienced Iranian immigrants. These countries are getting a 'free ride' from the education and expertise of the Iranian elite. Most of the Iranian immigrants in the US are working in fields such as education, engineering, medicine, and other professional services. Their work has important external social benefits for the host countries that are missed in Iran" (Torbat, 2002, p. 273).

Many Iranians took up residence in suburban Washington, DC, particularly Fairfax County, and have resided there for decades. How Iranians navigate their place within suburban space has become increasingly relevant in the atmosphere of heightened social and political attention to people of Middle Eastern descent following the September 11, 2001, terrorist attacks. In addition to facing similar linguistic and cultural barriers as other non-English-speaking suburban immigrant groups, Iranians are also troubled by the potential for institutional racism and other discriminatory practices such as racial profiling, which can pose barriers to suburban entry (counteracting their generally high incomes and educational attainment). Despite Iranians' historically, ethnically, culturally, and linguistically distinct heritage, many Americans may simplistically view Iranians as members of the Arab world, and consequently – in the post-9/11 political climate – potential terrorists. Farsi (and also dialects such as Tajiki/Dari), not Arabic, is the language spoken in Iran.

Profiles of Recent Movers in Suburban Washington, DC

The racial/ethnic composition of the most recent migrant cohorts in suburban Washington, DC, is largely unknown and can easily be masked by the overall growth of these suburbs. In this section I present summary statistics for a snapshot of suburban DC adult householders ages twenty-five to sixty-four, of various racial/ethnic groups, who moved to their current residence in the previous twelve months.

In suburban Washington, DC, the profile of recent movers reflects the broader regional socioeconomic inequalities along racial/ethnic lines. Table 2.3

---

[3] According to the NIAC study, the majority of Iranian Americans reside in California (159,016, or 0.47 percent of the state's population, concentrated in Los Angeles and Beverly Hills), followed by New York (22,856, or 0.13 percent of the state's population) and Texas (22,590, or 0.10 percent of the state's population).

TABLE 2.3. *Recent Movers in Suburban Washington, DC, Select Summary Statistics by Race/Ethnicity, 2010*

	Asian	Black	Latino	White
Socioeconomic Status				
HS or less	13%	38%	44%	14%
Some college	44%	47%	41%	51%
BA or more	43%	15%	14%	35%
Median income	$86,000	$52,700	$56,000	$74,000
Unemployed	15%	15%	11%	12%
Household Characteristics				
Homeowner	43%	24%	35%	44%
Married	76%	40%	60%	57%
Female headed	32%	59%	45%	42%
Age (years)	38	40	39	40
School-age children present	46%	46%	53%	37%
Foreign born	90%	24%	64%	11%
Period of Immigration				
In 1980s	17%	5%	21%	2%
In 1990s	30%	9%	26%	3%
In 2000s	43%	11%	26%	5%
Type of Move				
In state	66%	73%	80%	61%
State-to-state	25%	24%	16%	32%
From abroad	9%	3%	4%	7%
Observations	1,000	1,815	456	3,980

Notes: Tables represent the mean summary statistics, except where noted.
Sample population reflects adult householder. All data are weighted using household sampling weights.
Source: Integrated Public Use Micro-Data Series, ACS, 2000–2010 (pooled data).

shows that white and Asian recent movers are more likely, on average, to have completed a college degree, to earn higher median household incomes, and to own their own homes than are recent black and Latino movers. A 2010 study by the National Community Reinvestment Coalition showed that black and Latino homeowners in the Washington, DC, metro area were, respectively, almost 20 percent and 90 percent more likely to be foreclosed on or to lose their homes than were similarly situated whites in the region (Jayasundera et al., 2010, p. 3).[4] Higher unemployment rates and fewer financial resources to fall back on may account for these disparities. By the first quarter of 2010,

---

[4] This study uses regression analysis of a sample of loans with 2004–2007 vintages in the Washington, DC Metropolitan Statistical Area (MSA). It controls for borrower, loan, and neighborhood characteristics that precipitated subprime lending and foreclosure.

Prince George's County had become "ground zero" for foreclosures in the state of Maryland, accounting for 34.6 percent of the county's total home sales. Foreclosures accounted for about 20 percent of sales in the quarter statewide. This is lower than the national average of 31 percent (Robbins, 2010).

Three-quarters of Asians dwell in married-couple households, compared to only four-tenths of blacks; Latinos and whites fall between these two extremes, at 60 percent and 57 percent, respectively. A little more than half of Latinos have school-age children in the home, whereas a little less than half of blacks and Asians do, and somewhat more than a third of whites do. According to this sample, post-1980 Latino and Asian immigrants moved to suburban Washington, DC, at greater rates than did European and black immigrants. Of all immigrant groups, Asians arriving in the United States in the 1990s and 2000s were by far the most likely to move to suburban Washington, DC.

With this overview in mind, I turn now to focus group responses in order to drill down from summary statistics to individual experiences. Doing so allows a better understanding of disparities *within* the three counties of interest.

Sorting Out: Factors Driving Residential Selection, by Race/Ethnicity

This study uses data from five focus groups conducted in the DC metro area during summer 2005. Each group contained nine to twelve immigrants or domestic migrants, ages twenty-five to sixty-four years, of a specific racial/ethnic group: black, Latino, Chinese, Korean, or Iranian. The black focus group participants were largely African American, and lived in neighborhoods in Prince George's and Montgomery Counties. The Latino respondents were a combination of U.S.-born citizens and Mexican or Salvadoran immigrants residing in Montgomery or Prince George's Counties. The Chinese, Korean, and Iranian respondents mostly resided in Fairfax County. Detailed descriptions of the participants, recruitment methods, protocol, and discussion outline can be found in Appendix A.

Recall that spatial assimilation theory suggests that a rise in individual income and educational attainment increases the likelihood of exiting an urban ethnic enclave for a more heterogeneous suburban neighborhood (Alba & Logan, 1993; Charles, 2003). Place stratification theory suggests that residential mobility is a reflection of status in the social hierarchy, and that race/ethnicity continues to play a role in limiting an individual's residential choices (Alba & Logan, 1993; Logan & Alba, 1993; Logan & Molotch, 1987). For blacks and other groups with African phenotype, increases in socioeconomic status are *less* likely to translate into residential proximity to non-Hispanic whites than is true for other racial/ethnic minorities (Iceland & Wilkes, 2006; Massey & Denton, 1988a; Massey & Fischer, 1999). Finally, economic sorting (vote-with-your-feet) models (Tiebout, 1956) predict that individuals will sort out based on the areas offering those goods and services that meet their preferences (e.g., high-quality public education).

Several factors emerged as driving residential selection and subsequent interactions. First, in line with the spatial assimilation theory, income as well as affordable housing constrained suburban residential selection for some discussants, particularly blacks. Moreover, family-related factors drove spatial location patterns for some groups. Second, similar to place stratification theory, negative stereotypes and reported experiences of living in particular areas also influenced decision making, particularly for Latinos. Third, corroborating the economic sorting model, the perception of a county's delivery of goods and services (e.g., public safety, school quality) were influential in driving location decisions for most groups.

Latino Respondents

Most Latino focus group participants were foreign born and resided in Montgomery County although a few resided in Prince George's County. Recall from Table 2.2 that one in three Montgomery County residents is foreign born. The county has long enjoyed a reputation as open and welcoming to both legal and undocumented immigrants. The city of Takoma Park, in Montgomery County, has long been designated a "sanctuary city" for its protection of the rights of undocumented immigrants. In contrast, northern Virginia is known for its history of passing ordinances that crack down on undocumented immigration.

All but one Latino participant had lived in the District of Columbia prior to moving to the suburbs. Interestingly, they had moved to Montgomery County because they found housing more affordable there than in DC, which in recent years has experienced rapid gentrification. Most renters in Montgomery County reside in the southeastern areas of the county and have lower median incomes than residents in other sections of the county. These areas also house a large percentage of the county's immigrant populations. Yet one respondent noted that the rising cost of housing in Montgomery County made it difficult for "regular people" to achieve the dream of homeownership:

MALE: We didn't have our little girl, and we were thinking of moving to Fairfax, Virginia, which is also one of the counties that has a good reputation in the United States in terms of education. So, we bought a condominium there and when we decided to buy a house because we were expecting our little girl, we couldn't buy.... We couldn't buy in Virginia so we decided to move. We looked in Maryland, and Maryland at that time, four years ago, was still a place where you could buy. Now it is another story.... So it would be a good thing to find out what happened to the affordable homes for regular people.

Other reasons Latinos cited for moving to Montgomery County included better schools, green space, employment opportunities, safety, and public services. One man remarked: "We've looked through other houses but we come back because the neighborhood is perfect. There are like five parks, I mean, which is something good. Even though in Montgomery you pay a lot of taxes, but you can see the difference in the parks, the streets, the garbage gets picked up, all the services."

Another shared the following:

MALE: I started a little late in life having kids, and one of the reasons we decided to come to Montgomery County in Maryland was for the schools. Primarily because of the schools, but also the cost of housing, because in 1993 we were living in Washington, DC, and the prices were higher. Well, Montgomery is classified as one of the best counties in the education aspect in the United States. So that is an attraction for everyone. I mean, everyone wants their children to have an educational system that will develop them academically, that will give them opportunities and a good education.

Unlike many black discussants, most Latino discussants resided in racially diverse neighborhoods. While diversity generally seemed welcome, a few Latino discussants voiced racial tensions as an important factor in their decision to relocate. These respondents reported that Montgomery County generally presented a safe haven from perceived mistreatment, threats, or victimization by African Americans in Prince George's County. A Montgomery County Latino compared his experiences of living in Maryland versus the District of Columbia:

MALE: I lived for five years in Washington and I saw everything in Washington; everybody lived very crowded and there are a lot of black people that don't like you. And here in Maryland I can walk three to four blocks at night calmly, and I don't walk into any black people; I feel safe. It is safer than in Washington [DC], it is more peaceful, like she said. And where I live I can leave the door open, I can be in the yard and I can sleep in the yard if I wanted to; but not in Washington [DC]. I lived in Washington for five years, so I am telling you the truth. It is much safer here, less expensive, less smoke, more security for everyone. I have been here for ten years. Well, I have only lived in two places, in Washington [DC] and in Maryland. And the place that I have liked the best has been Maryland. I have been and seen other states, but where I live, here in Maryland, is very secure.

A Montgomery County Latina voiced similar concerns that extended to the comparison of Prince George's County and Montgomery County public schools:

FEMALE: When we were starting to figure out where we were going to go between those two [counties], we realized, of course, because of the schools, the type of the people that live in Montgomery County were really different from the people who live in PG county. So that was one of the factors that we took into account when we decided to go to Silver Spring [Montgomery County], like the stores, the restaurants, and everything is really different from PG County.

MODERATOR: When you say the people were different, exactly what do you mean?

FEMALE: I don't know. For me, it seems there was a lot more, the ones from Hyattsville on over, there are a lot of black people, and you don't see as many in Montgomery County. And it changes because also in the schools it's the same thing. My little girl was at a PG County school and had a lot of problems with them, and I did everything I could to get her over to a Montgomery County school.

MODERATOR: When you say problems with them, are you talking about that ethnic group?

FEMALE: Yes, also the teachers. We didn't have the same communication with them as we have now in the schools. It's a much better situation.... With my little girl and with my family, I have experienced racism. We've tried to avoid those places; we prefer to go to Rockville or Gaithersburg [in Montgomery County], even though they are so far, because we feel like we're going to be treated better.

The views of these Latino respondents raise questions about interethnic relations in suburban DC and the consequences of increasing physical proximity among some racial/ethnic groups. Blacks and Latinos have a shared history of discrimination in education, housing, and the labor market. Some scholars would contend that such commonalities may strengthen the prospects for coalition building, while others would suggest that they promote an atmosphere of contempt and competition between the two groups. For example, Bobo and Hutchings (1996) find that low-income minorities tend to see themselves as in competition with other minority groups. McClain and collaborators (2006) find that blacks view Latinos much more favorably than Latinos view blacks, and that there is a higher prevalence of negative stereotypes of black Americans among the Latino immigrant community than among whites.[5] Frasure-Yokley and Greene find there are multiple and often conflicting considerations regarding, for example, blacks' views toward proposed undocumented immigration policies (2013, p. 107). Blacks with lower levels of income are more likely to reject punitive policies such as deportation, while blacks who hold negative racial stereotypes about Latinos are more likely to favor punitive policies. However, attitudes about racial identity and perceived commonality with Latinos are important influences on blacks' views. They contend, "One the one hand, a shared history of marginalization might bring Blacks and Latinos together on common issues, especially if policies are seen as racially targeted. On the other hand, the perpetuation of persistent stereotypes could derail these efforts" (p. 107).

Price and Singer find that tension occasionally emerges between blacks and Latinos in Prince George's County over police enforcement of anti-loitering ordinances and restrictions against informal food vendors (*pupusa* trucks or fruit vendors, for example) (2008, 150). They also report that many immigrants in Prince George's County – which remains largely governed by black leaders – are frustrated by the lack of immigrant-related services and have expressed a need for a multicultural center to serve the immigrant population, like those found in Montgomery County.

According to a 2009 *New York Times* article, racial conflict cost Prince George's County a center for Latin American youth. The Roman Catholic

[5] The majority of Latino immigrant respondents felt they had the most in common with whites (78.3 percent) and the least in common with blacks (52.8 percent); meanwhile 49.6 percent of blacks reported feeling they have more in common with Latinos.

Archdiocese of Washington offered to build a $12 million service complex housing a church, clinic, gym, and youth center. However, the proposed site was occupied by a reportedly "foundering," predominantly black Boys and Girls Club whose club leader objected to the plans on the basis that "Latinos were trampling the rights of black youth." In 2006, the youth center eventually opened in a small, nondescript office suite in the county, under the name Maryland Multicultural Youth Center, rather than as the Latin American Youth Center (DeParle, 2009).

Black Respondents

Most black focus group participants resided in Prince George's County and a few in Montgomery County. Black discussants reported moving to Prince George's County for an overall lower cost of living, affordable housing, employment opportunities, and closeness to local institutions such as their church. Despite media and popular images of Prince George's as an elite, prosperous, black suburb, most residents, particularly blacks, would *prefer* to live elsewhere in the metropolitan area, such as Montgomery or Fairfax Counties, but cannot because of a lack of affordable housing in those counties. They verbalized the trade-offs of residing in Prince George's County rather than Montgomery or Fairfax Counties. Interestingly, black respondents focused less on racial tensions and more on their dissatisfaction with the lower-quality goods and services in terms of the perceived inferior public school system in Prince George's, as well as the retail shopping options, the service sector, and increasing neighborhood safety concerns – particularly when compared with neighboring Montgomery or Fairfax Counties.

A black Prince Georgian man, originally from DC, commented: "The past couple years, the people that have moved in are younger, more kids, noisy, loud, destructive, walk around ... smoking joints. Dropping trash, just don't care. And I'm constantly like, what's going down? ... Now it's just like I'm living in Southeast [DC]."

A black woman from Kentucky, who described her neighborhood as predominantly black, echoed concerns about neighborhood safety: "I get off the bus and I go directly into my apartment. But every night I swear I hear gunshots going off.... I always used to think 'maybe that's just cars backfiring' and that would be it, but they really are bullets.... But it's weird because I'm thinking I'm gonna hear something about this on the news or something. And that stuff does not get played on the news. It's just my little community or whatever." In short, the black focus group reveals that prosperity is very unevenly divided, depending on one's neighborhood in Prince George's County, and significant class disparities exist across the black population.

The finding that blacks' spatial location choices within the metropolitan DC area (e.g., Prince George's versus Montgomery County) continue to be constrained by income is important. Financial constraints can reinforce patterns of black segregation and the associated negative implications such as lower-quality goods and services (e.g., public education), and increasing social problems such as crime (Charles, 2003; Logan & Schneider, 1982).

Chinese, Korean, and Iranian Respondents

The Chinese, Korean, and Iranian focus groups were conducted in Fairfax County, largely among residents residing in this county. Most Chinese respondents resided in majority-white and Asian neighborhoods. The Koreans' neighborhoods contained a more balanced mix of Latinos and Iranians, but very few black families. Most respondents noted they rarely saw black people in their neighborhoods.

The homeownership rate and median value of owner-occupied housing units in Fairfax County are slightly higher than in Montgomery County (see Table 2.2). Yet affordable housing seemed to pose less of a spatial location constraint for these groups than for blacks or Latinos. Instead, family ties and often the desire to live close to people of their own ethnic groups more directly influenced their residence decision. One Iranian man explained that he followed family members who moved to the United States: "in Iran the path to success was paved with either thievery or payoffs, otherwise there was no way to succeed. So for that reason they [his family] sold all their possessions and made their way over here [to the United States]." An Iranian woman who followed her husband to the United States articulated another common immigrant experience. Her family moved to the United States to give the children more educational opportunities, and moved to Fairfax County because they had extended family members and friends already living in the area. The extended family, in turn, helped them to get established in their new country. Another Iranian man, pleased with his location decision, shared his reasons for choosing Fairfax County:

MALE: Fairfax County is one of the best counties to live in because of the services it provides, ranging from education, from police, from fire and rescue to health. Most people who reside here are from a higher income bracket than people from other areas; at the same time they have a higher education level and their lifestyle is more affluent. They are better able to understand and accept others who are of different backgrounds than themselves, especially of foreigners or people who look like foreigners. I think that moving to Fairfax County is one of the best things we have ever done – although we did not purposely move to here. It was just one of the best coincidences.

Another Iranian woman described her immigration decision and residential satisfaction within the larger context of better life opportunities for women in the United States than in Iran:

FEMALE: I'm happy here because of all the opportunities to improve one's life if they choose to do so; especially when you compare all the obstacles to succeed in other places like Iran, for women. By coming to America I have been able to complete my education and pursue many of my interests. My options have not been limited. Also in Iran, if you wanted to go to universities or good job opportunities then you had to go to a major city, whether it was Tabriz, Tehran, Esfahan, or Shiraz. But another benefit of living here in Fairfax County is that there are major universities ... and numerous job opportunities. You are not limited because you are not in the inner/ major city limits.

Most Korean, Chinese, and Iranian discussants were pleased with their current living situation in Fairfax County. All three groups perceived great differences between Fairfax County and Montgomery and Prince George's Counties, particularly with regard to public schools and public safety. Among these groups, some areas in Maryland were stereotyped as a very dangerous place to live, as an Iranian man stated:

MALE: The safety in Virginia is much greater than Maryland, without a doubt. There are some areas in Maryland that you can say without a doubt are slowly becoming as dangerous as the worst areas in Washington, DC. But Virginia, especially Fairfax, is really under police control. Their presence is felt everywhere you go, even in the neighborhoods where the minorities reside and there is a higher incidence of crime. Even those neighborhoods are still under police control.

This respondent offers an interesting perspective. He seems to be associating criminal activity with minorities and therefore dissociating himself from a minority identity. Other discussants had greater reservations about recent demographic changes in their neighborhoods. Some indicated that if possible, they would move, as an Iranian woman conveys:

FEMALE: Can I be honest? My neighborhood used to be more diverse but it changed in the last five years. The area is now called Little Korea. I don't have a problem with that except that so many of them live three to four families in a single townhouse. I know they are used to that type of living, but I think it's unclean. I don't understand how the county allows them to get away with that. Many of our previous neighbors have sold their homes and moved away because of this.

She also conveyed her dissatisfaction that large numbers of cars and trucks were parked on the street and on lawns. Another Iranian female and longtime Fairfax County resident echoed similar concerns:

FEMALE: Oh, God, these people and their work trucks. I live on a block of newly built homes surrounded by older homes. When we first moved there (this was fifteen years ago) our entire neighborhood, we were Americans. Now [I] have an Italian neighbor, an Indian neighbor, and people from other countries as well. I have never had any problems with any of them. But in these past few years Hispanic people have purchased the older houses around the neighborhood. Most of them are good people. But there are some who, like your Korean neighbors, live five families to a small house with ten work trucks. They seem to rent a room to each family. One of them has created two driveways, one on each side of the house, and still parks three to four more cars or trucks on the grass in front of the house. [They removed] the azalea bushes in the front yard and planted corn in their place. I live in the heart of Fairfax County, not on a farm in Central America. I know that they work hard, but so do we. They have no respect for other people or the property value of the local homes. Some weekends they play loud music until the morning, and the lawns are strewn with empty beer boxes and cans.

Overall, these findings suggest that while financial constraints limit suburban location opportunities for some groups, spatial location choices and the satisfaction with these choices are often influenced by racial/ethnic preferences. There seemed to be a sense of elitism, particularly among the Iranian suburbanites. They equate themselves with wealthy white Americans and seemingly resent the signs of working-class life creeping into their neighborhoods. Next, I turn to the demographics of respondents' current neighborhoods, how well they know their neighbors, and whether they engage in formal or informal activities together. Huckfeldt, Plutzer, and Sprague suggest that individuals make location choices "for good reasons on rational grounds, but in the process they also define – even if indirectly and unintentionally – the dimensions of their social experience" (1993, p. 380). Social environments and interactions within the neighborhood social context are likely to influence residents' participation, or lack thereof, in local affairs.

Suburban Neighborhood Interactions

Racial, ethnic, and class-based shifts in the suburban Washington, DC, area also raise several questions regarding the effects of physical proximity among various racial/ethnic groups: How do new neighbors of different cultural backgrounds interact with and perceive their suburban environment, and how are they perceived by out-groups? Respondents reported that lack of time and desire impeded their neighborhood interactions and engagement in activities outside of their immediate families. For many Chinese, Korean, and Iranian (but less so Latino) discussants, language and cultural barriers also curtailed their desire to participate in community activities (language access for Limited English Proficient adults will be discussed in greater detail in Chapter 5). Because of cultural and language barriers, many discussants reported that they did not know how to begin getting involved in community activities. Some of these factors are detailed later.

About half of the Latino respondents stated that they had friendships with their neighbors, and about half reported gathering frequently, both informally and formally. Most acknowledged that these interactions were mostly with other Latino neighbors. In the Latinos' case, lack of time and desire to interact with neighbors unlike themselves, more than language barriers, motivated their disengagement from the broader neighborhood. Latinos' involvement seemed to be largely in their children's school activities (e.g., PTA) or their church.

Most Korean respondents reported engaging in activities with their neighbors but feeling uncomfortable in such situations because of language and cultural barriers. Many would like to get involved in events that affect the entire community, but language barriers deter them. A Korean man recalled his frustration as a new immigrant many years earlier:

MALE: Because I couldn't speak English, when teachers invite[d] the parents to school, I wasn't able to go and participate. That's one of the most regretful things as a parent.

I feel that I couldn't fulfill the responsibility as a parent and feel really sorry to my children. When I first came here, there were not that many Korean kids, in 1974. It is now thirty years ago. There were so many difficult things [that] happened back then because we were Koreans and Asians. If I could have fulfilled the responsibility as a parent and [done] things for school and community, such hardships might not have been so difficult to bear. But because I could not do anything due to lack of English and cultural differences, I was extremely regretful and sorry. Even after we moved here, because we don't speak English so well, only thing that we could say to people was "hi" and "bye." When something happens in our town, neighbors come to us and try to help us out. Even if we understand their willingness to help, we cannot say or communicate with them, and express our gratitude due to lack of language skills. We could only say "that's ok." Especially, the American educational system and environment that our kids grew up [in] contain many things that parents like us could not embrace well. And that's really something that we feel sorry to our children. That's why we cannot balance out well with the community. Also, because there have been already many Chinese and Japanese, people used to make fun of us and call us Chinese or Japanese. So we had to tell them that we are not from China or Japan, but from Korea. But now that our kids are all grown up and we lived here for so long, no such thing happens anymore.

Several Korean participants discussed how cultural differences impeded their interactions with service providers and neighbors, as in this example:

MALE: When Americans visit our house for fixing something, I really cannot understand why they put their shoes on in the house.... I think if the customer wants it, they should do it. I think these Americans do not have such mindset. In Korea, it's so obvious for those workers to take off their shoes and fix whatever they came to fix if the customer asks for it. But these people just leave without doing their job if I ask them to take their shoes off.

Many Iranian discussants also expressed reservations about interacting with their neighbors because of time constraints and a general preference for sharing their free time with people from their own heritage and culture. Some Iranian women pointed out that their activities were limited to what their husbands permitted. Some discussants did, however, agree that children were typically less inhibited by language constraints or perceived cultural biases. The presence of children in the home often forced them to interact with other parents in the neighborhood, as an Iranian male articulated:

MALE: My wife and I are so busy with work, kids, and extended family that we have very little time to socialize with our neighbors. We spend our weekends taking care of errands and tending to the lawn and garden. Having said that, since the kids in the neighborhood all play together, they force us parents to interact with each other. We also have several block parties every year. The entire neighborhood celebrated the Fourth of July together this year with our own fireworks display.... Most of our socialization revolves around activities with our extended families and friends.... It's very important to continue our traditions and make sure our children understand and continue those traditions even though they are growing up in America. I want my children to understand that being Iranian does not just mean being born in a different country or speaking a different language, but that they come from a rich heritage with deep-rooted values and traditions.

The Iranian discussants perceived that their neighborhood interactions and broader relationships with those outside of their ethnic group had become more constrained and adversarial since September 11. Many discussants stated that it had become harder for them to access basic goods and services, much less gain American citizenship. Some discussants shared experiences of discrimination and intimidation that they had not previously shared in public:

MALE: I was in Home Depot one day, and another customer in line kept staring at me angrily. He came over to me and said: "You damn foreigner, go back home." I told him, "I am an American, I'm an American citizen." He said, "Shut up. This is not your home!" … I was so scared. He was huge, a redneck. I put my items down and just walked out. I was shaking from fear by the time I got to my car. I have never told anyone about this before, I was so embarrassed.

Similarly, Iranian respondents felt that government officials, particularly law enforcement officers, discriminated against them more now, and expressed conflicted attitudes about law enforcement as both a vice and a virtue. Some Iranians believed that local police had protected them after the September 11 attacks, whereas others felt that they or someone they knew were targets of undue harassment by local police, the former Immigration and Naturalization Service, or Homeland Security. An Iranian discussant communicated her gratitude for local police presence and protection immediately following the events of September 11:

FEMALE: My husband and I have owned several businesses, oriented to Iranians and other Middle Easterners, in the same shopping center for more than twenty-five years. I was nervous after 9/11 because the large neon sign for our business has the words "Iranian" and "Middle Eastern" written in both Farsi and English. A few days after the attacks, four police officers came into the store. I was nervous at first. The officers asked us if anyone had bothered or threatened us as retaliation for the attacks. We said no, that we were fine. The officers gave us their phone numbers and instructed us to contact them immediately if we had any problems. One of the officers used to come to our restaurant twenty years ago and said that he thought of us immediately and wanted to make sure we were all right. How can I explain what we felt at that moment? We really recognized that we are part of the community here, we are valued.

Discussion

The comments from these focus groups reveal that spatial location decisions were generally influenced by housing and employment opportunities, established family and co-ethnic ties, quality of the public school system, and neighborhood safety concerns. Housing costs posed a significant barrier to some groups aspiring to grasp a piece of the suburban American dream, particularly blacks. Racial/ethnic groups perceived substantial *intra*-metropolitan disparities in housing affordability and delivery of some local public goods and services.

These findings corroborate descriptive statistics for suburban Washington, DC, that underscore persistent racial/ethnic disparities in socioeconomic status and other family/household characteristics, differences that can be masked by the prevailing economic prosperity of some suburban jurisdictions in the metro area, such as (parts of) Fairfax and Montgomery Counties.

Housing constraints persist for some minority groups despite Montgomery County's fair housing ordinances, established in 1973. Montgomery County is often referred to as having the nation's first "inclusionary zoning ordinance" because of its creation of moderately priced dwelling units (MPDUs), designed to establish socioeconomically mixed neighborhoods and school districts.[6] Fairfax County did not adopt comparable affordable housing policies until 1990, nearly twenty years later. These focus group analyses are limited because we do not know whether participants were aware of MPDUs or any other affordable housing programs prior to renting or purchasing their homes. Also unknown is the extent to which affordable housing information is widely distributed, and to what extent it is made available in languages other than English and Spanish.

Moreover, the extent to which discriminatory practices may have played a role in steering some discussants toward renting or buying in specific suburban counties or specific areas within a county is unknown. A recent housing survey by Squires, Friedman, and Saidat concluded that "African American home seekers simply do not enjoy the same opportunities as whites in the metropolitan Washington, DC, area. Their priorities for neighborhood amenities differ from those of whites in part because they are more dependent on the provision of public services due to the fewer private resources they command" (2002, p. 171).[7] Furthermore, African American homebuyers, as compared to whites, are far less likely to obtain their first housing choice. Moreover, if black respondents perceive that they failed to receive their first housing choice because of discrimination, they are less likely than whites to

---

[6] Rusk offers a perspicacious account of Montgomery County's battle to "mix up the neighborhood" through MPDUs. "The level of economic integration is not the result of any progressive business ethic among local developers and builders (although several builders active in Montgomery County have become national champions of mixed-income communities). Montgomery County's neighbors have mixed-income housing because Montgomery County law requires it" (1999, p. 184). He continues, "by law, all new subdivisions in Montgomery County must contain a mix of housing of different income groups: 85 percent market rate (at whatever income levels the developer targets) and 15 percent priced for moderate-income households." Housing developers were rewarded for their compliance with permission to develop at higher densities.

[7] This study compared blacks and whites in metropolitan Washington, DC, including 921 adults (480 from DC and 441 from suburban Maryland and Virginia). The survey solicited responses from individuals about their experiences in searching for homes in metro DC, their satisfaction with their current neighborhoods, their experiences of perceived discrimination in their housing search, and their general racial attitudes.

report these claims to authorities because they believe such efforts would be pointless (p. 171).

These findings support the place stratification theory, which suggests that racial/ethnic factors continue to play a role in determining where an individual resides. In accord with this theory, residential mobility is a reflection of status in the social hierarchy (Alba & Logan, 1993; Logan & Alba, 1993; Logan & Molotch, 1987). Both descriptive statistics and some of the focus group results reveal a persisting social hierarchy by race. Racial/ethnic disparities were especially marked in SES and household demographic characteristics. These findings may imply a multiracial equivalent of white flight as the focus group discussions also exposed some level of racial tension, particularly Latinos having negative opinions of blacks and Iranians having pessimistic views of Koreans and Latinos. For example, to avoid close proximity to blacks, some Latinos reportedly decided to exit predominantly black suburbs in Prince George's County or to avoid moving there altogether. Many Asian participants noted having few if any black neighbors, particularly in Fairfax County.

These findings may also suggest the emergence of new ethnic enclaves in the suburbs and raise concerns about the extent to which multiracial suburbs are in reality racially segregated. This is especially important because, according to Charles, "Whether voluntary or involuntary, living in racially segregated neighborhoods has serious implications for the present and future mobility opportunities of those who are excluded from desirable areas. Where we live affects our proximity to good job opportunities, educational quality, and safety from crime (both as victim and as perpetrator), as well as the quality of our social networks" (2003, pp. 167–168). As Manning observes, "the metropolitan suburbs are not necessarily a panacea for the socio-economic mobility of US minorities. These suburban groups may find their lifestyle aspirations thwarted though segregated communities, job discrimination, and less desirable school districts" (1998, p. 349).

It is clear from these discussions that living in a so-called multiethnic area does not necessarily result in less segregation or isolation, particularly for blacks, whose income levels and housing options constrain their entry into select suburban neighborhoods. Ironically, the prestigious label Prince George's County holds as the wealthiest black county in the nation means little to black residents trapped in low-income rim suburbs just across the DC border. Moreover, Latinos and Asians have failed to embrace this label, adopting an all-encompassing view of Prince George's County as an area of high crime rates, low property values, and underperforming public schools, in contrast to the adjacent Montgomery and Fairfax Counties.

The focus group discussions also gauged what factors influence or deter neighborhood interactions. For some immigrant groups, language and cultural barriers also reportedly impede neighborhood interactions. Discussants also report a lack of time and desire to engage in neighborhood events and activities outside of their immediate families or racial/ethnic compatriots.

While outside the goals of this study, future research should examine the extent to which the lessons learned from the suburban Washington, DC, experience could provide insight into suburbs with growing minority populations. Several questions remain unanswered concerning the responsiveness of suburban Washington, DC, institutions to the influx of immigrant and racial/ethnic minority groups into their jurisdictions. It is very likely that each county has sought or been forced to reallocate local and state funding from one pot to another in efforts to address the needs of recent immigrant and ethnic minority groups. This raises further questions concerning how local suburban institutions negotiate local budgetary constraints and a suburban political environment likely to be averse to a change in the status quo. An important and often understudied component of minority suburbanization is the perceived responsiveness of local government to their needs and concerns. Moreover, the sociology of demographic change and persistent inequality and disparities between suburban areas remain important to consider for understanding the coalitions formed around the public policy concerns explored in Chapters 3–5. The next three chapters attend to these concerns through a reexamination of the political economy approaches used to study local governance, challenging traditional public choice and urban regime theorizations regarding constraints on local politics.

3

Educating Immigrant, Minority, and Low-Income Students in Suburbia

> We've got to do a better job of reestablishing an egalitarian society because this is a fundamental tenet of democracy. Democracy spins from an educated electorate. Well, if most of your electorate is going to be growing by immigrants or children who have historically been deprived of educational opportunities, then you've got to do something about it.
>
> Jerry Weast, Montgomery County Public Schools Superintendent (1999–2011)

For the first time in our nation's history, many suburban public school districts around the country are trending toward majority-minority enrollments, driven in large part by heavy immigration from Latin America and Asia. Yet to date very little research has examined how suburban school districts are responding to these demographic shifts, particularly in light of ongoing budgets cuts in public education and fewer resources from the federal and state levels to fund services for limited English proficient (LEP) adolescents and adults (but see Frasure-Yokley, 2012). This chapter examines such responses in the three counties that are the focus of this volume: Montgomery and Prince George's Counties, MD, and Fairfax County, VA. We know from the focus group findings in Chapter 2 that the perception of a county's delivery of local goods and services, particularly public education, was an influential factor driving residential location decisions for many respondents.

Among large counties nationwide Montgomery County is tied with Howard County, MD, for first in educational attainment, with 30 percent of residents having earned an advanced degree (Montgomery County Planning Department, 2012). Jerry Weast, Montgomery County Public School (MCPS) superintendent from 1999 to 2011, points out that public education remains the dominant local public good in suburban jurisdictions and that demographic changes in the student population are threatening an "unwritten compact" between officials and citizens:

What's really interesting is that while the community knew it was happening [i.e., increasing enrollment of LEP students], they weren't gearing up for it.... What we were doing when we put our administration together five years ago was forcing people to bring to the forefront the issue. The [LEP] issue had been there and had been evolving over a period of time, but there was a fear, in my opinion, of it being brought here, right on the table. The fear was, is that we'll promulgate flight, it will promulgate, have a negative effect on property values and won't have any laudable effect on improving anything but just makes things more confusing.... The problem they had is that from an academic point of view [MCPS] was a strong school system back in the '70s and '80s but had been holding its own for a period of time. With the demographics changing, it became imperative that everybody learned at the high rates. So it was a qualitative issue. That was even more important because the majority of the funding didn't come from the state; it came from the local district.

So the unwritten compact, if you will, is that you come here, there is no large buildings, traffic is not so good, your child gets a good education, and in return for that good education they will contribute to keep the system strong and viable in wages of teachers, etc. Now that compact was going to be threatened if you had an increasing number of African Americans [who] were born in Africa and many other places, an increasing number of Hispanics.... Africans and Hispanics were not scoring at the level that the Whites and Asians were.

Weast's comments speak directly to the contradiction between redistributing scarce funding and other resources to address the needs of a growing and disproportionately lower-income constituency while maintaining the unwritten compact that MCPS will provide a quality education to children of middle- to upper-income suburban voters. Public choice theorists would argue that explicitly serving LEP students whose parents are unlikely or ineligible to vote would induce flight among the district's long-standing, relatively wealthy constituents, who remain the primary revenue generators through property taxation. As Weast acknowledges, local decision makers' reluctance to confront the issue in his district was rooted exactly in this fear. Yet LEP and other programs to service immigrants and ethnic minorities are being expanded, although unevenly, in some jurisdictions. The reasons why warrant further examination.

Keeping the Social Compact through Social Investment

The logic of educating immigrant, minority, and lower-income children seemingly moves beyond the long-standing dichotomies in the urban politics literature of tradeoffs between equality and efficiency and economic growth and redistribution. Rather than redistribution being a nonissue, many of the elected, appointed, and nonprofit leaders I interviewed expressed a need for social investment in the future of children – regardless of their immigration status – as a positive investment in the future of their suburban counties. Following Stone, "social investment refers to programs for children and youths, ranging from prenatal care and early childhood education to after-school and youth-development programs" (2011, p. 125). Stone points to the assumptions inherent in this paradigm:

Social investment means that a current civic generation provides for coming generations through some form of collective action. First, this means politically that public and civic effort has to prevail over free-rider calculations. Second, it involves deferring to a future outcome that may be less than certain. The politics of social investment thus means something quite different from reliance on market efficiency to meet our needs. It calls for the construction of a set of political relationships capable of dealing with both a need for collective support and the risk of future uncertainty. (p. 127)

Not surprisingly, topics such as bilingual education remain contentious in suburban counties. Nor are actors who promote policies to help close the academic achievement gap necessarily altruistic. In fact, given local and state mandates, coupled with the economic downturn and the new political economy of fiscal austerity, many leaders were quite instrumentally oriented and deliberate in their goals to invest in poor-performing schools, which disproportionately serve minority and low-income children, as a local public good for the county as a whole (Jones-Correa, 2008).

The social investment initiatives described in this chapter, such as early childhood education and ESOL, faced several challenges, in particular the disconnection between policy time and political time (Stone, 2011, p. 128). "Political time" is inherently short term and keeps leaders focused on putting out the day-to-day fires at the local level and on seeking reelection or reappointment. The prospective long-term but not immediately apparent benefits of social investment initiatives require a reorientation to the longer time frame of "policy time." Stone further suggests that the "political feasibility of social investment is profoundly affected by the fragmented structure of metropolitan regions. With their highly uneven distribution of well-off and disadvantaged households, metropolitan regions make stand-alone municipalities ill suited for the pursuit of social investment. A large concentration of wealthy families provides a strong tax base but an electorate little disposed to support the policy aim. A concentration of poor people provides a supportive constituency but a weak tax base" (p. 141).

Jones-Correa (2008) examined several factors that may explain changes in education policy in suburban Washington, DC. He identified four factors external to the public schools – electoral politics, federal/state mandates, court decisions, and budgetary constraints – as well as two that are internal to the public school system – the interests of professionals such as ESOL teachers, and the role of professional norms (Jones-Correa, 2008). Each of these important factors influenced the policy responsiveness of school officials to rapid demographic change. He found, however, that with the exception of professional norms, none was sufficient to explain the direction in policy change toward expending greater resources on ESOL students. Instead, "the evidence pointed to bureaucratic norms and administrators' own ethos as being the key factors behind redistributive policy change" and further that "the language they used to describe their own positions in favor of redistribution are purely normative" (p. 318).

I agree with Jones-Correa's assessment, however, I argue that the relationships among suburban institutional actors are structured in ways that go beyond ideology and bureaucratic norms alone, and that the ways they are structured helps us understand, among other things, how public-nonprofit partnerships are necessitated, maintained, or dismantled through the development and implementation of policies to foster greater educational opportunities for immigrant, minority, and low-income children. For example, Frasure-Yokley's research in suburban Orange County, CA, public schools underscores the complexity of issues facing school districts that are, for example, borderline or that recently transitioned to majority-minority status (2012, p. 89). The study highlights the many ways administrators and school districts are far from autonomous institutional actors in suburbia. Suburban educational actors operate under conditions of severe budget cuts and scarce resources and amid internal and external pressures to adhere to several state (Prop. 209 dismantling bilingual education in California) and federal mandates (No Child Left Behind Act of 2001). Administrators must find common ground and a method of developing and implementing programs and policies to address an out-migration of the white student population and a subsequent in-migration of low-income, minority, and recently arrived immigrant students to their district schools.

Similarly, Marschall, Rigby, and Jenkins examined school-level responses to English-only laws (1987–2004), finding that the "enactment of English Only law reduces the likelihood that schools offer native language instruction and increases the likelihood that they either rely strictly on ESL methods or provide no special instruction for ELL students at all" (2011, p. 602). Their findings also "support a bureaucratic notion of control in which school-level agents identify as policymakers themselves ... Yet, this role is more constrained when state policy specifically targets the behavior of local actors (in this case educators), while state policies that are more vague in scope seem to allow room for street-level bureaucrats to interpret the policy in different ways to justify different efforts at implementation" (p. 605).

In this chapter, I show that suburban institutional interdependency (SII) (see Chapter 1) eases the burden of redistribution of resources in K–12 public education and helps to pave the way toward long-term social investments in suburban children and families. I examine the extent to which the SII model explains the development or implementation of educational policies and programs to foster the incorporation of immigrant and low-income minority children and families, focusing on two quite comparable public school districts, Montgomery County and Fairfax County, with some limited demographic comparisons to the nearby, predominantly black schools in Prince George's County, which are also seeing rising immigration. I draw on twenty-seven (out of 114) face-to-face, semi-structured, in-depth interviews conducted in suburban Washington, DC, with school board officials, administrators, PTA leaders, and other related education actors, as well as on quantitative data for the metro area's local public school systems and county governments.[1]

To set the context, I first review socioeconomic and demographic characteristics of public school students in the three counties of interest. Then, I examine the extent to which the SII model explains the development or extension of LEP programs and policies, focusing predominantly on Montgomery County, Maryland, and Fairfax County, Virginia, public schools, with limited comparisons to Prince George's County, Maryland, schools.

Student Demographics for the Three County School Districts

Fairfax County Public Schools (FCPS), Montgomery County Public Schools (MCPS), and Prince George's County Public Schools are referred to as the three "national capital" districts. Each is located in an "inner suburb" of the District of Columbia metropolitan region. All three districts are large, MCPS being the largest district in Maryland (141,722 students), followed by Prince George's County (127,039 students). FCPS is the largest district in Virginia, enrolling more than 175,000 students in 2009–2010 (see Table 3.1). It boasts a graduation rate of 91 percent, and more than 94 percent of graduates intend to pursue postsecondary education. The graduation rates in the MCPS and Prince George's County districts are nearly ten points lower than for FCPS, but are actually among the highest in Maryland.

MCPS is the most diverse of the three districts. Whites make up the largest proportion of the student population, at 38 percent, followed by blacks and Latinos at a little less than 25 percent each, and Asians at 15 percent (Maryland State Department of Education, 2010). Prince George's County Public Schools are, like the county population, majority black, at nearly three-quarters of enrolled students. The demographics have shifted rapidly in the past decade, however, as the Latino student enrollment in the school system has more than tripled, from about 7,000 students a decade ago to 23,683 students (20 percent) by 2008. White, Asian, and Native American students together constitute less than 10 percent of the student enrollment in Prince George's County. Remarkably, the two Maryland school districts, Montgomery and Prince George's, enroll 68.8 percent of the total LEP student population for the entire state of Maryland public school system (Maryland State Department of Education, 2010).

Underscoring the findings from Chapter 2, in addition to the variation in racial diversity, there is also substantial variation across the counties in terms of poverty. In Prince George's County 53 percent of students qualify for free or reduced-cost meals, compared to only 22 percent of students in Fairfax County.

---

[1] The author conducted these interviews together with Michael Jones-Correa of Cornell University and Junsik Yoon of George Washington University.

TABLE 3.1. *Student Population Statistics for Targeted School Districts, 2009–2010 School Year*

	Fairfax	Montgomery	Prince George's
Student Population			
Overall enrollment	175,296	141,722	127,039
Black	10.4%	23.2%	72.2%
American Indian/Alaska Native	3.0%	0.3%	0.4%
Asian/Pacific Islander	18.8%	15.6%	3.1%
Hispanic/Latino	18.1%	22.7%	19.6%
White	45.3%	38.1%	4.6%
Free/reduced meals	22.2%	30.7%	52.7%
English learners	12.1%	13.0%	10.7%
Average cost per pupil	$12,597	$14,969	$13,183
Graduation rate	91.2%	83.1%	84.4%
Graduates attending postsecondary programs (2009)	94.5%	92.8%	82.6%

Sources: Fairfax County Public Schools Statistics, 2009–2010; and Maryland State Department of Education Fact Book 2009–2010.

Montgomery County is in the middle, with 30 percent of students qualifying. The cost per pupil, or the funds spent on public education in relation to the number of students enrolled in school, is highest in Montgomery County (nearly $15,000), followed by Prince George's County (around $13,000), then Fairfax County ($12,500). Surprisingly, Fairfax County has the highest graduation and postsecondary education rates despite having the lowest average cost per pupil.

Whereas Fairfax and Montgomery Counties have proved willing to accept increasingly diverse immigrant populations, some counties farther from the District of Columbia have seemingly thrown up their hands. In Prince William County, which borders Fairfax County in Virginia, local leaders have started a "movement to deny some public services to illegal immigrants and to require police to check the immigration status of crime suspects thought to be in the country illegally" (Chandler, 2008). As a result hundreds of immigrant families have moved out, resulting in a 760-student drop in LEP enrollment in 2008. County records reveal that most of those students moved to other Virginia school systems, and Fairfax County received 623 LEP transfer students from Prince William (up from 241 in 2007).

Suburban Institutional Interdependency (SII) in Public Education

Issues of race, class, and growing inequality, already present in many suburban DC school districts, make limited English proficient (LEP) instruction in public schools an increasingly sensitive issue for school district leaders because of the widespread public perception that many recipients of these services are

undocumented or the children of undocumented parents and therefore undeserving of tax-funded services. Dan Domenech, FCPS superintendent from
1998 to 2004, commented on how he addressed the bilingual education issue
by, in essence, disguising it:

The word *bilingual education* is still not utterable in Fairfax County. So, I said, "Fine."
But I learned that we had some outstanding language immersion programs – which
are bilingual education, except that unlike the traditional bilingual education program
that's geared to the language-minority child, the language immersion program is seen
as an enrichment program, almost a [gifted] program for American kids who want to
speak a second language. [They] will be taught in that language and, in this case, it's
French, it's German, it's Japanese, and it's Spanish. Well, we used that opportunity to
take the Spanish component of that and create dual-language programs where we've
provided many of our Spanish-speaking students the opportunity to learn in Spanish
with their American counterparts who were learning Spanish while they continued to
learn English. We extended that program to the kindergarten level, and we have a number of dual-language kindergartens in the district, which are doing very well, and we're
still not calling it bilingual education.

Later in the interview Domenech describes the process of funding and creating parent buy-in for the dual-language program:

The strategy for implementing those programs was a carefully crafted one because it
meant that we had to divert resources within the school system. We weren't getting
any more money from state, federal, or county sources. So, to do these things, we in
essence had to reallocate resources to take [them] from one area to put it where they
were needed.... Our ESOL [English for Speakers of Other Languages] program has
expanded dramatically, as has dual-language and full-day K [kindergarten]. To do
all of these things, we in essence have to convince the community that in order for
Fairfax County to remain as a world-class organization and to have the average student perform ... we in essence had to bring the bottom up.

The kids who were the traditional white, middle-class community in Fairfax were going to
continue to perform wonderfully, but ... if one of the extremes moves, then that will either
bring your average up or down. In this case, the top wasn't going to go any higher, but the
bottom was definitely going to fall, and that was going to bring the average performance
of our students really down unless we shored up the bottom.... It's really by doing that,
that today's Fairfax County students have the highest academic achievement scores ever.

In the school system we have the highest SAT scores, highest performance in Advanced
Placement International Baccalaureate, highest performance on Stanford 9s, SOLs,
whatever measure we can use, and that was simply a matter of taking our at-risk population of students and addressing their needs so that their performance would increase....
The community bought into that concept, some of them more willingly than others.

When asked how he persuaded people to take this path in a politically conservative county that generally opposes tax increases and redistribution, he
commented,

I did a lot of political head banging. Some of the politicians, if not all of the politicians,
in this area will tell you that I had no business ... doing what I was doing. In essence,

what I was doing ... was being a very vocal advocate on behalf of the schools and I was basically using my role as a community leader to ... get the parent community, the business community, the staff from the school system to exert political pressure on our elected officials to free up as much money from county and state levels as I possibly could.... So, every year I squeezed them for every penny I could get out of them, and they don't like that. They didn't like it then, and they don't like it now, and they're probably not very sorry to see me go.

Because the school budget remained more or less constant during his tenure, Domenech was forced to reallocate funds from one area to another. When asked if he encountered resistance from schools or parents at more privileged schools, he replied,

Yes, I did get some of that, although not beyond just the grumbling, never organized. It was always the occasional remark at board meetings or letters to the papers, etc., that, well, here at Great Falls while we are paying all of these taxes, our roofs are leaking and we don't have the new computers and we don't have all these wonderful things that Domenech is putting into all those other schools. They were right. They didn't. But those kids were coming to us from homes that these other kids could only dream of. Those kids were coming to us with a background and preparation that these kids would never have. And, so, yes, we are diverting resources from your kids and from your schools but, you know, when the quality of education in Fairfax County starts to slide, the first ones that are going to put their homes up for sale to get out is going to be you folks, because these other kids have no place to go. They are here. They don't have much choice. So the quality of the education that everyone is getting and the quality of these schools is dependent on our ability to do what we do. And, so, that worked.

Montgomery County Superintendent Jerry Weast faced similar challenges and became both celebrated and reviled for his sweeping responses to demographic change in his district. Since the late 1990s, the English language learner population increased 103 percent and the free- or reduced-lunch population increased 44 percent. Soon after he took office in 1999, Weast and his administration hired demographers to divide the MCPS into zones. After reviewing the demographic data in the district, Weast stated, "A big blind spot that we uncovered is that when we put all of our students on a map of our county – we are about a million strong in the county and about 141,000 students – we found that there was a defined territory where 80 percent of our students on free and reduced lunch and about 75 percent of our minority children lived. It comprised an area with about 67,000–70,000 students, which would make it one of the top sized school systems in America if it were a stand-alone system" (2009) (also see Childress, Doyle, & Thomas, 2009; Childress & Goldin, 2009; Mapp, Thomas, & Cheek, 2006a, 2006b). The result was a map dividing the district into a majority-white, middle- to upper-class "green zone" to the west and a red zone disproportionately made up of black and Latino lower-income students to the east (see Figure 3.1). Many of the red zone schools were failing to meet both district and state academic achievement standards, whereas

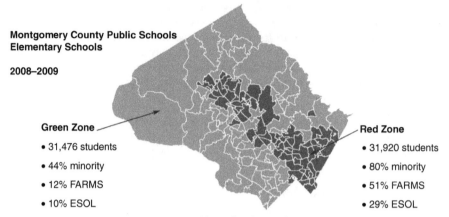

FIGURE 3.1. Montgomery County Public Schools "Red Zone/Green Zone" Map. *Source:* Montgomery County Public Schools. "FARMS" refers to free and reduced meal students.

most of the green zone schools were flourishing and were largely labeled high performing. During my interview with Weast he affirmed,

But what was really astounding, and we unveiled this over a three-year period, and now it's fully unveiled, this represents 75 percent of all of the minority kids in the elementary schools ... close to 85 percent of all the kids who don't speak English, and it represents 70 or more percent of all racial group diversity. Interesting, there's 20 some percent of this population in this [zone] that is Caucasian, but over 60 percent of the Caucasians [live] in poverty. So it's poor. It's diverse. It's mobile. They talked about mobility, where is the mobility? It moves around right in the same area. Then ... they talk about it hitting everywhere but [when] you map it out and put it on a GIS system and circumscribe it, you're going to find the density of poverty, the density of diversity, the density of language difficulty, even the mobility, it's all like in the same areas and it makes sense because that's where your wrinkles are. It makes sense because that's where your transportation routes are. It makes sense because that's where your clinics are and that's where their services are available.

Weast's administration set out to target additional resources for the red zone schools. His focus on minority achievement foreshadowed the 2001 No Child Left Behind Act. The targeted efforts started with the Early Success Performance Plan, which implemented full-day kindergarten beginning with the red zone schools and then in all MCPS elementary schools. Elementary schools in the red zone also received a class size reduction to a student-teacher ratio of fifteen to one. Then red zone schools added after-school and summertime extended learning opportunities from kindergarten through fifth grade. The four-week summer program included four hours of instruction each day, transportation to and from school, free meals for students, and continuing ESOL classes for LEP students (Childress et al., 2009; Marietta, 2010). Weast certainly received pushback from the parents in the green zones, but responded with an egalitarian logic:

If you came in to me and said, "Look, I'm a big-time taxpayer, my kid is 1 to 23 in a kindergarten, and you don't pay much taxes and you just got off the boat and your kids are going 1 to 15 all day. Don't you get it who votes and who doesn't, here, Jerry?" My answer would be back, "Yes, I get who votes and who doesn't and I know you do, but let me tell you, do you get it what your property value is based on? It is based on MCPS' quality, not just your individual child's quality. Have you lost all of your egalitarian feelings for everybody and do you not understand this little mathematical equation called Simpson's paradox[2] and aren't you willing to help put a blunt on some of the urbanization of your county by lifting people before it becomes too late?" ... So we just worked on it. People supported it. They voted board members in that supported the initiatives and we've been successful in keeping them pushing for five years now.

Since 2000, the share of black students in the red zone who graduate with a passing score on at least one advanced placement test has doubled, and the percentage-point gap in reading pass rates for black and white students has narrowed from thirty-two points to fourteen. During his tenure, countywide SAT scores also increased substantially (Birnbaum, 2010a). After implementing these sweeping changes, the district has improved the proportion of third graders reading proficiently/at grade level or above to 88.9 percent and lowered its third grade reading achievement gap between red and green zones by twenty-nine percentage points. The number of students taking at least one advanced placement exam increased from 25 percent to 61.5 percent – two and a half times the national average. At the start of his administration, Weast set a goal of 80 percent of students being college ready by 2014 as determined by an ACT score of 24 or a combined SAT score of 1650 or higher. This goal was already nearly achieved by 2009, when 77 percent of all graduating high school seniors enrolled in college.

During his twelve-year tenure Weast focused on closing the achievement gap between the red and green zones. Of course much work remains to be done. Although MCPS's graduation rates are among the highest in the nation, the disparity in graduation rates by racial/ethnic group remains stark. Graduation rates are still lower for blacks (84 percent) and Hispanics (78 percent) than for whites and Asians (95 percent) (de Vise, 2009).

Arguably, Weast lasted through three terms by forging alliances with school board members, employees, and a wide array of elected official leaders. Observers claimed he "transform[ed] staff meetings into hand-holding motivational sermons, spinning stories with a Midwestern twang and evangelical zeal" (de Vise, 2009). He established a close relationship with the teachers' union and established a peer-review system by which the school system identified struggling teachers, then worked with the union to either help them improve or dismiss them (de Vise, 2009). On the flip side, his

[2] Wagner (1982) "Simpson's Paradox in Real Life." *The American Statistician*, 36(1), 46–48.

detractors saw him as narrowly focused and unwilling to compromise or to work with other constituencies, particularly those representing special-needs populations or the gifted and talented (the last being highly unusual for a suburban county).

Superintendents Domenech and Weast provided strong leadership that drove changes in the bureaucracies of their school districts, but they could not develop or implement such changes alone. Each actor needed to build local partnerships to accomplish their goals. School officials built community support by holding language-specific parent outreach meetings, hiring parent liaisons with fluency in specific languages, and outsourcing to community-based organization leaders to defray some of the cost of disseminating information about school and district programs to LEP parents. The next section illustrates the interdependent local public-private–nonprofit relationships that developed among school officials, parents, local organizations, and business leaders to address the needs and concerns of LEP, minority, and low-income children and parents.

Interdependency Increases Access to Resources

Forming partnerships gives CBOs access to programmatic funding and resources available in the public sector. A primary incentive for suburban nonprofits to form interdependent relationships with local government agencies and officials is the latter's access to resources. CBOs often rely not only on direct funding from local governments, but also on institutional resources that government agencies control (e.g., meeting spaces, photocopiers, materials) that can reduce their overhead costs. In MCPS, as Superintendent Weast and his administration worked to develop (financially and politically) low-cost avenues to provide resources to underperforming schools disproportionately populated by ESOL students, they reached out to various organizations for support. A few of the public-nonprofit partnerships are highlighted here, in brief, to provide a sense of the kinds of nonprofits receiving public support.

The Ed Bohrer Parent Resource Center, housed in a trailer behind Gaithersburg Elementary School, is an example of the services that resulted. In 2003 the mayor of Gaithersburg, Superintendent Weast, and a host of other leaders recognized the center for its local service delivery to the immigrant community. Bohrer is a long-standing collaboration between MCPS, the nonprofit Family Services Inc., the City of Gaithersburg, Montgomery College, and the Barbara Bush Foundation for Family Literacy. It offers basic literacy classes in Spanish and English, adult ESL classes, basic computer skills, citizenship classes, and parenting skills workshops. It also provides services and referrals in English and Spanish, including interpretation and translation services (e.g., for parent-teacher conferences); advocacy for families and individuals; clothing; food and furniture programs; counseling and mental health referrals; legal assistance referrals; and medical, dental, and eye clinic referrals. All of these services are offered free of charge to the public, regardless of immigration status.

In 2002 the mayor of Gaithersburg and the city council authorized the city manager to provide additional services at the Ed Bohrer Parent Resource Center in the relatively small sum of $20,724 in conjunction with the Montgomery County Public School system. These funds were expended from the city council's operating budget. Also in 2002, the City of Gaithersburg in partnership with the MCPS received a third consecutive year of funding for the Even Start Grant Program from the Maryland State Department of Education to serve low-income families of the Gaithersburg community by providing family literacy, parenting classes, and early childhood education at the Ed Bohrer Parent Resource Center. The city council adopted a resolution that authorized the city manager to execute a memorandum of understanding (MOU), which provided the city with funds in the amount of $96,238 expended from the city's operating budget through the Maryland State Department of Education Grant (City of Gaithersburg, 2002). In 2004, the center also received a $30,000 grant from the Montgomery County Department of Health and Human Services to continue its programming (City of Gaithersburg, 2004).

Another nonprofit organization, called Identity, was established in 1998 to serve Latino youth (both immigrant and native born) in the Washington, DC, metropolitan area. After opening a branch in Montgomery County in 2003, Identity collaborated with MCPS to provide an after-school and evening program for youth and their parents in about a dozen schools located in heavily Latino areas, with the schools allowing use of their space free of charge. MCPS Board of Education member Gabriel Romero also serves on the board of Identity. Romero was one of the first ESOL students to graduate from MCPS in 1976 and believes the MCPS-Identity partnership is vital in supporting the growing population of Latino youths in Montgomery County.

Linkages to Learning is another collaborative initiative among MCPS, the Montgomery County Department of Health and Human Services, and private community-service providers. It was developed in 1991 to address the complex social and mental health needs of the increasingly diverse, transient, and impoverished population in Montgomery County. The program provides social and mental health services to thousands of families at twenty-five schools and centers. The initiative provides a variety of programming for at-risk children and their families, including counseling, health care, education, tutoring, and mentoring. The programs at Linkages to Learning aim to provide the basic necessities families require for their children to succeed in school (e.g., food, housing, and health care). In addition, some services are geared to immigrants, such as translation, assistance with completing financial and medical assistance forms, and community outreach and prevention programs. The organization also provides adult ESOL and literacy classes. Linkages to Learning facilities are provided by MCPS on a 50/50 cost-sharing basis with Montgomery County. MCPS provides these facilities rent free and also pays for utilities and custodial care. With its placement of centers in school facilities, Linkages to Learning seeks to provide greater access to health and social services and referrals for at-risk children and families who may otherwise not receive or seek such integrated services (MCPS, 2003).

Interdependency Increases Legitimacy and Lowers Transaction Costs

Schools in many districts face similar challenges in reaching out to parents from other languages and cultural backgrounds. More than 140 languages are spoken in school communities in the inner-ring suburbs of these three counties. The size and growth of this population is fed by in-migration from abroad and from other U.S. locations, as well as by children born into linguistically isolated households; that is, households where no one over the age of fourteen is proficient in English (Singer, 2009). Former Montgomery County School superintendent Jerry Weast acknowledged during our interview that "between 30 and 40 percent of the kids who are here [in the Montgomery school district] that don't speak English *actually were born in America*, many of them in this county. Because the communities are so insular, there is no need. They hear Hispanic radio, they stop and go to a Hispanic restaurant, the church is a Spanish-speaking church. There is no need for them to learn English" (emphasis added).

In 2007 Montgomery County Public School District received the highly coveted Magna Award from the National Association of School Boards for its work to improve communication with LEP parents and increase their participation in school activities. In 2006 the district established a unit with four full-time staff members who translate school documents into Spanish, French, Chinese, and Vietnamese. General school information is available in seven languages on the district's Web site. Contract interpreters also are available upon request to assist school personnel during events ranging from parent-teacher conferences to special education assessments to administrative hearings. The school district fulfills more than 5,000 requests for interpreter services annually (Wang, 2009).

Several school administrators interviewed noted that many foreign-born parents do not participate in school activities or contact teachers. In some cultures, parents speak with teachers only if something is wrong. Fairfax County Public Schools board chair Kathy Smith stated, "That's the biggest challenge: cultural differences. People come from different cultures where the parents never got involved in the school. I think one of the best things they've done in Fairfax County is the Parent Liaison Program they have." FCPS's Parent Liaison Program, at a relatively low cost to the school district, provides trained, part-time employees belonging to a variety of cultures, languages, and races. They work to link families to schools by breaking down communication barriers and involving families that otherwise would be unlikely to take part in school activities. The liaisons can also help recent-immigrant and non-English-speaking parents access county programs and resources that they may not know about, orient the family to the school system, and provide information. Simultaneously they familiarize school staff with the student's family and culture. In 2002, MCPS ESOL parent specialist Teresa Wright concurs that "cultural differences can make it appear that parents don't care about their child's education," even though most in fact do value education but do not understand what is required in terms of regular attendance, parent involvement, required courses, and so forth. She continued:

I think it's also my job to partner, to make connections, to network with other agencies, with other people, in order to bring services to their parents. It means I have a very good relationship with the police department; they have a center that's called Community Outreach Division, in which, when I give the workshops, I talk about academics. I talk about how you come and talk to a counselor, to a principal, or whatever, and I talk to them about, for instance, how many credits your kid needs to graduate from high school. And how important it is that they are not absent. Because that's another thing that Hispanic parents do not understand, that right now you cannot go on a vacation and I'm going to go to El Salvador or Mexico or Nicaragua, no, no, no, because you lose the credits.

Another way MCPS addressed this problem with Latino parents was to reach out to the local Catholic church, enlisting the priest's support to hold workshops after Sunday mass "not to talk about religion, but just to talk about education." MCPS also attempted to build similar relationships with community churches of other denominations. As a part of these efforts the Spanish Catholic Center provides services for the poor, at-risk immigrant newcomers, and persons with mental and developmental disabilities. They offer many programs that meet emergency and long-term needs, including medical care and employment training. Four educational resources assist LEP people to learn vital life and work skills: ESL courses focused on teaching conversational and workplace English; the Family and Literacy Program, which supports parents and families in an English-speaking environment; the Spanish literacy program, for native Spanish speakers with limited or no formal education in their home country; and the Bridge Program, which helps nonnative English speakers master English so that they can prepare for higher-paying jobs or further their formal education.

Interdependency Leverages Public Resources

For local school districts, allocating funds to local nonprofits facilitates addressing the needs and demands of a new population by shifting the burden of service provision onto CBOs and in some instances the business community. As school budgets continue to shrink, school districts are also imposing more and more fees directly on students.

One aim of the Education Foundation for Fairfax County Public Schools is to eliminate or defray some of those costs by utilizing the resources of the business community. A partnership of the Fairfax County Chamber of Commerce and FCPS, the Education Foundation is designed to provide educational opportunities and resources to students through school-business partnerships. The foundation connects schools in need to resources in the business community, which donate clothing, school supplies, glasses, and other essentials students' families are unable to provide. In addition, the foundation helps defray the costs of advanced placement and International Baccalaureate exams taken for college credit, and of participating in sports and other extracurricular activities. For low-income families, these additional fees erect barriers to completing the advanced classes and activities necessary for a strong college application. Another foundation activity is to identify potential underrepresented and first-generation college attendees in the seventh grade and offer them college preparatory experiences in partnership with George Mason University.

In Montgomery County, an MCPS collaboration with the nonprofit organization Montgomery County Business Roundtable for Education (MCBRE) was established in 2001. The operating budget in 2003 was $992,000, primarily by grants through the MCPS; only about $200,000 came from participating businesses, which included Lockheed Martin and Marriott International of Bethesda.[3] The MCPS, the nonprofit MCBRE, and the Montgomery County Chamber of Commerce have established "Study Circles" to address racial and ethnic barriers to student achievement and parent involvement. The program brings together parents, teachers, and students from different backgrounds. Trained facilitators guide participants to build relationships, learn about each other's cultures, have honest conversations about race, and develop strategies to help all students succeed. The goals of the program are to give parents information on how to help their children, while giving teachers a greater understanding of the effects of race and culture on teaching and learning. In addition, action teams are formed to address issues raised in the circles. Having a space for dialog and relationship building can be especially valuable in schools and districts undergoing marked demographic shifts. New entrants to the community have a space to address their concerns and build relationships with established community members. Study Circles seek to foster a unified group of diverse parents and teachers who understand the challenges and needs of a diverse school.

Ruby Rubens, a longtime Montgomery County resident and NAACP community organizer, helped to develop Study Circles. She discussed her views on their development and the community's need.

You have self-segregation and the fact that you must begin to understand other people before you can be comfortable and build relationships, build trust, and I think we're beginning to do that.... Study Circles have brought people to the table that have never

---

[3] In 2004, the MCBRE's new executive director, Jane E. Kubasik, began a concerted effort to raise its own funding for the coming fiscal year and to "wean" itself from public school funding; and in turn give businesses a larger role in helping schools prepare students for the workforce (Bond, 2004).

been together before, who never began to understand each other's cultures.... It's affording opportunity, I think, for people of different backgrounds and beliefs and cultures or races of at least having a conversation, getting the dialogue going, and affording a space for that to happen. Until we do that and find out that we are not the enemy, and we are going to have to work at this together if we're going to solve the problems of education, of housing and jobs, and all of that in the economy that it's going to take, and I think that the grassroots efforts are taking some tiny steps. I know we can't deal with the power structure, but I think we can deal with where we live.

Regarding Superintendent Weast's goals in developing the collaboration, Rubens commented: "[Weast] said he wanted the Study Circles to target the so-called 60 low-performance schools, or the schools that could improve. They could improve by, in his view, talking about the issue of race, bringing parents who normally would not be at the table to come." She also openly discussed a variety of perspectives related to the complex issues concerning immigrant newcomers, noting, "So many of the Latino parents say, 'I don't become involved in this and that because I would have been prohibited from doing it in my country. It was just unthought of.' There are cultural reasons why we are not on the same page. There are language reasons. You certainly have the conflict of English only versus having taxpayers' money spent to translate everything and to teach kids in their native language. This is an issue." When asked how she believes the local constituency views providing funding for services directed toward immigrant newcomers, which often entails diverting funds away from other school or community programs, she noted:

Well, I certainly support the ESOL part of it. I support the money because most of our newcomers are taxpayers too. But, I can make a distinction between, and because we look at, say, in my day, growing up in New York we had many, many immigrants in our community. I'll never forget the community that I grew up in, there was an influx of Puerto Ricans at one point. Although they were of American territory and they learned English in school to some extent, they did not speak the language, but they were relatively educated. They were literate, at least, in their own language.

What we're facing today is you're having families and immigrants who are not even literate in their own language. So, that's the dilemma. I certainly, truly believe that if you have a highly literate child in Spanish, that child can be immersed and it's proven. It's been done. Immerse them in English and they will get it. But, for a child who comes here at the age of a ninth grader or eighth grader, with a third-grade literacy level, you certainly have to bring them up to the level of literacy in their own language. I have to believe that that's necessary to do. But that's not to say that there are those who don't see that as a solution.

Well, it's like just about every year in the General Assembly ... you had a bill [proposed] that Maryland is an English-only state. It's failed every year, but it keeps coming back.... So, I think that ... the minority groups, if you will, or those unempowered groups are going to have to partner, they're going to have to collaborate, and they're going to have to become more involved in order to gain that power if they are going to make decisions about their own life because now the same people are making the decisions about my life and your life and the newcomers' life, and they feel they know better.

The Stability and Limitations of Institutional Interdependency in Suburbia

Several factors can limit the stability of public-nonprofit partnerships in the suburban educational arena. Some critics may note that the cases in this chapter are "the cream of the crop" and question whether similar phenomena can be generalized outside the wealthy suburbs of Washington, DC, or without the strong leadership of the superintendents. Indeed, the MCPS budget increased to more than $2 billion during Weast's administration. However, it is unlikely that the vast array of services provided and the number of children and families affected could not have happened by the county acting alone. The outsourcing of scarce resources from state, county, and local budgets to nonprofits helped leaders in the public school system accomplish what none could do acting alone.

Some have also pointed to the unusual stability of MCPS during Weast's twelve-year term (Birnbaum, 2010c). The average superintendent serves only three years before being driven out by school board politics or the teachers' union, or moving to greener pastures in another school district (Birnbaum, 2010c). During Weast's tenure, FCPS had two superintendents, Prince George's County had five, and the District of Columbia had six (de Vise, 2009). On the other hand, building and maintaining relationships with the county executive and council was not always easy for Weast, particularly during fiscal downturns. In 2010, a bitter battle erupted between MCPS and the county council when the district's budget was cut for the first time in memory. Weast and school board members even threatened to sue the county. This dispute severed long-standing bonds between Weast and several council members (Birnbaum, 2010b). Both MCPS district leaders schools garnered numerous accomplishments and awards – Harvard researchers even produced a book and series of policy reports heralding the MCPS district as a model for the nation. Yet, when Weast decided to step down after twelve years, many were ready for new leadership, and the same was true when Domenech departed from his district.

A second limiting factor involves establishing and maintaining coalitions that reach across race, ethnicity, class, and political party (Garcia Bedolla, 2012; Hero, 2005). Numerous local leaders suggested the need to diversify their local PTA and school board memberships and the county council. As FCPS Assistant Superintendent Michael Glascoe commented,

In the old days we used to talk about parent involvement across the board, and to us, parent involvement was, you sat on the PTA, you baked cookies, you showed up for everything. Well, that's not going to happen. You got some parents holding down three jobs and, at the same time, what are the PTAs like in Montgomery County, in Fairfax County? Take a look at the PTAs. What's the makeup? PTAs in these two school systems are white middle-class females. I charge you to go out and find the different ones. It's a clone. It's a closely-knit organization. The soccer moms, if you call it, ... they've got the slate of candidates lined up and they just bore right through....

... We're not user-friendly. We have to figure out ways in which to do that. When I was at Einstein High School, we changed that. It was a battle at first. In fact, a group of my white middle-class parents called it ... reverse discrimination. We had a Hispanic Advisory Council. We had an African American Advisory Council. I said, "You're not going to have these councils unless you have one, two, or three people from those councils who will sit on the regular PTA and report back to the regular PTA and vice versa." They agreed. These two groups became powerful, so powerful that they banded together and had their own slate and crashed the elections and had an African American male as the PTA president for two years, and following him came a Hispanic. After two years, the whole community embraced that whole idea. We became one. It was wonderful. That was the group that came together as a community and painted the interior of the school. You should have seen it. People from all walks of life right there, inside, painting that building because "this is our school, we love it, and this is what we're doing."

MCPS school board member Reginald Felton echoed these sentiments.

If African Americans build their voting bloc, and Asians build their voting bloc, and Hispanics build their voting bloc, and start coming together on two or three major issues, it will be okay. Because they'll have the votes to say, "If you want to be re-elected, we need your support for this." But it's not going to come naturally. It won't [happen] because [of] the goodness of hearts of the politicians, because they want to survive. It's not their heart, it's if you want to be re-elected, these folks vote, these folks don't vote, who I rely on to get re-elected at least will be those who vote.

However, making school boards more diverse is only the first step. As Browning, Marshall, and Tabb remind us, "the concept of political incorporation concerns the extent to which group interests are effectively represented in policy making" (1984, p. 25). What mechanisms do minority school board members have to ensure they are more than symbolic representatives? Does their representation on the board increase responsiveness to minority interests?

Weast stated that the problem is that because voter turnout is lower for minorities than whites in the county politicians do not feel the pressure to extend resources to the needs of this constituency:

[Y]ou've got to remember at the bottom of most political equations is the ballot box, and, so, this group [minority populations], ... I keep visiting with them about getting organized and some of the lessons I've learned from them [about] how difficult it is to get organized because there is nothing monolithic about the Hispanic community, nothing monolithic about the Asian community. The folks will tell you that it's quite open warfare about leadership positions and ... old cultural issues from the old countries and how that really affects things. There's nothing monolithic about the African American community because it comes from all over. And, frankly, there isn't anything monolithic about the Caucasian community either. Everybody has known those things, but they seem to think every other community is monolithic. So when it comes down to paying the bill and providing the access and dealing with things in an equitable way, it's very difficult.

Arguably, in some suburban jurisdictions such factors must be viewed within the context of multiracial coalitions operating in multiracial areas.

Rogers contends that "racial commonalities are not enough to generate an alliance of minority groups; indeed, appeals to racial unity actually may privilege some interests over others and thus heighten divisions among non-White groups. What is more, the institutional design of a city's electoral system may exacerbate these differences. To avoid these perverse effects, political leaders looking to foster race-based alliances must turn to neighborhood and community institutions" (2004, p. 31). Rogers further suggests that community institutions generate an "institutional framework to identify shared issue concerns, acknowledge distinct interests, and generate dialogue" (p. 31).

While many respondents in suburban DC – elected, bureaucratic, and non-profit actors alike – acknowledged the potential mobilizing effects of multiracial group organizing, they asserted that such coalitions, if they are to be efficacious, should operate within a de-racialized, issue-based framework. Interviewees from all camps attempted to divert attention from potentially divisive race-based or immigrant-based issues toward broad issues thought to affect larger (usually voting-eligible) constituencies. MCPS Board Member Felton provides an interesting assessment of how race influences campaigns and electoral outcomes in suburbia:

Well, obviously, there was a major segment in the population, African American as well as non–African American, that realized that there ought to be, that this ought to change. But, of course, when you are there campaigning and you have to campaign countywide, because in Montgomery County, even though we may have districts, the entire county elects you. So you can't say, "Well, I live in the 'hood, and therefore, as long as I get my community to support me, I can win." That's not the case in Montgomery County; you actually have to run countywide. So the strategy obviously was [to] focus on educational issues, and I did that. Secondly, because the county is so large, and because there is at least the perception that there will be people who will not vote for you because you are African American, I used in my artwork, the photographs reflected a diverse group of school-aged kids. So my name was there, [but] the first thing you saw when you picked up the literature was, I think it was, "Because we care about their future" or something like that. So people picked up the material and then, of course, you read the bio and it says NAACP and Howard University, you could figure it out if you wanted to.

Former councilmember Tom Perez noted in our 2004 interview that although he did not receive much support from Montgomery County elites, such as the county executive, he was supported by the teachers' union (which had a large, diverse base), the African American Democratic Club, and the Coalition for Asian Pacific American Democrats. CASA de Maryland could not formally endorse Perez, but many of its members volunteered for his campaign. Motivating his interest in electoral politics is his belief that there needs to be greater inclusion of minorities in county institutions to reflect diverse perspectives during decision making. Perez's goals as a county official always reflected his understanding of Montgomery County's shifting demographics (Perez, interview with the author). When we interviewed him in 2004 Perez stated, "The more I looked at the local electoral landscape, the more evident it was to me that it didn't reflect the new Montgomery County, and our county got sick of hearing people say, 'Well, you know, there really aren't qualified minorities to run.' I don't think that's accurate."

As a member of the county council, Perez pushed for more coalition building between minority and white low-income communities. During our interview, he downplayed division between the county's African American and Latino communities. He dismissed black sentiments that the influx of Latino immigrants in Montgomery County infringes on African American opportunity as well as Latino claims that slots in the Head Start program disproportionately go to black children. Interestingly, Perez noted that much of the tension in Montgomery County politics occurred over language access (not traditionally a black-Latino issue), noting that more than half of Maryland's ESL population resides in Montgomery County. Montgomery County leaders spearhead most statewide immigration-related legislation.

Moreover, he remarked that Latinos in the county were often ignored because politicians assumed most were undocumented. He added, however, that in recent years more Latinos had become citizens and many had registered as independents. He stressed that, unlike African Americans, Latinos in Montgomery County cannot automatically assumed to be Democrats. Still, despite demographic changes, he contended that "the voting demographics ... still don't mirror what the county has become. And that's a huge challenge, and if [you are] looking for reasons why we are where we are it's because that [Latino voting demographics] hasn't caught up yet."

This chapter underscores that administrators like Superintendents Domenech (FCPS) and Weast (MCPS) were the leaders who forced changes in the organizational culture of their education bureaucracies in order to better serve low-income and immigrant children, but that was only the beginning. Sustained partnerships were necessary to bring their goals to fruition. Interdependency breeds a division of labor and resources that facilitates the process of getting things done in the face of tightening budgets. Through information dissemination, building trust, and facilitating norms of reciprocity (classic social capital argument), interdependency can also reduce public resistance to redistribution – by wrapping it in the language of egalitarian principles to some constituents and the language of protecting private property to others. Interdependency of local actors can function as an oversight and monitoring mechanism for feedback and accountability – two factors often missing in the metropolitan fragmented arena of suburban government structures.

4

The Politics of Institutionalizing Day Labor
Centers in Suburbia

The influx of substantial numbers of day laborers into suburban locations poses a new set of policy issues for suburban governments and service providers. Whereas a growing number of sociologists, urban planners, policy makers, and activists have examined the impact and policy implications of this largely immigrant segment of the low-wage workforce (del Carmen Fani, 2005; Espenshade & Calhoun, 1993; GAO, 2002; Gordon & Cornell, 2008; Griffin & Newman, 2007; HPRP & Casa de Maryland, 2004; Maher, 2003; Sassen, 1999, 2000; Waldinger, 1986; Waldinger & Lichter, 2003), fewer studies have examined how local receiving institutions respond to the needs and demands of this population.

Addressing this gap, this chapter examines how local governments respond to the burgeoning low-wage, largely Latino, day laborer population in suburbia.[1] Drawing on data from more than 100 face-to-face, semi-structured, in-depth interviews and participant observations among state and local elected or appointed officials, bureaucratic service and regulatory agency administrators, and community-based organization leaders, I examine the extent to which suburban institutional interdependency (SII, see Chapter 1) explains how institutional interdependencies play out as institutional actors attempt to implement programs to address the needs and concerns of lower-income immigrant and racial/ethnic minority groups in suburban areas undergoing rapid and dramatic demographic shifts.[2]

---

[1] Parts of this chapter first appeared in my doctoral dissertation, Frasure (2005) "We Won't Turn Back: The Political Economy Paradoxes of Immigrant and Ethnic Minority Settlement in Suburban America," University of Maryland-College Park. Parts of this chapter have been revised from Frasure and Jones-Correa (2010) "The Logic of Institutional Interdependency: The Case of Day Laborer Policy in Suburbia." *Urban Affairs Review* 45: 451–482, and appear with the permission of *Urban Affairs Review*.

[2] I conducted these interviews, together with Michael Jones-Correa of Cornell University and Junsik Yoon of George Washington University.

Borrowing from Valenzuela and Meléndez, I define a day laborer "as someone who gathers at a street corner, empty lot or parking lot of a home improvement store (e.g., Home Depot), or an official hiring site, to sell their labor for the day, hour or for a particular job" (2003, p. 1). The authors identify three types of pick-up/drop-off sites. *Connected* sites are related to some industry, such as painting, landscaping or gardening, moving, or home improvement. *Unconnected* sites lack a connection to a specific industry. Finally, *regulated* or "formal hiring sites [are] either controlled by the city or county ... or managed by a community-based organization" (Valenzuela & Meléndez, 2003, p. 5). I focus on attempts by local suburban jurisdictions to manage day labor by creating regulated sites, which I refer to as institutionalized settings for day labor.

Two factors make day labor an issue of heightened concern and contention in both urban and suburban jurisdictions. The first is that day laborers are particularly vulnerable workers in the labor force. In this often underground economy, "day laborers have an informal relationship with the labor market, often working for different employers each day, being paid in cash, and lacking key benefits, such as health or unemployment insurance" (GAO, 2002, p. 1; also see del Carmen Fani, 2005; HPRP & Casa de Maryland, 2004; Valenzuela, 1999, 2000, 2006; Valenzuela & Meléndez, 2003). The 2002 GAO report found that day laborers are routinely subjected to hazardous work environments and workplace abuses, such as underpayment or nonpayment for their services. In addition, many day laborers are unable to file complaints because of language barriers or lack of legal documentation and fears of deportation. The second factor is that the increased presence of day laborers may lower the perceived quality of life that makes suburbia an attractive location for many residents. By most accounts day laborers have resided in parts of Montgomery, Prince George's, and Fairfax Counties for nearly twenty years, yet had gone largely (or at least officially) unnoticed until the recent stark increase in their numbers. The emergence of new informal day laborer sites – such as convenience stores or home improvement stores where day laborers wait for employers to drive by seeking temporary labor – has raised public safety, health, quality of life, and other concerns among suburban residents and business owners who assert laborers (particularly those who may be undocumented) have no right to appropriate these public spaces.[3] Both the location of informal day labor sites and the creation of formal sites often run into what is called the "NIMBY" (Not in My Back Yard) problem. Residents and business owners do not wish to see day laborers – literally or figuratively – in their own backyards. They may

---

[3] Notably, the interviews in this study, collected from June 2003 to August 2004, preceded the immigrant rights marches of 2006, where thousands of immigrants (both documented and undocumented) from Los Angeles to Atlanta came "out of the shadows" to voice their grievances concerning several national comprehensive immigration reform bills proposed by the 109th and 110th U.S. Congresses. These interviews also preceded many of the later developments related to the day labor center in Herndon, Virginia, as discussed in detail here.

support the local government establishing a formal labor pick-up site to meet the needs of day laborers – as long as it is not in their neighborhood.

Suburban jurisdictions have various means of handling informal day labor sites. Law enforcement officials may be called in to "dismantle" the sites (even though some argue that such tactics are often ineffective and short-lived), and some jurisdictions have gone so far as to outlaw informal pick-up sites (Calderon, Suzanne, & Rodriguez, 2005; Espenshade & Calhoun, 1993). In most cases, however, suburban residents and business owners raise outcries about day laborers "loitering" in public and want to see them removed from the immediate vicinity, but do not support a complete ban. On the other side of the coin, some jurisdictions have moved to create formal, regulated centers designated as job pick-up sites, where day laborers can also receive shelter, job assistance, the means to report unscrupulous practices by employers, advocacy support, and if necessary restitution through legal channels. The rise of institutionalized day labor sites challenges suburban norms regarding the use of both public space and public funds, as well as attracting charges from illegal immigration watchdog groups, such as the Minutemen Project and the Federation for American Immigration Reform, that public dollars are being misappropriated for the benefit of undocumented immigrants. These issues of contestation over public space, complaints that day laborers are illegitimately using public space, and resistance to the location or relocation of either formal or informal day labor sites have all surfaced in Montgomery County, Maryland, and Fairfax County, Virginia.

Suburban Institutional Interdependency (SII) in Day Labor

In the introduction, I described a 2005 press conference held by a group of Montgomery County public and nonprofit actors to mark the groundbreaking of a second day labor site in that county. The range of political figures present at the event revealed a significant degree of political backing in Montgomery County for public-private initiatives and coalitions to address the integration of immigrants and in particular day labor issues. Such initiatives are, however, hardly run of the mill, and are neither uncontroversial nor costless. In fact, voters in nearby Herndon (Fairfax County), Virginia, revolted against a city-sponsored day labor site, removing from office in 2006 all the local lawmakers who had approved the initiative. This raises questions about how interdependent relationships among institutions develop more readily in some jurisdictions than others.

Any policy to address day labor is bound to involve multiple local actors, both public and private, entailing the usual complications of collective action. Each suburban sector – elected officials, bureaucrats, and community-based organizations – holds certain tangible and intangible resources at its disposal, but also has constraints on these resources. So how do these actors pool their resources and build symbiotic relationships that generate additional leverage to address issues like the NIMBY problem? In addition, the introduction of immigration issues into suburban politics requires some reallocation of public resources. How is this accomplished? The case study in this chapter underscores the *institutional logic* behind collective action to address issues that require redistributive policy solutions. Three facets of the logic of SII are explored here: increasing access to resources, increasing legitimacy and lowering transaction costs, and leveraging public resources.

Interdependency Increases Access to Resources

One of the main incentives for suburban nonprofits to form symbiotic relationships with local government agencies and officials are the latter's access to resources. Community-based organizations (CBOs) often rely on local government agencies not only for direct funding, but also for institutional resources (e.g., meeting spaces, photocopiers, materials, etc.) that can reduce overhead costs.

Given the resources at stake, local CBOs have a vested interest in cultivating good relationships with local governmental actors because these relationships translate into access, and access can translate into resources. For instance, during a 2005 interview, Elmer Romero, director of education for CASA de Maryland, detailed CASA's relationship with the local government, particularly former Montgomery County executive Doug Duncan (1994–2006) and former Prince George's County executive Jack Johnson (2002–2010).[4]

Duncan is always in touch with this organization, and when we need him for any specific issue, he will be open-minded to hear [our concerns] and try to get some solution. In addition, [the county will] provide money to resolve a specific issue. For example, they support this employment center, because they support the day laborers' central issues. And in addition, for education, I've received some money through the county to develop, for example, literacy classes in Spanish, literacy from the ESOL program, and for citizenship training. So the county, really, is a real support for us. But, obviously, it depends, [on] who is the executive, because now, [with] Jack Johnson in Prince George's ... we have good relationship, but in the past, the last executive, the relationship [was not nearly as good] ... because, they were not comfortable with immigrants ... I would say, probably they were not really sensitive about this issue. But now, the relationship with ... Duncan and Jack Johnson is really good. And they are in touch with us and, for example, they support us in new legislation. When we had this anti-immigration bill, they went with us, to support us, to Annapolis, and to talk to the media, and support immigrants.

As this quotation illustrates, good relationships with local government executives can mean support across a number of different arenas, at both the local and state levels. But perhaps more important for CBOs, support on policy

---

4 On November 12, 2010, Johnson and his wife were indicted on federal charges as part of a larger political corruption scandal in the county. On May 17, 2011, Johnson pleaded guilty to extortion and witness- and evidence-tampering (Castaneda & Miranda, 2011; Castaneda & Thomas, 2010).

issues from key local elected officials can translate into financial support. CASA de Maryland, the largest Latino CBO in Montgomery County and one of the primary movers behind the establishment of institutionalized day labor sites in the county, is a prominent example of how local political backing has translated into budgetary support.

CASA de Maryland. Founded in 1985 by Central American refugees and North Americans, CASA was originally known as the Central American Solidarity Association of Maryland. A registered 501(c)3 nonprofit, CASA is the largest Latino and immigrant service organization in Maryland, according to its Web site. Although active in advocacy and assistance throughout the state, it primarily serves Prince George's and Montgomery Counties and the City of Baltimore.

Since 1985, CASA has rapidly grown from its modest beginnings in the basement of Takoma Park Presbyterian Church. In 1991, when as many as 150 day laborers began congregating daily at a street corner in the Langley Park area of Montgomery County, CASA set up its first formal day labor site in a construction trailer to provide shelter as well as social and employment services for workers. CASA also aggressively provided legal aid for day laborers who encountered difficulty being paid. This trailer is where I interviewed several staff members in 2004. Since then CASA has moved to a newly restored multimillion-dollar space in the former McCormick-Goodhart Mansion in Langley Park. The 21,000-square-foot, twenty-eight-room, three-story building holds historic preservation status in the state. It serves as a multicultural center as well as housing the offices of several other nonprofits (Listokin, Lahr, & Heydt, 2012). Meanwhile CASA's budget has grown from $500,000 to $6 million, and its staff from five to sixty-five employees (plus thirty part-time English teachers). CASA also reports that 10,000 members pay $25 in annual dues to the organization.

The organization presently operates five social service and employment centers, called welcome centers, in Prince George's and Montgomery Counties and the City of Baltimore. In recent years its client base has also expanded beyond Latinos, and currently as much as 25 percent of CASA's clients are immigrants from African countries. In addition to providing workforce development for day laborers, CASA provides comprehensive support services to more than 20,000 low-income immigrants every year, including English classes, information concerning citizenship, health care, job training, and mediation services between workers and employers. In 2010, CASA clients filled nearly 19,000 temporary jobs and 250 permanent jobs. CASA also employs a host of immigrant rights lawyers who closed more than 1,000 cases during that year.

Progressive activists, especially those in immigrant rights, celebrate CASA as a national model for immigrant advocacy and assistance. However, the five welcome centers are highly controversial. Detractors constantly scrutinize them and would like to see them closed permanently because they are funded in part by tax dollars and do not screen clients for their citizenship status (Londoño,

2007; Seper, 2007). In 2007, an arson fire was set at a welcome center that had opened only months earlier in Shady Grove. Montgomery County police classified the fire as a hate crime (Montes, 2007).

Currently, a mix of public and private dollars funds CASA. In 2010, the agency reported receiving $4,739,096 in individual, corporate, and foundation support. Even some of its private funding has been controversial, however. Examples include a 2002 grant for more than $300,000 to fund the Workers' Rights Legal and Organizing Center in Baltimore from philanthropist George Soros' Open Society Institute, and a $1.5 million donation in 2008 from CITGO, the Venezuelan state-owned petroleum corporation, to fund educational, training, and economic development programs (Lazo, 2008). Many conservatives and other opponents suggest that both donations solidify CASA's political agenda as radical and communist or at least leftist.

The controversial welcome centers are run by CASA under contract with the governments of the counties where they are located. Major sources of government funding include the Montgomery County Department of Health and Human Services (DHHS), Montgomery County Department of Housing and Community Development (DHCD), Montgomery County Community Development Block Grant (CDBG), Prince George's County CDBG, Prince George's Special Appropriations Funds, Takoma Park CDBG, and the City of Takoma Park. The amount of public funding has increased over time, and as of 2010, nearly half of CASA's budget comes from government contracts, whose value has skyrocketed from $685,803 in 2003 to $4,966,948 in 2010 (CASA de Maryland, 2003, 2010). The amount of funding CASA receives from government sources may be unusual, but the *share* of public funding it receives as a percentage of its total budget is less unusual: nonprofits, particularly those with ethnic orientations, either receive public funding or are simply very small.

The most controversial project to date has been the renovation of the Georgian Revival McCormick-Goodhart Mansion, constructed in 1924 as a private residence on a 565-acre estate. The Sawyer Realty Holdings real estate company sold the property to CASA for just one dollar in 2007. Sawyer's president, Gregg Clickstein, owns apartment units near the mansion and was once the target of a tenant protest organized by CASA Executive Director Gustavo Torres to call for better living conditions. According to Clickstein, "So, Gustavo and I end up over a bowl of pickles at the Parkway Deli.... He starts talking about his vision for CASA. What was interesting to me was, Gustavo was really talking about America. This nation of immigrants ... and this new wave of immigrants, and having the opportunity to assimilate and be great Americans. And it really just touched me" (Montgomery, 2011). The two began to work together to improve tenant conditions, leading later to the virtual donation of the mansion property. The 2012 Historic Tax Credit Coalition (HTCC) report details the total cost of renovating the mansion for office space at $13.7 million. Of that cost, the project received $963,384 in federal HTC; $1,176,624 in

Maryland HTC equity; $64,700 in federal energy tax credit equity; and more than $4,000,000 in Federal New Markets Tax Credit (NMTC) loan monies, which are targeted for revitalization efforts in low-income and impoverished communities across the United States. The project also generated 90 construction jobs, 121 permanent jobs, and $705,800 in state and local taxes (Listokin et al., 2012).

On October 3, 2007, CASA kicked off a multimillion-dollar fundraising campaign to renovate the rundown mansion. Several government and private-sector leaders gathered to lend their support. Montgomery County executive Isaiah Leggett, a Democrat, said, "Maryland is very inclusive," and "Part of our strength is our diversity.... The center is just one of the ways that shows how Maryland has more 'enlightened leadership'" (i.e., than neighboring Virginia, where anti-immigration measures were passing (Izadi, 2010). Governor Martin O'Malley, a Democrat, affirmed Maryland as an inclusive state: "in our Maryland, there's no such thing as a spare American" (Izadi, 2010). Tom Perez, assistant attorney general for the Civil Rights Division of the U.S. Department of Justice, also attended the fundraiser. He stated in reference to CASA's opponents, "Since the beginning of our nation there's been nationalists and others, who have railed against immigrants from the Italians and the Irish on.... The good news is they have never been successful. That's why the Know Nothing Party vanished into history. There will always be those forces of gloom and doom that want to divide us. What a difference a year makes. A year ago we had a governor who said multiculturalism is bunk. Now we've got a governor celebrating a multicultural center" (Ford & Montes, 2007).

Perez, a longtime advocate of the day labor centers, had come under fire earlier in 2007 for stating, "Labor centers are the most cost-effective investment of government money I can imagine.... We're providing employment, addressing public safety by creating an orderly process, keeping people from street corners and protecting workers" (Brewington, 2007, p. 1). These remarks, which Perez made regarding the opening of a new center in Baltimore, while he was serving as secretary of the Maryland Department of Labor, Licensing, and Regulation, were scrutinized during his 2009 Senate confirmation hearings. Senator Jeff Sessions of Alabama criticized Perez for his brief stint on the CASA board of directors. Sessions accused Perez and CASA of "promoting illegal immigration" because the organization had published a pamphlet informing undocumented immigrants about their legal rights in the event they were caught in an immigration raid (Seper, 2007; Serwer, 2009). On March 18, 2013, President Barack Obama nominated Perez for U.S. secretary of labor. The nomination has been held up several times by Senate Republications because of his decision not to intervene in a whistleblower case (*Magner v. Gallagher*) and, again, because of his association with CASA. After a lengthy and controversial confirmation hearing he was confirmed as secretary of labor for the Obama administration in July 2013. Conservative leaders and organizations have subjected other former CASA board members – such as Maryland State Delegate Ana Sol Gutierrez and Cecilia Muñoz, director of intergovernmental affairs for the Obama administration – to scrutiny.

Across the Potomac in Virginia. The institutionalization of day labor sites in Fairfax County is more recent, and finding a location for a center has generated much greater controversy, particularly in the town of Herndon. Nonetheless, the growing informal congregations of day laborers at convenience stores throughout Fairfax County began raising public safety, health, and quality-of-life concerns for longtime residents and business owners, provoking numerous complaints. Heightened concern about the issue forced Fairfax County to address the problem, as Fairfax County Deputy County Executive for Human Services Verdia Haywood noted:

We got the day laborer issue, and by the way, it is growing significantly in our community.... Now, if you can't get a driver's license where you drive to work, chances are you are going to have to depend more on things like the day laborer's market.... [W]e have seen in just a period of two months a threefold increase in one of the day laborer sites in the number of people going to that site, trying to get access to the economy and earn a living so that they can support their families.... A three-fold increase. And guess what? That has implications for the businesses in that community. It has implications for the citizens in that community. It has public implications. The whole issue now, for example, in our day labor site where the sensitivity to the police involvement has compounded some of the problems that we already have.... It's almost like after September 11th ... [the] level of consciousness about immigration [has] increased dramatically, and when that happens, it [means] that politicians are going to try to do something about it.

Fairfax County took longer than Montgomery County to recognize and respond to day labor issues, but by the early 2000s the issue had become too visible – and too politicized – to ignore. In response, county officials conducted a small-scale survey of the experiences of day laborers in the county in 2000, and undertook a more detailed survey in 2003. Staff from the Department of Systems Management for Human Services, the Department of Community and Recreation Services, the Fairfax County Fire and Rescue Department, and a member of Reston Interfaith (a faith-based organization) working as a liaison at the informal day labor site in Herndon, collaborated to conduct the 2003 interviews in Spanish.[5] David Ellis, director of the Fairfax County Day Labor Taskforce, remarked:

looking at just the demographics of Fairfax and recognizing that we have had some rapid demographic changes ... suddenly some of the issues out in neighborhoods and

---

[5] The survey found that day laborers in the county tend to be Hispanic men between eighteen and thirty-five years of age. Moreover, "Over 80 percent of respondents are from Central America (37.4 percent from Honduras, 26.3 percent from El Salvador, 16.8 percent from Guatemala, and 2.1 percent from Nicaragua). South American countries of origin reported include: Peru (9.5 percent), Bolivia (2.1 percent), Chile (0.5 percent), and Colombia (0.5 percent). The remaining 4.2 percent of respondents were from Mexico" (DSMHS, 2004, p. 6). According to the report,

communities don't necessarily fit in [any] one agency's area ... day labor is a perfect example.... For years the police department was the agency that really [was at] the forefront [on this issue], because they were the ones receiving the complaints ... [but recently] we recognized that it was just more than a police issue, more than a human services issue, it is really a community issue. You need to have discussion, you need to have representation for the business community, the residents, as well as the day laborers. [Y]ou need to find a way to kind of bring folks together and develop some type of consensus on what would be the best approach.... [T]he demographic changes in the county ... [are] not going to go away.... [The county's] probably going to have more day labor sites ... we currently have four sites, but we probably picked up three of those sites [recently], or they have become more noticeable in the last five years.

These remarks emphasize the heightened visibility of the day labor issue in the early 2000s, and the realization that any one institutional actor could not resolve it.

Similarly, Verdia Haywood described how Fairfax County government funds were being used to support local nonprofits involved in serving ethnic minorities, particularly through community development block grants from the federal government. These block grants are prized for their flexibility because each locality can set its own priorities for spending and support:

We actually created on our own, in Fairfax County, what we call a community funding pool, which really, truly, is a community investment pool.... [W]e allocate roughly $10 million annually to community-based organizations, and allow those community-based organizations to leverage other funding streams, including federal funding streams and grants and foundations, to contribute to the community. And a significant portion of the community funding pool is now going to ethnic minority groups.... They are ... newly emerging organizations, they have excellent vision in terms of energy, drive, and commitment; a lot of them leverage the help out of communities around them.

In Fairfax and Montgomery Counties, local ethnically oriented CBOs are receiving greater shares of public funding, which indicates that governmental actors are recognizing new issues arising from the demographic changes taking place in their jurisdictions, are receiving new demands from residents and CBOs, and are responding by allocating resources. These public resources provide a significant incentive for these organizations to seek out and maintain good relationships with local governmental actors.

"The majority of respondents (over 90 percent of respondents who provided zip code information) reside in Fairfax County.... The majority of respondents live within walking distance of the site where they were interviewed and most respondents live within a few miles of the day laborer site where they were interviewed. Of all of the respondents, two-thirds walk to the site. The average distance to the site for those that walk is less than one mile. For those respondents that drive or use public transportation to go to the site, the average distance is 4.9 miles. On average, respondents reside 2.4 miles from the day laborer site where they work" (DSMHS, 2004, p. 7).

Interdependency Increases Legitimacy and Lowers Transaction Costs
While CBOs seek relationships with elected officials who control public funding, local governments have their own reasons to actively seek out partnerships with nonprofits. Verdia Haywood succinctly summarized the changing relationship of local government to CBOs in Fairfax County:

> One of the dramatic changes that has taken place ... [is] a shifting of responsibility ... to the local level. [The county] didn't have a major human services function that was institutionalized in government ... because our social services [were funded by] the state ... but ... in the early part of the '80s, [responsibility for human services] was shifted from the state government to the local government. And not only was the shift policy-wise, the shift was resource-wise, and the shift was also service design-wise. In other words, we started trying to figure out what was the best mix and combination of services that we needed in our community.... And as a result, we greatly enhanced ... the levels of service, and the one thing that we did very strategically was beginning to look more at community-based organizations as a part of the solution ... to the issues.... [W]e leveraged some federal funds there. We leveraged some state funds; we put in some local dollars there. We've obviously lost almost all of the federal dollars in the anti-poverty area [but] they've been ... enhanced three times over by the locality.

What Haywood describes is a process of devolution of responsibilities from the state (Virginia) to localities (Fairfax County) in the 1980s, during which localities took over much of the social service provision previously funded and administered through the state or federal governments. In this process, localities lost funding streams they had relied on, but also gained greater control over service provision, arguably becoming able to target their aid more precisely. The funding shifts and greater flexibility in program design led them to work with nonprofit CBOs rather than setting up programs of their own. However, these public-nonprofit partnerships are not driven solely by the desire to leverage reduced funding.

By building alliances with CBOs, public agencies can lower the transaction costs associated with overcoming language and cultural barriers between newcomers and longtime residents. CBOs have expertise and networks in this area that governmental agencies simply do not have. Janet Hubbell, Fairfax County regional manager for community affairs, explains how county bureaucratic agencies are grappling with the issues new immigrant residents have raised:

> You have to ... go back to our three core areas, access to services, service provision, and community capacity building, and we do that by influence.... [I]t's not like I can advocate on behalf of immigrant [or] refugee populations, but I can maybe be influenced in some way by having access to those populations and bringing them in. I think, just in the five years that I have been here, everybody's struggling with it. There isn't one county agency that isn't trying to figure out how to be a better public servant when we are dealing with a population that doesn't speak our language.

Hubbell's comments reveal that local governments are behind the curve in responding to the demographic changes that have taken place in their jurisdictions, and are, as she puts it, "struggling" with how to serve the new immigrant and ethnic populations in suburbia. However, instead of trying to work independently to build the necessary expertise and trust with local immigrant and ethnic communities, local governmental agencies can turn to nonprofit actors to serve as a bridge to these constituents. Haywood further discusses how CBOs help county agencies to reach out to immigrant newcomers:

[W]e have obviously had to reorient our services.... And that is a great challenge. I mean, trying to gain confidence ... and trust [from immigrants]. [T]hat population ... particularly the Hispanic population, you know, where you've got all of the issues of ... immigration and the issues associated with that, and can I trust [government] ... In a lot of areas they came from ... they came here because they couldn't trust their government. Now you all of a sudden [are] going to access the services that you need from government. Who knows, they may report you and you may get deported. All of those issues ... are dramatically taking place [and] we have to rethink ... how we deliver [services], and we found, quite frankly, that a significant vehicle ... is to partner with community-based organizations that are part of those cultures.... I think we are just now beginning to touch the surface of the need, quite frankly, to do that, and that's what I mean when I say the basic structure of services has had to change as a result.

Haywood's comments underline the symbiotic relationship between ethnic nonprofits and governmental actors. Tim Freilich, an attorney at the Virginia Justice Center, amplifies this point:

As long as you're filling a need that the county is looking for – I mean, that's one of the other things that we've been able to offer from the beginning. Even though we don't limit our services to Latinos, all of our staff is bilingual English/Spanish, and so ... we've been able to say, "Hey, we have bilingual staff." You know, there's a tremendous need in northern Virginia for Spanish-speaking attorneys. And human services workers, for that matter. And so that's been a good selling point ... you know, we were able to use our experience representing migrant farmworkers to say, "Hey! This is an area of expertise that we can very readily just shift over to day laborers." You know: [they have] a lot of the same issues, as far as language access ... lack of familiarity with workers' rights.... Plus, we have ... contacts with folks who work with [the] Latino population throughout the state, that we were able to sort of tie into the efforts and ongoing organizing efforts in northern Virginia.

For the most part, county agencies have been slow to hire bilingual staff to interface with the new immigrant residents they must serve. What CBOs like the Virginia Justice Center offer local governments is access to a readily available pool of experienced staff with specialized language skills, strong ties to the immigrant community, and a broad range of contacts with similar actors throughout the state. The expertise of nonprofit CBOs can lower the transaction costs governmental agencies face in dealing with new issues raised by the presence of immigrants. And by entering into partnerships with CBOs, public agencies gain access to "trust networks" that facilitate their interactions with these newcomers.

Interdependency Leverages Public Resources

From the perspective of local government, funding allocated to local nonprofit agencies is money well spent. There is a practical benefit to their support of local CBOs: the public funds they allocate make it easier to address the needs and demands of a new population by shifting the burden of service provision onto CBOs. There's also a political payoff: state and federal funds, channeled through localities to particular community-based interests, whether ethnic or otherwise, are a form of selective incentive that local political actors can provide in exchange for presumed political support. In this respect, the channeling of public funds to local nonprofits is not far removed from the machine politics of the past, which also served to incorporate ethnic newcomers (see Chapter 1). Erie (1988) argues that even mature political machines did not have sufficient resources to reward all their adherents and supporters; likewise, contemporary suburban governments are usually operating under strict fiscal constraints. Whether couched as offering services or rewarding potential supporters, the incentives local governments can offer are, in fact, quite selective.

Although local governments are aware of the issues raised by changing demographics, it is not clear that they have the funds, or the political will to raise additional funds, to address these issues effectively. What local governmental actors therefore seek to do is to leverage their funds, to multiply their effect, through partnerships with nongovernmental actors. Consider again the case of CASA de Maryland. Robert Hubbard, director of permitting services for Montgomery County, describes how his agency facilitated the establishment of CASA's first day labor site:

Initially ... the problem was identified as a community problem, a loitering disruption ... people out here soliciting for jobs or whatever. And like I said, CASA stepped up, so there wasn't real police enforcement or zoning enforcement needed. So they said, "Well, we'll organize, but we need space to do this." And the [Latino] community was helpful in terms of initially finding the site.... CASA found a trailer that [the day laborers] could operate out of, so we had to permit the trailer, we had to inspect the trailer. CASA, like I said, does not have a lot of money. They're a nonprofit organization. So there are regulatory requirements and the permitting process, like the requirement for architectural seal and signature on plans, that we had to look at and decide whether it was necessary and all. We had the expertise in-house that we could waive some of those requirements....

And then once this became a popular site, it again became a nuisance to surrounding businesses and CASA was asked to move, and so we were constantly looking for areas that complied with the zoning requirement or didn't. And it ended up that they're [i.e., the day labor site] on government property right now, they're on property that's owned by the Maryland National Capital Park and Planning Commission. So they're basically exempt from the zoning requirement as [it's] a public use.... It's just fortunate that CASA was able to find this site [and] get Parks and Planning to agree to [let them] use it. And now, you know, they've satisfied their zoning requirements but we're still working with them on some of the building code issues and making the space work for them on a daily basis.

Hubbard describes a process by which bureaucrats and CBOs identify a common problem, then the specific implementation is left up to the CBO while the government eases regulatory and political roadblocks. In this case, once the need for a day labor site was identified, CASA was left to find a workable site. Once the site was found, a bureaucratic process of complying with government regulations had to be surmounted. Montgomery County governmental agencies could at this stage easily have stymied CASA's initiative by placing bureaucratic obstacles in its way, but instead facilitated CASA's passage through the permitting process. Later, once the initial site became too successful to remain where it was, public agencies, in this case the Parks and Planning Department, once again cooperated with CASA to smooth the relocation process, helping to acquire public land that was exempt from the zoning process. At every stage, however, it was the CBO that took the initiative in implementing the policy and public agencies that responded to problems encountered in those initiatives.

This case highlights two aspects of the relationship between public agencies and nonprofits. First, even when local government officials and nonprofit agencies agree on the issue at stake and the possible solutions, the nonprofit may be left to work out the actual solution. Second, the kinds of resources that government agencies allocate to support the CBO's efforts are often non-material (i.e., aid-in-kind or expertise) rather than financial. It may be that leaving much of the legwork to the CBO allows local governmental actors to gain credibility with a particular constituency while simultaneously distancing themselves from any potential political fallout. On the other hand, if things go well, their ties to the CBO allow them to claim part of the credit for the success (see Mayhew, 1974).

Best of all, local governments can gain these benefits relatively cheaply. From housing to education, and from zoning to law enforcement, bureaucratic service providers and local governmental regulatory agencies are often the "first responders" of suburban municipal government for immigrants and other suburban newcomers. Such agencies are responsible for providing local public goods and implementing programs/services that directly affect the daily lives of suburban newcomers, particularly among the most vulnerable populations. However, despite being on the front lines of service provision, local agencies are constrained by their financial resources. They are likely to have few or no additional funds available to address increases or shifts in social needs, even should they wish to.

Alliances with nonprofit groups allow local bureaucrats to minimize outlays of their scarce resources for evolving needs. The primary cost outlays for any agency initiating a new program is typically personnel related, so minimizing staffing through building partnerships with local nonprofit agencies is a major way to keep costs down. What occurs in these partnerships is that governmental agencies essentially outsource their response to a particular issue (e.g., day labor) to nonprofit groups, thereby keeping down their personnel and benefits costs as nonprofits typically do not offer the same benefits package as governmental agencies.

In return for programmatic funding, access to public facilities, and agency support, nonprofits essentially absorb the costs of hiring specialized personnel, such as staff with particular specialties (e.g., immigration law), skills (e.g., bilingual abilities), or access to networks (e.g., of undocumented immigrants) developed through long-term relationships built on trust (see Figure 1.1). What we see in the Washington, DC, metropolitan area is that local governments are responding (albeit slowly) to the needs and demands of immigrant and ethnic new arrivals to the suburbs, but they are outsourcing much of the effort to nonprofit agencies, while still taking credit for the programs these CBOs initiate, maintain, and staff.

Unlike during the earlier era of mass immigration to urban centers, when political machines were built on the votes of immigrant groups in exchange for patronage jobs and other benefits that helped some immigrants move up the social mobility ladder, the direct beneficiaries of programs and policies directed at day laborers are largely nonvoters and noncitizens. For example, CASA's 2012 report states 1,762 legal permanent residents completed the citizenship application process; 432 community members became citizens, and 100 percent of citizenship micro-loans were repaid (CASA de Maryland, 2012).

The Stability and Limitations of Institutional Interdependency in Suburbia

I set out to analyze how local political actors seek to address issues like day labor in suburbia despite the difficulties of collective action, particularly around policies requiring redistribution of public resources. The fact that local actors often address these redistributive issues through institutional coalitions formed among elected officials, bureaucratic agencies, and CBOs suggests that some tenets of public choice and urban regime theories are in need of revision. The logic of institutional interdependency overcomes the obstacles to collective action and allows local actors to leverage a combination of public and private resources to address the needs of documented and undocumented immigrants in suburbia, even though these newcomers are unable to bring much pressure to bear on local political actors through electoral politics.

Given the difficulties of maintaining coalitions or partnerships in other social and political arenas, it might seem puzzling that the relationships between local governmental agencies and CBOs should even occur, or that they can prove stable. Yet a powerful logic is at work behind these relationships that lends them stability: as this study has shown, each set of actors benefits from the relationship. The most obvious aspect of the relationship is the funding and support nonprofits receive from local governments. But the relationship is far from one-sided: local governments profit as well from this symbiosis through

increased legitimacy and lower transaction costs as they attempt to grapple with new issues and problems. In addition, by leveraging their resources
through partnerships with nonprofits, governmental agencies can outsource
much of the work, particularly human resources expenses, keeping their costs
lower while also insulating themselves from risk but allowing themselves to
share in any success.

The relationship between these actors may prove a win-win solution for
all involved. However, this analysis also raises several important empirical
and normative questions concerning suburban democratic governance and
accountability worthy of future study. On one hand, institutional interdependency can yield a division of labor and resources that facilitates the process
of "getting things done" in the face of tightening budgets. On the other hand,
for CBOs, forming interdependent relationships with local governmental and
public-sector actors can blunt their potential for advocacy, limiting options for
political insurgency at the grassroots level. In urban areas, political insurgency
has typically been necessary to change the status quo, particularly in the areas
of civil and human rights (Piven & Cloward, 1977). If the facilitation of local
governments enables CBOs to provide immigrant newcomers with the human
services and resources they need to "get started" in suburbia – and if regulatory
agencies adopt policies that generally appease these groups – why would constituents bother rallying in the state capital, attending PTA or neighborhood
association meetings, applying for citizenship, registering to vote, or casting
a ballot on election day? In other words, to what extent do CBOs risk being
silenced when they form interdependent relationships?

Second, local governments often have the power to turn controversial issues
into non-decisions or nonissues (Bachrach & Baratz, 1962) by taking them off
the collective decision-making table. In suburbia, the nonissues are as significant as those issues that make their way to the fore. Elected officials can select
which constituency issues or CBOs to support and which to shut out. Factions
favoring the "non-decision or nonissue" can hinder change efforts, particularly where weak or ambivalent leadership is present – as witnessed in Fairfax
County's slow efforts to address day labor concerns and the eventual stalling
of these efforts in Herndon in the face of entrenched anti-immigrant sentiment
(Alonso, 2007; Dwyer, 2005; Hobbins, 2006; Osterling & McClure, 2008;
Singer et al., 2009; Turque, 2006; Turque & Brulliard, 2006). The Herndon
story unfolded as follows.

On August 17, 2005, the Herndon mayor and city council approved a
publicly funded institutionalized day labor hiring center. The local government, in collaboration with local churches (particularly Reston Interfaith)
and community-based leaders, including the HEART organization (Herndon
Embraces All with Respect and Tolerance), organized Project Hope and
Harmony to facilitate the setup of the center inside a former police station.
Reston Interfaith lobbied for and secured a grant from Fairfax County for
the center's operating costs. In September 2005, the conservative political

watchdog group Judicial Watch filed a lawsuit against the town of Herndon and Fairfax County for using taxpayer funds to establish the day labor center. Less than a year following the opening of the center, Herndon voters rejected local officials who supported it, unseating Mayor Michael O'Reilly and several council members and replacing them with new politicians who openly opposed the center's establishment.

Unable to withstand persistent local and national public outcry, coupled with strong opposition from anti-immigrant groups such as Help Save Herndon and the local chapter of the Herndon Minutemen, as well as lobbying from 2006 Republican gubernatorial candidate Jerry W. Kilgore, the day labor center closed in September 2007, after operating for only twenty-one months (Alonso, 2007; Dwyer, 2005; Hobbins, 2006; Singer et al., 2009; Turque, 2006; Turque & Brulliard, 2006). Osterling and McClure aptly describe the influence of anti-illegal-immigration groups like the Minutemen in the local debate:

Rather than staging mass marches, the Minutemen chose to target day laborer sites, along with social service funding and housing occupancy regulations in very small areas within the DC area. By deploying a physical presence of their members and using national funding, the Minutemen were able to change the composition of the city council in Herndon, Virginia, where the day laborer site controversy became the focus of national attention. (2008, p. 27)

It's clear from the Herndon example that whereas the institutional interdependency of governmental and nongovernmental sectors is important to getting a project off the ground, the stability of these relationships varies greatly both across and within political jurisdictions, particularly if such policies become highly politicized, provoking local opposition (Hopkins, 2010).

A growing list of conservative and right-wing opponents and anti-illegal-immigration organizations, such as Help Save Maryland, hold CASA de Maryland in great disdain, calling it "the biggest promoter and facilitator of illegal aliens in Maryland" (Help Save Maryland, http://www.helpsavemaryland.com). Organizations such as the Immigration Reform Law Institute (IRLI) charge CASA regularly lobbies the state on legislation, endorses political candidates, and supports Democrats through get-out-the-vote volunteer efforts, all while taking tax-deductible donations as a nonprofit (Simpson, 2011). Monique A. Miles, a staff attorney for IRLI, states that "IRLI wants the IRS and state agencies to cut off CASA's source of tax-exempt money and state funding, so it can't use taxpayer money for political purposes.... CASA thinks it's too big and well-connected to fail, like ACORN did, but there are watchdog organizations like IRLI who are looking out for taxpayers' best interests" (quoted in Dinan, 2012, p. 1). One of CASA's chief opponents is Maryland Republican State Delegate Pat McDonough, who voices concerns that nearly half of CASA's $6 million budget comes from local, state, and federal tax dollars, and that CASA uses those dollars to aid undocumented immigrants. In reference to CASA's growing political power in the state, McDonough states,

"Gustavo [Torres] has created a sanctuary state.... The governor does his bidding. The politicians who control power in the State of Maryland do his bidding.... And his success has caused financial and personal heartbreak for the State of Maryland" (Dinan, 2012, p. 1).

To address these concerns, in 2010 Torres spun off a sister organization called CASA in Action, which engages in direct political action, endorses candidates, and facilitates greater electoral and campaign engagement by Latinos and immigrants in Maryland by providing them with political education and getting them to the polls. Incorporated under a different section of the tax code (501(c)4), this arm of CASA is allowed to take political stances. According to its Web site, "During election years, CASA in Action engages voters through political debates, questionnaires to candidates and candidate endorsements, Spanish-language media, voter registration, and Get-Out-the Vote activities. When CASA in Action endorses a candidate, it bases that decision on the candidate's position on priorities chosen by our members. Our members vote for those candidates who align with their vision for a more just society. And that endorsement is communicated to Latino voters." CASA in Action's operating budget of $100,000 is reportedly funded without taxpayer dollars (CASA de Maryland, 2013).

However, the formal establishment of CASA in Action raises concerns because it blurs the line between lobbying efforts and nonprofit work toward the incorporation of immigrants in suburbia. The "Social Justice" section of the 2012 Annual Report of CASA (the nonprofit arm), boasts that twenty-eight anti-immigration bills were defeated in the Maryland state legislature in 2012 "thanks in part to CASA's advocacy"; and that 300 community members participated in a June 2012 "No Displacement, No Deportation" march through Langley Park and Long Branch (CASA de Maryland, 2012). The report also boasts of the biggest success in CASA's lobbying efforts to date: the March 2011 passage of Maryland's Development, Relief, and Education for Alien Minors (DREAM) Act. This act allows minors without legal documentation to live in the United States and receive local tuition rates at Maryland community colleges and in-state tuition rates at public universities. When Governor Martin O'Malley signed the act into law in April 2011, Maryland became the eleventh state to approve this type of legislation. Opponents then launched a successful petition drive to block the law, and CASA sued to block a 2012 referendum on the issue, which the opponents called for (marking the first time state DREAM legislation has been put to popular vote). In November 2012, Maryland voters passed the measure 58 percent to 42 percent. An undocumented student said of the bill's passage, "The Maryland DREAM Act is a dream come true. For me it means fairness and equity. Finally I can say I'm a Marylander; for once in my life I feel truly American" (CASA de Maryland, 2012).

5

Lost in Translation

Language Access at Government Agencies in Suburbia

An immigrant newcomer's first contact with government is likely to occur at the municipal level, be it for health care and government services or police/fire protection and emergency preparedness. For limited English proficient (LEP) individuals, those who do not speak English as their primary language and have a limited ability to read, speak, write, or understand English, language access is an integral part of assistance, communication, and incorporation into American metropolitan areas. Three federal laws are particularly applicable to language access for LEP persons: (a) Title VI of the landmark Civil Rights Act of 1964, which prohibits discrimination based on race, color, or national origin; (b) Section 203 of the Voting Rights Act of 1975, which mandates language assistance if more than 10,000 or more than 5 percent of the citizens of voting age in a jurisdiction are members of a single language-minority group who do not speak or understand English adequately to participate in the electoral process; and (c) Executive Order 13166, Improving Access to Services for Persons with Limited English Proficiency, issued by President Bill Clinton in 2000 (described later in this chapter).

The efficient provision of government services to LEP individuals serves the public interest and facilitates the provision of local public goods and services. A 2002 U.S. Office of Management and Budget (OMB) report found, "Improved access to a wide variety of services – ranging from delivery of health care and access to food stamps to motor vehicle licensing and law enforcement – can substantially improve the health and quality of life of many LEP individuals and their families. Moreover, language-assistance services can increase the efficiency of distribution of government services to LEP individuals and may measurably increase the effectiveness of public health and safety programs" (pp. 3–4).

By 2010, 25.2 million people, or 9 percent, of the U.S. population over the age of five years were LEP, an 80 percent increase since 1990 (Pandya, McHugh, & Batalova, 2011). The majority of LEP individuals are concentrated in six traditional immigrant-destination states, California (27.3% of the U.S. LEP population), Texas (13.3%), New York (9.7%), Florida (8.4%), Illinois (4.6%), and New Jersey (4.1%) (Pandya et al., 2011). However, new immigrant gateways such as the Washington, DC, metro area have witnessed more than a doubling in their LEP populations since 1990. More than a quarter of DC residents speak a language other than English at home, and as of 2010 the LEP population exceeds 10 percent in the national capital counties of Montgomery County, Maryland (15.2%), and Fairfax County, Virginia (15%), and nearly so in Prince George's County, Maryland (9%).

On the other hand, immigrants in the DC metro region are on average better educated and more proficient in English than immigrants nationwide. Forty-five percent of Montgomery County's immigrants over the age of twenty-five hold at least a college degree, compared with less than 30 percent nationally. An estimated 42 percent of the county's immigrants are LEP, compared with 52 percent nationwide. Those from Europe, South Central Asia (South Asia and the Middle East), and Africa are the most English proficient while those from Central America and Eastern Asia are the least proficient (LEP Leadership Team, 2011). Seventy-three percent of South Asian and Middle Easterners in Montgomery County have at least a college degree and only 25 percent are LEP (LEP Leadership Team, 2011). These numbers, however, mask the intragroup language and cultural barriers that exist (Junn, 2007), particularly for some Asian-origin groups such as Vietnamese and Cambodians, as well as for LEP senior citizens who are often vulnerable and underserved. English language proficiency varies widely by country of origin and is often concentrated in certain areas of the county.

Not all LEP populations have "meaningful" or "equitable" access to language assistance when accessing government services. This is primarily why the issue of language access has galvanized a broad spectrum of immigrants in the Washington metro area, beyond the well-organized infrastructure of the Latino community, incorporating the voices and concerns of Asian, Middle Eastern, and African language minority groups.

Some observers may take a more narrow view, which argues that states and the federal government mandate these services, therefore leaving little variation left to explain concerning local service delivery. If history is our guide, particularly in American suburbs, simply because the federal or state governments mandate a public policy does not mean it will be enforced or monitored at the local level. The responsibility for implementing language access varies greatly by jurisdiction. Some counties merely comply with state and federal mandates, whereas others exceed those standards and move toward the implementation of language access measures tailored to the needs of their LEP population. In some suburban municipalities, the county executive's office oversees compliance with language access policy whereas other areas have separate subdivisions to monitor the assessment and provision of language access resources (Wang, 2009).

Others might look to ideological explanations for the implementation of language access policies. For example, Virginia is viewed as traditionally more conservative, adopting an English-only law, while Maryland is viewed as more liberal. In this chapter, I find support for the role of ideology as well as the possible role of state mandates, such as English-only laws in Virginia. However, Fairfax County (Virginia) and Montgomery County (Maryland) have similar demographics and both have leaned more liberal and Democrat in recent local and national election cycles, yet they vary in language access policies, practices, and level of implementation. These factors deem the case of suburban language access in need of evaluation.

This chapter examines how local suburban institutions respond to the needs of LEP populations in the face of local budgetary constraints and a suburban political environment that may to be hostile to any redistribution of resources to support the needs of LEP residents (e.g., by hiring bilingual staff, contracting for translation and interpretation services, and providing specialized support services at government agencies), particularly if such resources are suspected of aiding undocumented immigrants. As the anti-illegal-immigration Federation for American Immigration Reform wrote in a 2009 report called "English Learners and Immigration":

The rapid increase in students who struggle to comprehend and communicate in English is an unwelcome cost burden for Maryland taxpayers. Furthermore, the money spent to teach students basic English-language skills depletes the resources available to fund educational programs for the children of native-born Marylanders.... Not to be lost in the discussion of the dollar cost of LEP education is the impact that non-English speaking students have on the quality of education for the children of native-born Marylanders. While this is hard to quantify, it is a question that should not be ignored. (Ruark, 2009)

Yet despite political opposition and tight budgets, some jurisdictions, through strong leadership and public-private-nonprofit partnerships, have reached out to the LEP community. As I did in Chapter 3 with public education and Chapter 4 with day labor, in this chapter I challenge traditional theorizations regarding constraints on politics and redistribution at the local level. Public choice theories argue that local municipalities should refrain from advocating for redistributive policies for fear of driving out the long-standing middle- and upper-income populations. Language access initiatives are presumed to result in costly redistributive programs generating little immediate political payoff for elected and appointed officials because the recipients are disproportionately lower-income, nonvoting suburban newcomers. In contrast, I invoke SII to explain the development, or lack thereof, of public-private-nonprofit partnerships, and how such partnerships vary across and within jurisdictions. This chapter draws on data from both the focus group discussions described in detail in Chapter 2 and the semi-structured, in-depth interviews conducted in suburban Washington,

DC, as described in Chapters 3 and 4.[1] In the next section, although I discuss
federal and state statutes regarding language access policy in order to provide
context, the bulk of the analysis focuses on language access at the local level.

Federal, State, and Washington Metro Area Language Access Legislation

Title VI of the federal Civil Rights Act of 1964 prohibits discrimination on
the basis of race, color, or national origin in programs and activities receiving federal financial assistance such as Medicaid, health care, or human services (Federal Register, 2000). To confirm his administration's commitment to
Title VI and to promote greater compliance at the state level, on August 11,
2000, President Clinton signed Executive Order 13166, "Improving Access to
Services for Persons with Limited English Proficiency." Following an extensive
cost-benefit analysis by the OMB,[2] President George W. Bush affirmed his commitment to Executive Order 13166 via a memorandum issued on October 25,
2001. This executive order requires all federal agencies to establish and issue
to their funding recipients LEP guidelines to ensure that the programs and
activities they normally provide in English are accessible to LEP persons and
do not discriminate on the basis of national origin. In addition, federal agencies
must work to ensure that recipients of federal financing provide "meaningful
access" to their LEP applicants and beneficiaries. To assist federal agencies in
carrying out these responsibilities, the U.S. Department of Justice (DOJ) issued
a policy guidance document, "Enforcement of Title VI of the Civil Rights
Act of 1964 – National Origin Discrimination against Persons with Limited
English Proficiency" (Federal Register, 2000). Subsequently, in 2001, the Civil
Rights Division of the DOJ developed a four-factor test for "reasonable steps
to ensure meaningful access":

1. The number or proportion of LEP individuals eligible to be served or
   likely to be encountered by the program;
2. The frequency with which LEP individuals come in contact with the
   program;
3. The nature and importance of the program, activity, or service to individuals' lives; and
4. The resources available to the grantee/recipient and costs of providing
   LEP access.

According to the DOJ guidelines, quality interpretation and translation services
may be provided by multilingual staff, telephone interpreter lines, written language services, or community volunteers.

---

[1] The author conducted these interviews together with Michael Jones-Correa of Cornell University
and Junsik Yoon of George Washington University.
[2] The OMB report was entitled "Assessment of the Total Benefits and Costs of Implementing
Executive Order: No. 13166: Improving Access to Services for Persons with Limited English
Proficiency" (Office of Budget and Management, 2002).

At the state level, comprehensive language access policies usually require most or all public agencies within a state or local jurisdiction to have the capacity to communicate with and serve LEP residents (Wang, 2009).[3] Since 1973 five states (California 1973, Minnesota 1985, Maryland 2002, Hawaii 2006, and Illinois 2006) have enacted comprehensive language access policies requiring their public agencies to make their programs accessible to LEP individuals. California was the first state to adopt comprehensive language access but also one of the first to adopt an English-only law (in 1986). Importantly, because federal law supersedes state or local laws, local or statewide English-only laws do not relieve federally funded entities from their responsibilities to comply with Title VI and other nondiscrimination statutes, although agencies can refuse federal funds (Department of Justice, 2013).

Many jurisdictions have established language access policies similar to the federal model. In the District of Columbia, the DC Language Access Coalition (an alliance of forty-one community-based and civil rights organizations that came together in 2002) played a significant role in pushing the DC city council to pass the 2004 Comprehensive Language Access Act. The founding member of this coalition was the Asian Pacific American Legal Resource Center (APALRC), established in 1998 to address the lack of linguistically and culturally appropriate legal services for the growing number of Asian Pacific Americans in the DC metro region. The 2004 Comprehensive Language Access Act holds covered agencies accountable for providing limited and non-English proficient (LEP/NEP) DC residents with greater access to and participation in their programs, services, and activities.[4]

[3] According to Wang, the details of these policies differ, but they share a number of common elements aimed at overcoming language barriers, including that public agencies must (a) assess their constituents' language needs by identifying commonly spoken languages in the locality, especially by people likely to participate in their programs; (b) assess their capacity to communicate with and serve LEP constituents and identify areas for improvement (e.g., hiring more bilingual staff members, improving signage, developing multilingual telephone capacity, translating vital documents); (c) develop language assistance plans to improve communications with LEP individuals; (d) train staff members in how to implement the agency's language assistance policy; (e) establish centralized resources or offices to provide technical assistance and monitor the implementation of language assistance plans; and (f) conduct outreach to publicize the availability of language assistance services (2009, p. 4).

[4] APALRC also filed the first language access complaint against a DC law enforcement agency and received one of few pro-language-access rulings in the country. APALRC, joined by CASA de Maryland and the Maryland Legal Aid Bureau, filed a friend-of-the-court brief in support of Ms. Nonceeya, an LEP Thai immigrant, in the matter of *Nonceeya v. Lone Star Steakhouse* in 2008 (APALRC 2009), where Ms. Nonceeya had been deposed in English without access to an interpreter. The brief focused on the differences between written and oral English proficiency and highlighted the impact of LEP on individuals' abilities to fully participate in legal proceedings, including deposition hearings. In response to the brief, the court ruled that statute requires the presence of an interpreter at depositions unless the deponent waives interpretation services in the presence of an interpreter. Kerry O'Brien, senior manager of the legal program at CASA de Maryland, stated, "We believe that having interpreters at all stages of legal proceedings is

As demographics shifted rapidly in the state of Maryland, the Democrat-controlled Maryland state legislature sought to strengthen state compliance with Title VI and DOJ guidelines for serving LEP residents. The legislature commissioned the National Foreign Language Center at the University of Maryland to examine how well state agencies were providing information to and serving new residents with LEP needs. The report, released in 2001, found that "almost all state agencies interacted with LEP residents, yet 28 percent of the surveyed agencies reported that these individuals experienced significant delays in receiving services because of language barriers" (Wang, 2009). In addition, the report also raised the concern that in some departments, children served as interpreters for their parents.

As a result of federal compliance pressures and growing language access needs, immigration lawyer and state senator Perry Sfikas (representing Baltimore's District 46, 1995–2002), sponsored SB 265, enacted in 2002 as the Maryland Equal Access to Public Services Act. In part this legislation required government agencies to provide written translation of all documentation. Reaffirming Executive Order 13166, the act mandated, "State departments, agencies, and programs shall provide equal access to public services for individuals with limited English proficiency; requiring vital documents to be translated into any language spoken by any limited English proficient population that constitutes 3% of the overall population within a specified geographic area under specified circumstances; establishing a schedule for the implementation of specified requirements of the Act" (Sfikas, 2002).

A major concern with this act is that it does not provide a clear criterion for when state agencies must provide *oral* assistance in non-English languages, only that they have a duty to provide "reasonable" access. Given the limited language resources at most Maryland state agencies, oral interpretation assistance is likely to be available only in frequently spoken languages such as Spanish.

In 2008, Governor Martin O'Malley issued Executive Order 01.01.2008.18 establishing the Maryland Council for New Americans to assist the governor and state agencies in facilitating immigrants' integration in the state. The New Americans Initiative (part of the Maryland Council for New Americans) is a regional effort of CASA de Maryland, Tenants & Workers United, and Maryland New Americans Partnership (a coalition of more than thirty-five organizations) whose goal is to bring together nonprofit organizations, educational institutions, businesses, unions, and faith communities in Maryland that are committed to supporting eligible immigrants in their efforts to become U.S. citizens and active members of their communities post-naturalization. Their goals were to build the capacity and effectiveness of existing CBOs that

essential to achieving the full participation of Maryland's immigrant community in the justice system, and that immigrant voices must be heard throughout the justice system to prevent further abuse and exploitation" (APALRC, 2009).

I speak Korean.
I need language assistance.

If your facility receives government funds, the law requires you to ensure equal access to services, including oral interpretation and written translation services.

For more information about the federal law:
http://www.hhs.gov/ocr/lep
(800)368-1019

District of Columbia law:
Office of Human Rights
(202)727-4559

Maryland law:
Office of New Americans
(410)767-8970

영어를 잘 하지 못하십니까?
통역자를 원하시면 카드의 뒷면을 보여주십시오.

당신은 아래 사항을 요청할 수 있습니다:
•무료 통역원 서비스.
•한국어로 되어있는 정보 안내지.

가족이나 동반자가 통역을 위해 동행하지 않아도 됩니다.

정보가 더 필요하시거나 불편사항이 있으시면, 아래에 있는 연락처를 이용해주십시오:

La Clinica del Pueblo
(202)464-0158
www.lcdp.org

CASA de Maryland, Inc.
(301)270-8432
www.casademaryland.org

FIGURE 5.1. "I Speak" Card (Korean Version) with Contact Information. Cut on the dotted lines and fold on the solid line to create your own "I Speak" card. *Source*: District of Columbia, Office of Human Rights, Maryland's Office of New Americans, La Clinica del Pueblo, and CASA de Maryland.

assist LEP persons in the naturalization process through integrated citizenship services.

The mission of the Maryland Council for New Americans is "to promote full immigrant integration into the economic and civic life of Maryland" (Maryland Council for New Americans, 2009). The development of this council is strategic in that it creates a government body that serves as a watchdog for immigrant issues in the state, most importantly relative to language access. Council members state that "the onus is on government to help bridge the language gaps" offering as an accessibility analogy the fact that in the Americans with Disabilities Act "the government doesn't ask the disabled to build their own ramps up stairways."[5] The council helps to promote distribution and use of "I speak" cards in various languages (Figure 5.1). Their distribution is a concerted effort by several agencies including the DC Office of Human Rights, Maryland's Office of New Americans, La Clinica del Pueblo, and CASA de Maryland.

A 2009 Maryland Council for New Americans report stated the limitations on enforcement of the state language access statute:

Unlike other language access laws, Maryland's does not require each agency to develop implementation plans to increase access for LEP individuals. The law directs the state's

---

[5] Quotation from the meeting minutes of the Maryland Council for New Americans, Government Access Working Group meeting, held in March 2009, at the Bethel Korean Presbyterian Church (Lee, 2009).

Department of Human Resources (DHR), in consultation with the Attorney General's office, to provide coordination and technical assistance to agencies. Since the law took effect, DHR has issued model policy guidelines applicable to its local social service offices and contractors, provided training to public contact staff of various state agencies, and shared promising practices. However, the statute does not provide DHR or any other state entity with monitoring or enforcement powers. Without guidance and resources devoted to implementation, the promise of Maryland's language access law will likely be unrealized. (p. 40)

This limitation is particularly important because Montgomery County is bearing the brunt of state LEP requirements: more than one in three (39%) residents ages five and older speaks a language other than English in the home, and one in seven (15 percent) is considered LEP; these figures are the highest in the state of Maryland (A. L. Taylor, 2010). The county sought to build on the Maryland Equal Access to Public Services Act by tailoring a language access plan to meet county residents' needs. In 2009 County Executive Ike Leggett appointed the LEP Leadership Team, made up of senior managers and staff with expertise in language access, to provide leadership and guidance on the county's compliance with its own policy and with federal LEP guidelines (Montgomery County, 2011).

In March 2010, Leggett issued Executive Order 046-10, Access to Government Services for Individuals with Limited English Proficiency (LEP). Modeled after executive orders in several other jurisdictions, it mandates that (written) translation and (oral) interpretation services be made available to help county staff communicate with customers in their native languages. The executive order gave the Montgomery County LEP Leadership Team executive oversight over all aspects of the county's language access efforts.

Each department director must designate a department liaison, a staff member who reports to the LEP Leadership Team on the department's compliance with federal guidelines and county policy on language access. Among the department liaisons' key responsibilities are developing a written LEP plan for the department, ensuring proper staff training, communicating to management and staff about language access expectations and measurements, assessing the department's capacity to provide language assistance, collecting applicable LEP data, and reporting progress on and issues related to serving the LEP population (Montgomery County, 2009). Executive Order 046-10 also makes the Office of the Chief Administrative Officer responsible for the county's overall compliance with language access laws and policy, for providing oversight and support to all departments, and for developing accountability mechanisms (Montgomery County, 2009).

The most important and controversial aspect of this policy is that it requires government agencies to provide language services to *all* residents, not just those making up 3 percent or more of the population, which implies that government agencies must extend their services to cover even the most infrequently spoken languages. Although Montgomery County's policy provides guidelines and designates support organizations, Executive Order 046-10 has led many residents and officials to question who will pay for increased language access services and the extent to which county tax dollars should be utilized toward this end.

The situation in Maryland overall and in Montgomery County in particular contrast starkly to that in Fairfax County, Virginia. Language access services in Fairfax County are considerably less coordinated. In May 2002, the county created a new language access coordinator position to oversee county LEP efforts. Because of budget constraints, however, the position was cut in 2008, yet each department maintains a contact person for language resources. There is one singular language policy in the county, according to the county's Procedural Memorandum 02-08 (August 30, 2004). "No person will be denied equal access to county services based on his/her inability, or limited ability, to communicate in the English language." The primary protocol is that county departments/agencies must use professional, paid vendors for all official translations.

Very little information regarding the initiative appears on the Fairfax County public Web site, and (as of 2014) under the Office of the County Executive there appears no formal governing body to lead implementation, monitoring, or oversight of Fairfax County's language access policy. In fact, without having an informal and off the record conversation with a Fairfax County employee I would have been unaware of the County's internal Web site called Fairfax Net, which hosts, among other internal resources, language services and support tools to aid county employees in providing language access to LEP clients. The Web site provides resources and links to the U.S. Department of Justice language access materials and other resources including: comparable rates for face-to-face or telephone interpretation and translation services; Public Event Transmitter Equipment (PETE), a glossary of language terminology, and a county glossary of common county titles, department, and program names in Spanish and Korean for vendors and others to use in the translation of official county documents. The county provides a stipend for bilingual employees who meet certain requirements. Bilingual employees are encouraged to join the Translation Verification Team (TVT), where county employees are trained, by paid vendors, as volunteer verifiers through the Office of the County Executive, to review accuracy of all county translations for public distribution (flyers, brochures, video scripts, information packets, and form letters).

Neither the state of Virginia nor any jurisdiction within the commonwealth has a law similar to Maryland's Equal Access to Public Services Act that affirms compliance with federal Executive Order 13166. In 1981, Virginia passed a law proclaiming English the official language of the commonwealth, which aligns ideologically with the state's limited allocation of funding for a foreign language initiative. As noted, the federal law, Title VI, supersedes the Virginia state English-only law and thus applies to any Virginia entity receiving federal funds, including Fairfax County.

Fairfax County has the largest LEP population in Virginia (15% of residents, very close to Montgomery County statistics), so its lack of coordinated language services calls into question whether the county (and Virginia as a whole) is in compliance with federal law. It also raises concerns that Virginia municipal governments are placing language access policy on their political agenda at a strictly symbolic level, rather than taking serious steps to incorporate their LEP populations. The internal Web site with resources for county employees to better serve LEP constituents raises concerns about the extent to which Fairfax County's LEP residents, without prior knowledge of the resources internally available, are largely left to navigate language access on their own or to find their way to a nonprofit organization or religious institution offering language access.

Strong leadership in Maryland at the state and local levels pushed the adoption of language access policies, but these measures would not have passed without the collective efforts of leaders and activists in the public, private, and nonprofit sectors who laid the foundation for them. The next section illustrates the interdependency (or lack thereof) of relationships between state and local officials, bureaucrats, and local private/nonprofit organizations to address the needs and concerns of the LEP community.

Suburban Institutional Interdependency (SII) in Language Access

Interdependency Increases Access to Resources

As described in Chapters 3 and 4, access to the greater resources found in the public sector creates an incentive for suburban nonprofits to form partnerships with local government and bureaucratic agencies. Nonprofit organizations may benefit not only from direct funding from local governments, but also from their institutional resources (e.g., meeting spaces, photocopiers, materials), which can reduce overhead costs. In Montgomery County, the community partnerships for language access include the county executive's Ethnic Advisory Groups (Asian Pacific, Middle Eastern, Latino/Hispanic, Caribbean, African, and African American); immigrant-serving organizations like APALRC; and the Montgomery Coalition for Adult English Literacy (MCAEL). MCAEL offers one model of a public-private-nonprofit partnership and illustrates the role of interdependent relationships in suburban language access.

MCAEL is a community coalition of more than seventy business, nonprofit, and public partners aiming to expand opportunities for English language and literacy instruction in Montgomery County. MCAEL's mission is to strengthen the countywide adult English literacy network with resources, training, collaborations, and advocacy to support a thriving community and an optimal workforce (Montgomery Coalition for Adult English Literacy). In 2002 Montgomery County Council members Mike Subin, Marilyn Praisner, and Blair Ewing commissioned Montgomery College, Montgomery County Public Schools (MCPS), and the Center for Applied Linguistics to study the current system of adult ESL programs in the county. Over a six-month period several focus groups, interviewees, and other community leaders convened to review and offer insight into existing county programs. Following the study, council president Mike Subin appointed council member Tom Perez to chair the Adult ESL Task Force. Perez worked with MCPS, Montgomery College, community- and faith-based organizations, Montgomery County public libraries, business leaders, community activists, and others to address language access and develop a strategic action plan for improving the current system of delivery.

In 2003, the county council and Montgomery College collaborated to open an adult English literacy coalition office with a full-time staff person under the auspices of Workforce Development and Continuing Education with the Montgomery College Foundation as the fiscal agent. Within a few years, the coalition incorporated as a 501(c)3 nonprofit under its current name, Montgomery Coalition for Adult English Literacy (MCAEL). Many participants in the former Adult ESL Task Force formed the inaugural board of advisors. Now, the Montgomery County Council outsources to MCAEL the task of awarding grants to support adult English literacy programs across Montgomery County.

During fiscal year 2012, MCAEL awarded $508,225 in grants on behalf of the Montgomery County Council, supporting sixteen out of eighteen applicants and seventeen different programs, including three pilot micro-grants for smaller/emerging programs. The objective of MCAEL's grants program is to increase the availability and quality of adult English literacy services offered to diverse populations. CBOs funded through the grants have served more than 3,000 English language learners on average each year since the grant program began in 2006 (Montgomery Coalition for Adult English Literacy, 2013a). Table 5.1 summarizes the grants awarded, the program enrollment for winter/ spring 2012, and the total instructional hours delivered for fiscal year 2012.

For fiscal year 2013, the county council awarded MCAEL $716,058 to fund its administrative costs, English literacy promotion efforts, and grants program, an increase of $34,098 over the previous year's funding level. MCAEL also received $5,000 or more in funding from the following partners: the Housing Opportunities Commission, Lockheed Martin, Morris & Gwendolyn Cafritz Foundation, United Way of the National Capital Area, Verizon Foundation, and the Community Foundation for the National Capital Region.

Overall there seems to be no formal network similar to MCAEL in Fairfax County, and nonprofit or other organizations focused on language access do not have as strong or coordinated a presence there. Despite no longer having a language access coordinator (position cut in 2008), Fairfax reportedly remains part of the Local Government Language Access Coordinators (LGLAC), established in 2004, which includes a group of language access coordinators from various jurisdictions within northern Virginia, Maryland and the District of Columbia. LGLAC meets regularly to "review the impact of limited-English proficient (LEP) customers on government and public services in their

TABLE 5.1. *Summary of MCAEL Grants Awarded, Program Enrollment, and Instructional Hours Provided, FY 2012*

Organization	Grant Amount	Enrollment Winter/Spring 2012	Total Hours of Instruction, 2012
Casa de Maryland – Evening ESOL	$122,770	683	43,456
Thomas Shortman Training Fund	$82,853	410	17,109
Community Ministries of Rockville	$55,700	210	6,304
Spanish Catholic Center	$51,740	498	12,937
Literacy Council of MC ESOL classes	$42,500	194	10,611
Silver Spring Team for Children and Families	$27,678	111	3,769
Mental Health Association – Families Foremost	$22,379	24	993
Casa de Maryland – Workers' Center ESOL	$22,000	94	13,328
MCPS Foundation – Linkages to Learning	$21,013	200	3,654
Workforce Solutions Group of Montgomery City	$18,525	12	857
Rockville Seniors Inc.	$15,860	112	1,322
Muslim Community Center	$9,000	22	329
Boat People SOS	$6,151	34	773
Korean-American Senior Citizen's Association	$5,056	34	1,676
Caribbean Help Center	$2,000	60	1,460
Seneca Creek Community Church	$2,000	53	610
Korean Community Service Center	$1,000	7	168

Source: MCAEL FY12 Final Report, 2013.

jurisdictions, discuss demographic trends and explore resources to better assist in the provision of quality customer service to an increasing population of LEP residents in the metropolitan area" (LGLAC Mission Statement).

Most efforts in the county are targeted at increasing awareness of LEP populations and meeting their immediate needs, particularly in terms of interpretation and translation necessary to access legal and medical services. Many LEP individuals in Fairfax County have been unable to communicate with law enforcement in critical situations and in some cases LEP patients received hospital discharge papers in English (Alfisi, 2009).

The Community Legal Interpreter Bank, which offers a wide range of immigration and family law assistance, as well as social service support for all immigrants, is a notable exception in Fairfax County. In 2005, the DC Access to Justice Commission, motivated by the DC Court of Appeals, lobbied for city funding to address the lack of language access among legal services providers. The commission secured $3.2 million from the DC city council, which was used to found the Community Legal Interpreter Bank through a collaborative effort between the Access to Justice Commission, the DC council, and the nonprofit organization Ayuda. Other professional associations, such as the DC Bar Association, have since contributed funding to the bank, which was first piloted in 2008. Managed by Ayuda, Fairfax County's Community Legal Interpreter Bank has twenty-six legal services providers and fifty-one legal interpreters who speak about twenty languages. Ayuda's Web site proclaims the Interpreter Bank as "the first interpreter program in the US to provide professional training to interpreters targeted to the attorney-client relationship" (AYUDA, 2013).

Interdependency Increases Legitimacy and Lowers Transaction Costs

For county governments, the value of multiethnic nonprofits is that they are uniquely positioned to reach vulnerable, isolated, and hard-to-reach LEP communities that public-sector agencies working alone cannot effectively reach. Some immigrants may consume less in public assistance and become more able to help themselves through social networking among co-ethnics. The focus group discussions first introduced in Chapter 2 examined an important and often-understudied component of minority suburbanization – the perceived responsiveness of local governments to minorities' needs and concerns. The focus groups solicited discussants' positive and negative experiences with their county or municipal government, language and cultural barriers to participation in civic and political activities, small business regulations (particularly among Korean business owners), gaining U.S. citizenship, social services, and affordable health care.

For example, Korean discussants noted having strong social ties to places of worship such as the Presbyterian Church, whereas Chinese discussants noted the role of Chinese language schools that their children attend in order to maintain their language and cultural heritage; both groups described how these entities facilitated their transition into the existing suburban infrastructure by teaching them some of the "rules of the game" and where to find resources and support. Lagdameo and Ortiz point out, "Coming from different countries, immigrants often do not know the services and resources available to them or the rights they have (i.e., patient rights, tenant rights). As newcomers to this country, immigrants often turn to friends, family members, and organizations they trust before they turn to the local public health department or the state's Web site for information.... This is especially true for immigrants who come from countries where the government has been oppressive" (2009, p. 41). Some immigrant groups are hesitant to overtly seek services from the government or participate in government-sponsored activities.

To address some of these concerns, in 2001 Montgomery County opened the Charles Gilchrist Center for Cultural Diversity "catering to the needs of immigrants at various steps in their lives" (Gilchrist Center for Cultural Diversity, 2011). The center offers programs and services, including, among others, ESL and citizenship test preparation classes, basic legal assistance, informational seminars on a variety of topics, such as small business development, and an extensive information and referral system to county and CBO programs and services. During a 2004 interview, Alexandra Teaff, director of the Gilchrest Center, discussed what she tells her staff about gaining the trust of immigrant clients:

all we need is for whoever comes through our doors to get the service that they need in a ... nice, respectful way ... and they [the client] are our best marketing tool. You know, within a lot if not most of the immigrant communities, word of mouth is what works. You can print as many flyers as you want, but word of mouth is where the trust comes. If my mom or my neighbor or my co-worker or my cousin or whoever it is that I know tells me, "I went to this place, and they were nice, they were patient, they were able to give me this service program or find this service program in the county that I needed; they made sure that that's where I needed to go, or ... they weren't able to find a service or program for me, but they explained why, or they're looking for it and will get back to me." You know ... I think it's also a demeanor ... the way you interact with the person that's asking the information, and it just takes time. And thank goodness we've ... come this far, and people seem to have that trust.... So, like I said, word of mouth ... I'm always touched when somebody comes through our doors and, two minutes later, is telling me their life story; it's, a reflection of, we're doing something right.

Teaff also noted that the look and the feel of the building helps clients feel comfortable, relating the remarks of an older gentleman "who came in; he sort of stood in the reception area, and he looked around, and he looked around, and he said, 'This doesn't look like a government building.' And I thought, 'That's a good thing, I guess.'" The Korean, Chinese, and Iranian focus group participants were particularly vocal about language access whereas this was less of a concern for Latinos because many of the materials at government and health facilities are available in Spanish. Although some discussants praised law enforcement officers for helping to secure their neighborhoods or letting them out of an occasional speeding ticket, across all racial/ethnic groups, most participants' negative experiences with local governments occurred during interactions with local law officers and were perceived to result from racial or cultural biases.

Chinese respondents generally believed that because of their accent, outsiders were less likely to treat them fairly. One Chinese respondent from Fairfax County stated that his fear of being stopped by police officers, particularly if no one was present to interpret for him, was heightened by his inability to communicate adequately in English. Even immigrants who spoke English well reported often relying on their children to accompany them to county agencies or when handling government-related business. An Iranian woman from Fairfax County stated that although her English was fine for everyday purposes, she still preferred to have one of her children accompany her when communicating with government officials: "There have been times when they have used terminology that I'm not familiar with. It's comforting for me to know that there is someone with me who will make sure that there are no misunderstandings or mistakes if I have difficulty communicating with the representative." (This echoes an issue also raised in the University of Maryland report commissioned by the state legislature.)

An Iranian male articulated a similar point:

MALE: Well, our concerns are the same as those of other communities. We are concerned with employment opportunities, the economy, health, and our children's education. I think it's difficult to have the authorities to respond to our community's needs because we are not as populated or organized as the Hispanic community. We must follow their example to become a united group with enough power to apply political pressure.

Notably, some immigrant discussants chose to remain isolated from local government. One Korean discussant who does not speak English adamantly stated,

MALE: In my case, I could say that I do not have any bad experiences. But it's because I have never tried anything. I just work hard on my own and try to finish things in advance. Because I live like that, I do not have any direct contact with government whatsoever. Of course, I cannot speak English. But because I live in such a way that I get some distance from government and public affairs, I neither benefit from government nor harm the society.

The Chinese, Korean, and Iranian discussants voiced concerns that the local government addressed the needs of Latinos to a much greater extent than was true for other ethnic groups in the county. They perceived these differences to be associated with the political mobilization of local Latinos, who were notably more organized and were willing to pressure the local government to respond. Several Korean discussants felt the local government should reach out more to the Korean community, particularly regarding the translation and dissemination of public information. Such materials, they contended, should be more widely available in languages other than English and Spanish:

FEMALE: In my case, my mom just came here as well as myself, so when we want to travel somewhere and find some information about it, we couldn't understand the information written in the site well. It takes so long to just look up the dictionary and find the words. I found this site that allows the visitor to choose the language. It was really helpful. So I think that if it is possible for the county to provide such service, it would be really helpful for those who just came to America.

MODERATOR: Especially, translation at the place, of the materials and Web sites, you mean?

FEMALE: Right.

MODERATOR: You are talking about the Web site in Korean so that you can access it easily and understand the information better?

FEMALE: I think, in that way, we can obtain greater amount of information easier.

Overall, Chinese, Koreans, and Iranians reported that language and cultural barriers, sometimes compounded by perceived bias, hindered their communication with local agency officials over the phone and in person, particularly when interpreters or translated materials were not available.

In Fairfax County, Chong Ho Yuk serves as vice president of the Korean-American Association of Virginia (KAAV) and principal of Korean Vocational School, established by KAAV and housed in a county-owned building alongside a multicultural center that provides LEP programs for immigrants. During our interview, she described the need for the center:

Under 18, they [Koreans] go to public school. But over 18 adults ... there is no proper place for them to have education. This school is for that kind of adults. If Korean immigrants first come here, they need to learn American social systems, new language [English] and job training education to settle down in the U.S. And also all the people need lifetime education. They already have enough education in Korea but they also need another education in the U.S. in order to survive here. That's why we exist, for these needs.

Interdependency Leverages Public Resources

One of the most contentious issues surrounding language access policy at the local level is who will pay the cost of providing oral interpretation and written translation services to LEP adults seeking government services. In Montgomery County alone, the cost of providing LEP services was $414,547 in 2011, down nearly $40,000 from $451,086 in 2010 (County of Montgomery, 2011).[6] Government partnerships with nonprofit organizations are one effective strategy for providing low-cost translation and interpretation services. The Montgomery County–run Volunteer Language Bank provides free language services to both registered nonprofits and public agencies as a supplemental service. The county government also taps into community in language media and service providers to distribute translated materials in order to maximize exposure and save printing costs (Qi, 2013).

---

[6] Available Montgomery County language access services include interpretation (verbal) resources, certified bilingual employees, over-the-phone interpretation (contracted, instant access), on-site interpretation (contracted, prior arrangement required), translation (written) resources, Schreiber Translations, Inc. (contracted), automated Web content translation in the top five languages on the county Web site, multilingual public service video about LEP (on the LEP Web site), staff training on LEP through the Office of Human Resources training management and registration system, and a translated documents archive.

Noting some of the continuing limitations in language access provision, the Montgomery County Annual Report on LEP Policy Implementation (2011) stated, "Because of the budget limitations, departments are increasingly turning to the County's internal language resources, such as bilingual employees and even volunteers, before using a contractor. These 'borrowed' employees have been a great value added in assisting with multilingual services. A couple of departments have also effectively partnered with community organizations to provide additional multilingual services" (LEP Leadership Team, 2011, p. 6). To cut costs, county departments have focused their efforts on internal staff training to certify the hundreds of existing bilingual county employees instead of contracting out interpretation services to private companies. Utilizing bilingual employees who are certified in translation to help train other staff is more cost-effective than having untrained bilinguals translate documents in terms that may not be up to government standards. Departments have also partnered with nonprofit agencies to expand their services and outreach to even the smallest populations. Overall, the most notable advantages of this policy are improved relationships between immigrants and the government and increased access to language services for speakers of all languages (Montgomery Coalition for Adult English Literacy, 2009). The interdependent relationships forged via the MCAEL grants program leverage public resources by outsourcing to nonprofits to help to bridge the gap between available resources and potential clients. Here I highlight four of the seventeen nonprofit or faith-based recipients of fiscal year 2012 MCAEL grants funded by the county government (see Table 5.1).

CASA de Maryland was granted $122,770 to provide an evening ESOL program focused on improving participants' listening, speaking, reading, and writing skills so that they could become more financially independent, increase their employability, better integrate into American society, and achieve their personal goals. Figure 5.2 provides an example of the kind of English and Spanish publicity CASA de Maryland uses to advertise their evening adult English literacy classes. This program enrolled 683 participants who attended 43,456 hours of instruction and service provision. CASA also received a smaller grant for $22,000 to support the operation of the welcome center/day laborer ESOL program at three locations – Wheaton, Shady Grove, and Silver Spring – designed to help adult learners improve their employment prospects and increase their earnings. The welcome center ESOL program enrolled ninety-four participants who attended 13,228 hours of instruction and service provision.

The MCPS Foundation Linkages to Learning Adult English Literacy Program received $21,013. Linkages to Learning is a collaborative school-based partnership among the school district, Montgomery County DHHS, public and private agencies, families, and communities. The grant supports an adult ESOL program, offered at schools during school hours, to assist parents in achieving self-sufficiency in order to improve the well-being of their children and families. The 200 participants attended 3,653 hours of instruction and service provision.

The Spanish Catholic Center offers medical and dental clinics, job training programs, English classes, a food pantry, and case management services

126

FIGURE 5.2. CASA de Maryland English at Night Flier, English and Spanish Versions.

Source: CASA de Maryland (2013) Education and Leadership Department.

in one location in DC and three in Maryland. The multicultural staff of the center speak more than eight different languages and have experience working with individuals from more than seventy-two different cultural contexts (SCC Web page). The center received a $51,740 grant to support an ongoing ESOL program, located in Gaithersburg and Germantown, focused on increasing the language and literacy skills of low-income, LEP members of the growing immigrant and Hispanic communities. This program enrolled 498 participants who attended 12,937 hours of instruction and service provision.

The Korean Community Service Center of Greater Washington (KCSC) received a micro literacy access grant for $1,000 to support an English conversation club for Korean American stay-at-home mothers. KCSC enrolled seven women who attended 168 hours of English conversation. KCSC is a 501(c)3 not-for-profit human service organization established in 1974 by a group of Christians to meet the growing needs of Korean immigrants in the DC metro area. Headquartered in northern Virginia, KCSC has served more than 50,000 Korean American immigrant families and currently provides services to about 600 Korean Americans a month at four office sites: three locations in Maryland and one in northern Virginia. KCSC provides comprehensive social services to low- to moderate-income individuals and families to "promote self-sufficiency and to be contributing community members." Bilingual staff members assist clients with translation and interpretation, immigration services such as filing immigration documents and enrolling in citizenship preparation classes, job readiness, social services, and referrals for food stamps and government subsidized housing. In 1991, with support from the U.S. Department of Housing and Urban Development (HUD), the KCSC-sponsored University Garden Senior Apartment opened as the first Washington metro area apartment community for low-income seniors. Since then KCSC has received another $3.8 million from HUD to add twenty-seven more units to the existing building (Korean Community Service Center of Greater Washington, 2013).

These are but a few examples of the more than 3,000 LEP individuals served through MCAEL grants in fiscal year 2012 alone. Acting alone local governments could never reach this number of individuals.

The Stability and Limitations of Institutional Interdependency in Suburbia

Language access varies greatly between Montgomery and Fairfax Counties. Montgomery County passed legislation directly mandating language access. Its Web site has pages dedicated to its LEP policies and provides evidence of their implementation through government leadership teams, hierarchies of coordination, lists of community partnerships, government resources for training curricula, community involvement, and volunteerism, as well as annual reports detailing the budget, strengths of the program, and recommendations for the future (LEP Leadership Team, 2011).

No similar legislation exists in Fairfax County and its sole language access initiative appears moribund (Sicola, 2004). Fairfax County government does not appear to hold a central assessment or reporting system for LEP issues. Some departments in the county do conduct LEP assessments, but these are not systematic and are department specific.

Montgomery County frontline staff are mandated by County Executive Order 046-10 to participate in LEP and cultural sensitivity training yearly. Additionally Montgomery County offers year-round language access support to departments through their language access Web site. Fairfax County lacks comparable measures in place to ensure that its staff are adequately trained to meet LEP needs.

The effective implementation of language access at the county level presents many challenges. First, in an effort to save time and money, government agencies often rely on bilingual staff members to communicate with LEP clients and to translate official documents. Although this practice may save money and employees are often trained by vendors, it can result in incorrect interpretation and faulty translation of government documents. Moreover, departments are warned against the less than ideal strategy of using an LEP individual's family members or friends as interpreters when immediate language assistance is needed. However, there is little knowledge of the extent to which this practice still takes place.

Second, local government departments need improved outreach to LEP adults to inform them of available language access services and ESL classes. Although LEP individuals have accessible mechanisms to communicate with government agencies, it is much more difficult for the agencies to reach out to clients who might need their services but be unaware of them or uncomfortable contacting government entities. As a result, LEP services are not being utilized to their fullest potential.

Third, local governments face many challenges incorporating the needs of immigrants and LEP residents into the emergency planning process. Wang contends:

Newcomers are especially vulnerable when disaster strikes due to isolation, limited English skills, and/or limited knowledge about information and resources available during emergencies. The experience of the Vietnamese-American community in the aftermath of Hurricane Katrina, where many families did not know whether to evacuate or where to turn for assistance and safety, was a highly visible reminder of the importance of incorporating newcomers' needs in emergency planning (2009, p. 31, n. 74)

Unlike in Fairfax County, Montgomery County views the provision of LEP services "not [as] a special initiative, but rather a way of doing business for a local government whose constituency is as diverse as what we have in Montgomery County" (LEP Leadership Team, 2011). The Virginia counties' current priorities seem to be strategic planning of LEP services and efficient data collection on these services relative primarily to the health and legal arenas (Alfisi, 2009). Much work remains to be done in Fairfax County, although some new efforts seem to be under way. In December 2012, Fairfax County and Arlington County jointly hosted the first annual Language Access Leadership Conference. The county offices partnering to put on the conference were the Fairfax County Community Services Board, Alexandria Department of Community and Human Services, Loudoun County Government, Arlington County Division of Human Rights–Office of the County Manager, and Virginia Department of Behavioral Health and Developmental Services. Workshop topics included the LEP responsibilities of local jurisdictions, health and human services providers, the implementation of LEP plans and policies, and how to measure effectiveness of language access services. Workshop presenters included a refugee services manager from Lutheran Social Services, a compliance manager in the Human Rights Division for Arlington County, and language testing and training specialists at CBOs such as Northern Virginia Area Health Education Center (AHEC). This collaborative effort is a step in the right direction and highlights the fact that Fairfax County has a lot more to do to meet federal requirements under Title VI.[7]

In this case, it appears that the differences in responsiveness to LEP populations, between Montgomery and Fairfax Counties, may be attributed in part to outgrowths of their political ethos or ideologies. Montgomery County views the effective incorporation of LEP immigrants as ultimately benefiting the public good by helping these people become more self-sufficient, better employed, and eventually civic-minded citizens who contribute to local society. Fairfax County, in keeping with the state's English-only law, seems to be keeping much of its information on language access "in house" rather than forming public-nonprofit partnerships, specifically around language access to better serve the needs of its growing LEP population. This raises questions about the extent to which Fairfax views LEP services as an undue burden that diminishes the county's level of services to native-born citizens; or if fears of more public attachments to language access programs/policies on the face of county government (e.g., public Web site, collaborative public-partnerships) would attract unwanted attention. It also remains to be seen whether the rapidly changing demographics and recent trend toward more a liberal-leaning constituency will influence the direction of language access in the county. Ultimately, will these factors push the county to see immigrant and LEP services as a win-win or as a win-lose? Where the prevailing political will sees a win-win, then SII can provide the mechanisms for government to serve LEP immigrants more cost-effectively and less controversially by collaborating with the nonprofit sector.

[7] Also see Department of Justice (2013), Commonly Asked Questions and Answers Regarding Executive Order 13166.

Conclusion

To better explain how local institutional actors respond to and implement policies to address the rapidly changing demographics in American suburbs, I first set out to understand the factors that influence immigrant and native-born racial/ethnic minorities to move to or within a multiethnic suburb. My findings indicate that racial and ethnic factors continue to influence where an individual resides. In line with place stratification theory, residential mobility continues to be a strong reflection of status in the social hierarchy of U.S. society (Alba & Logan, 1993; Logan & Alba, 1993; Logan & Molotch, 1987). In fact, both descriptive statistics and data from five focus group discussions reveal a persisting social hierarchy by race. Descriptive statistics revealed racial/ethnic disparities are especially marked in spatial assimilation factors, such as educational attainment and income, as well as household demographic characteristic, marital status, and homeownership.

Also evident is the extent to which multiethnic suburbs are in fact racially divided in a type of "segregated diversity" (Nicolaides & Wiese, 2006, p. 99). Although a suburb may be characterized by significant economic and class heterogeneity, affluent and low-income areas within the suburb remain clearly distinct and, most important, starkly divided by race and ethnicity. Moving beyond the metropolitan statistical area as a unit of analysis to examine county-level differences within the multiethnic metro of Washington, DC, helps reveal the extent to which residential mobility is influenced by sorting out according to race/ethnicity, class, and other factors. Like many of the nation's larger metropolitan areas, metropolitan Washington has experienced rapid demographic changes over the past few decades. Deindustrialization and population decline in the urban core of the District of Columbia has coincided with rapid expansion of socioeconomically and politically fragmented suburban jurisdictions. Suburban growth and pockets of wealth within the melting-pot suburbs in Fairfax County, Virginia, and Montgomery County, Maryland, serve to mask some of the underlying factors driving suburban residential selection processes, as well as neighborhood interactions and perceptions of local government responsiveness (related to local goods and services), among particular racial/ethnic groups.

A series of native-language focus group discussions among adult black (English), Chinese (Mandarin), Iranian (Farsi), Korean (Korean), and Latino (Spanish) settlers in suburban Washington, DC, unveils a fascinating story of life in the "new suburbia." Not surprisingly, for these immigrant and racial/ethnic minority residents, suburban residential decisions are generally influenced by the perceived or actual quality of a county's delivery of goods and services (e.g., good schools, safe neighborhoods, reasonable quality and affordability of housing). Other important considerations are employment opportunities and established family ties. However, the findings reveal a more complex set of concerns, as discussants aspired to a piece of the American dream, their neighborhood selections were constrained by income, particularly for blacks. The respondents perceive substantial intra-metropolitan disparities in housing affordability as well as the delivery of some local public goods and services. The focus group discussions reveal that living in a so-called multiethnic area does not necessarily result in less segregation or isolation, particularly for blacks, whose income levels and housing options limit their entry into select suburban neighborhoods.

To some extent, the segregation appears self-imposed, in that discussants honestly expressed fears of or actual negative encounters with "undesirables" of different racial/ethnic backgrounds. Particularly salient were negative perceptions of outgroups. Some Latinos reported having exited predominantly black suburbs in Prince George's County, or having avoided moving there altogether, in order to escape close proximity to blacks. Some Fairfax County Iranians expressed their dissatisfaction with increasing numbers of Koreans and Latinos moving into the neighborhood and disrupting the quality of life by overcrowding housing units and parking vehicles on the lawns, for example. Notably, discussants' concerns often centered less on explicit racial bias toward a particular group than on behaviors alleged to be upsetting the status quo. However, such unwanted behaviors carried specific implicit racial/ethnic/class overtones and were generalized to entire racial/ethnic groups.

In terms of factors deterring access to government services, Chinese, Koreans, and Iranians frequently reported that language and cultural barriers hindered their communication with local agency officials, particularly when translators or translated materials were not available. For some immigrant groups, language and cultural barriers also reportedly impeded neighborhood interactions. Discussants also expressed a lack of time and desire to engage in neighborhood events and activities outside of their immediate families or with racial/ethnic outsiders.

Interestingly, across focus groups, the discussants generally agreed that the suburban library system was one of their most favored and valued local

services. Public libraries are traditionally viewed as a noncontroversial allocative rather than a redistributive type of public good. Local libraries offered the
discussants a welcoming, safe, quiet place to gather information and resources,
as well as to relax with their families. Discussants praised local library staff
for helping them to read maps and to find information concerning employment, transportation, and educational opportunities; as well as for providing
programming for their children (such as puppet shows, story times, and other
activities). For low-income individuals, the library also offered easy access to
computers and the Internet.

Local libraries also reportedly served as community "meet and greet" locations. Because of the challenges of motivating newcomers with language or
cultural barriers to come out and participate in formal activities designed to
increase awareness, enhance neighborhood interactions, or improve quality of
life, it is important to meet these people "where they are." Given residents' time
constraints and general apathy, holding informational meetings or seminars in
easily accessible, "neutral" spaces could prove important. Because they already
feel comfortable in and regularly frequent the local public library, libraries
could be excellent places to hold community meetings, open to all but targeted toward immigrant and ethnic minority newcomers. Workshops on topics
such as homeownership, public safety, and how to access local government
resources – held in a variety of languages – could lower some of the language
and cultural barriers suburban newcomers face. Increased dissemination of
information and knowledge could also temper the simmering racial/ethnic ani-
mosity that surfaced in the focus groups.

Despite fifty years of theorizing about the proper role of local governments
as either allocative or developmental, in seeking to "get things done" many
local actors find and implement redistributive policy solutions in response to
the issues immigrant, minority, and low-income groups raise. They do so in
the face of changing demographics, local budgetary constraints, and a suburban political environment likely to be averse to a change in the status quo. Yet
any discussion of gearing services specifically to immigrant and racial/ethnic
minority groups inevitably raises concerns about the suburban political economy dilemma facing contemporary suburban institutions. Large numbers of
these suburban newcomers are low-income noncitizens, ineligible to vote yet
nevertheless in need of local public goods and services. Local governments and
suburban residents have expressed widely divergent attitudes and responses to
the influx of new residents, and efforts to provide services to meet their needs
have often proven controversial, particularly when the intended beneficiaries
are suspected of being undocumented immigrants.

The case studies revealed varying levels of commitment and results between
counties; the suburban institutional interdependency (SII) framework helps
to explain the formation of coalitions of local actors – specifically, elected
officials, bureaucratic service and regulatory employees, and nonprofit or
faith-based leaders – to address the needs of immigrant and ethnic minority

newcomers. Local public and nonprofit institutions build partnerships based on reciprocity, repeated interactions, and the exchange of selective incentives for cooperation. Moreover, institutional interdependency in suburbia entails a division of labor and resources that facilitates "getting things done" in the face of rapidly changing demographics, tightening local budgets, and a lack of redistributive dollars from the federal government. SII explains how suburban institutional actors have responded to three public policy issues: (a) public education; (b) day labor; and (c) language access at public agencies. These case studies underscore the importance of symbiotic public–nonprofit relationships in suburbia.

I also highlighted how local government leaders' partisanship and their ideological sense of right and wrong influenced the actors interviewed. The case studies suggest that suburban institutional interdependency changes the way we should think about government actors' partisan and ideological decision making around redistribution in American suburbs. Similar to Stone's classic 1989 study of Atlanta, I also found that partnerships between unlikely collaborators did not necessarily grow out of a shared ideology. While ideology or preexisting state mandate may have influenced decision makers, governmental and nongovernmental actors joined together based on specific common goals, purposes, and selective incentives to cooperate (Stone, 1989, 1993, 1998, 2005). In the face of rapidly changing demographics and scarce fiscal resources to address new public policy concerns from the unyielding influx of immigrants and ethnic minorities to suburban jurisdictions, such explanations alone do less to explain how public-nonprofit partnerships are developed, maintained, or dismantled during the development and implementation of policies/programs.

Local actors often address redistributive issues through institutional partnerships among elected officials, bureaucratic agencies, and, most important, immigrant-serving nonprofit and faith-based organizations. To do so, suburban governments may direct public funds to a nonprofit organization, which acts as both service provider and intermediary between government bureaucracy and newcomers. The logic of SII overcomes some of the obstacles to collective action and allows local actors to leverage a combination of public and private resources to address the needs of documented and undocumented immigrants as well as minority and low-income groups in suburbia. There is a powerful logic at work behind these relationships that lends them stability: each set of actors benefits from the relationship. The most obvious aspect of the relationship is the funding and support nonprofits receive from local governments. But local governments also profit from this symbiosis through increased legitimacy and lowered transaction costs as they attempt to grapple with new issues and problems they are ill equipped to deal with. In addition to partnering with nonprofits, governmental agencies can leverage their resources by outsourcing much of the work, which lowers their costs and to some extent insulates them from risk while still allowing them to share in any success.

However, such symbiotic relationships have varying degrees of longevity and dynamism. Whereas some collaborative efforts endure beyond the specific public policy concern that precipitated their formation, others are volatile and are often disrupted by changes in local leadership or citizen attitudes. Moreover, by passing responsibility to nonprofit-sector organizations, local government thereby empowers these organizations to make decisions about who shall be served and how those services are to be provided. This raises the question of who assumes oversight responsibility for and evaluates the performance of the nonprofit partner receiving government funding. A second question is whether being beholden to government funding reduces a nonprofit's autonomy and commitment to its original goals, especially in the volatile arena of immigrant and racial/ethnic minority rights. Focus group discussants as well as government and nonprofit interviewees cited several additional challenges to the stability of local suburban coalitions. The next section examines some of these challenges regarding government outsourcing to nonprofits in suburbia.

The Persistent Challenges of Government Outsourcing to Nonprofits: Growing Suburban Poverty and Limited Nonprofit Capacity

By 2010, the suburbs of America's biggest metropolitan areas housed the largest and fastest-growing poor population in the country. Suburbia became home to 1.5 million more people in poverty than their primary cities and almost one-third of the nation's poor overall (Kneebone & Garr, 2010). Few suburban communities have an adequate social service infrastructure to address this challenge. Inner suburbs, in particular, are characterized by racial, ethnic, or economic segregation and older housing and infrastructure (Allard 2004; Orfield, 2002). Such areas are also experiencing a rapid economic shift from middle-income or working-class to lower-income and increasingly poverty-stricken residents, bringing with it many of the social and economic concerns of the neighboring central cities. These factors increase the demand for social services, especially those involving financial assistance, and place tremendous strain on suburban nonprofits (M. Hirsch, 2005). For example, a 2004 study of metropolitan Washington, DC, nonprofits found that in neighborhoods with rising poverty, the mean number of social service providers within a one-and-a-half-mile radius was only 6 in suburban areas versus 31.6 in the District of Columbia (Allard, 2004).

Nonprofit social service providers are increasingly asked to help rising numbers of low-income families with tighter budgets and fewer resources. Suburban social safety nets rely on relatively fewer service providers that are stretched over much larger service delivery areas than their urban counterparts. Thirty-four percent of nonprofits surveyed reported operating in more than one suburban county, and 60 percent offered services in more than one suburban municipality (Allard, 2004).

Suburban nonprofits witnessed significantly greater demand, and nearly three-quarters (73%) of suburban nonprofits are seeing more clients with no previous connection to social safety net programs. Needs have changed as well, with nearly 80 percent of suburban nonprofits surveyed seeing families with food needs, and nearly 60 percent reporting more frequent requests for help with mortgage or rent payments. At the same time, revenue streams have decreased. Sixty-six percent expect cuts in government funding and 47 percent expect philanthropic dollars to decrease (Allard, 2004).

While the relationship between the government and nonprofit social service organizations spans decades (J Alexander, 2000; J. Alexander, Nank, & Stivers, 1999; de Graauw, 2008; Salamon, 1999, 2002; Salamon, Hems, & Chinnock, 2000), it has largely been understood from an urban or central city context. The Great Society programs of the mid-1960s and the federal community development block grant program, enacted in 1974, solidified the relationship between the federal government and nonprofit sectors in providing services to urban poor, minority, and immigrant communities (de Graauw, 2008).

The Welfare Reform Law of 1986 further encouraged CBOs and faith-based organizations to become formal providers of social services through government outsourcing (Nightingale & Pindus, 1997). The Personal Responsibility and Work Opportunity Reconciliation Act of 1996 transformed the inter-organizational environment of nonprofit social service providers and their relationship to the public sector. The nonprofit sector was central to the implementation and operation of the Temporary Assistance for Needy Families (TANF) program initiated with the implementation of the 1996 welfare reform act. TANF is a block grant program designed, at least in theory, to help move recipients into work and turn welfare into a program of temporary rather than long-term assistance. TANF replaced the former Aid to Families with Dependent Children (AFDC), Job Opportunities and Basic Skills Training (JOBS), and Emergency Assistance (EA) welfare programs. The law ended federal entitlement to assistance and replaced it with TANF block grants that funnel federal funds to states, territories, and tribes each year to cover benefits and services targeted to needy families (Department of Health and Human Services, 2013).

Reisch and Sommerfeld, during interviews with service providers in the aftermath of the 1996 Welfare Reform Act, found "a general sense emerged that the public sector had abdicated much of its responsibility for the care of low-income populations to nonprofit organizations" (2003, p. 41). Although outsourcing may provide an opportunity to reduce costs without losing service quality, cost saving is usually not the primary objective of government outsourcing (Luna, 2006). Instead, the typical goals are to increase expertise related to the client/program/policy and *improve* overall service quality (Luna, 2006). Outsourcing allows bureaucracies to access a pool of talent, energy, technological resources, and innovation present in the private sector (Freeman & Minow, 2009).

As the case studies in this book reveal, immigrant-serving nonprofits and faith-based organizations offer social services, cultural preservation programs, language classes, workforce development programs, legal services, and often a safe, welcoming meeting place for immigrants and ethnic minorities. It is generally assumed that CBOs and faith-based organizations are less likely than government bureaucracies to skimp on quality services in an effort to cut costs, and hence are better suited to provide human services like LEP programs whose quality is difficult to verify (Werker & Ahmed, 2008). Yet some detractors fear that because of the lack of checks and balances, nonprofits could provide minimal services, hire underqualified staff, and otherwise misuse government funds (El, 2007). Poor oversight and lack of transparency and accountability can lead to corruption and profiteering, driving governments deeper into debt (Nichols, 2010). Outsourcing arrangements maybe unsuccessful because of lack of specific goals, a single point of accountability, and information systems to track services and outcome measures (Freeman & Minow, 2009; University of Tennesse, 2006). Government agency staff may be poorly resourced and trained for outsource management, leading to an absence of rules, meaningless oversight, and breakdowns in accountability structures between the agency and its private-sector partners (Freeman & Minow, 2009). According to Nightingale and Pindus (1997), the effectiveness and performance of outsourcing activities is dependent on the accountability, clarity, and structure embedded in the implementation phase. A successful framework for outsourcing implementation contains six components (which are not easily maintained): (a) political leaders as champions/advocates; (b) a formal structure for implementation; (c) a reduction in allocated resources to encourage change; (d) reliable data on costs; (e) strategies to deal with workforce transition; and (f) ongoing monitoring and oversight.

Another concern is the possibility that contracting out public services may cause job loss for public employees. As a result of outsourcing, the job growth rate in the public sector has experienced some shrinkage since the mid-1970s (Nightingale & Pindus, 1997). The number of federal civilian employees has expanded modestly – from 2.5 million employees in 1962 to 2.8 million in 2011 – in comparison to the expansion of the government sector. Outsourcing can be seen as a cause of this phenomenon whereby the federal government has increased its spending without adding many employees (Pierson, 2013).

The size and capacity of the nonprofit social service sector vary widely across suburbs. Competition among nonprofits remains a primary concern (de Graauw, 2008; de Graauw et al., 2013). Imbalanced and unfair competition can be caused by asymmetrical information. Reisch and Sommerfeld found "organizations were facing strong competitive financial pressures even during a period of abundance [referring to the 1990s]. This competitive environment disadvantages smaller organizations, because unlike their larger and more mainstream counterparts, they have less access to critical information, less flexibility in developing alternative staffing patterns, and fewer options to generate new resources" (2003, p. 42).

Racial and ethnic groups in suburban Washington, DC, differ in their degree of institutional strength and organization. For example, predominantly Latino-serving CBOs in suburban Washington, DC, have significantly more power than those serving predominantly African American, Asian, or Middle Eastern populations. For example, the NAACP is still active in suburban DC, but it cannot match the financial and human capital resources and support available to CASA de Maryland, the largest Latino immigrant organization in Maryland. This great imbalance in institutional resources between the two organizations has hindered their recent attempts to forge alliances. Moreover, negative stereotypes, racism, and language and cultural barriers further impede the formation of cross-ethnic coalitions. In order to overcome some of these limitations the incipient CASA-NAACP alliance has hosted community meetings that address stereotypes and racism, as well as jointly sponsoring candidate forums. CASA has also purchased translation equipment to enable participants to speak in their preferred languages, and has hired a staffer in Prince George's County to serve as a liaison with NAACP chapters (Grant-Thomas & Sarfati, 2009).

Perhaps the CASA-NAACP alliance can thrive and become a model for other rapidly changing suburbs to follow. This is especially important as Latinos, blacks, and other racial/ethnic groups "compete for space" (Logan & Stearns, 1981) on suburban school boards and other positions of power in places where one racial group remains the majority population, such as Prince George's County. Persistent racial and economic inequalities between and within suburban jurisdictions, the perceived threat of racial change in some areas, and increasing suburban segregation and avoidance in others can make it difficult for diverse groups to form coalitions or alliances and to pool their social and political capital. Where racial avoidance occurs, the prospects for forming alliances to gain greater social, economic, or political incorporation in suburbia are severely weakened. Although SII provides some insight into how public-nonprofit collaborations may form, a greater understanding of how suburban racial/ethnic groups create and maintain viable coalitions is warranted. Densely populated and increasingly racially bifurcated suburban jurisdictions can impede coalition forming among groups with social or political capital to wield.

Citizens cannot vote out a CBO in the same fashion as they can vote out public officials. Hence, they are essentially "held hostage" to a set of service-delivery programs implemented by the selected nonprofits, at least for the length of one funding cycle. Furthermore, some scholars suggest that embedded in the CBO structure are greater direct incentives to manage donor satisfaction versus beneficiary welfare and concerns (Werker &

Ahmed, 2008). Guaranteeing competition by developing an effective request for proposal (RFP) process and outsource contract monitoring protocols, and by addressing political opposition, could help increase the cost-effectiveness of outsourcing (Bandoh, 2003).

Some scholars suggest that government outsourcing to nonprofits challenges the integrity of nonprofits, as they become extensions of and dependent on government funding. As a result of outsourcing many nonprofits may cease to be private avenues that serve the public interest and instead become co-opted by the government (Pierson, 2013). Yet de Graauw makes a clear distinction between interest group organizations and nonprofits. She contends that whereas immigrant-serving nonprofits are similar to interest groups in that they "speak for, act for, and look after the interests of their clients or constituents in the political process," they differ in that "immigrant nonprofits are subject to more government restrictions and regulations on their political activities; less partisan; more exclusively informational power; more likely to serve the public (rather than special) interest" (2008, p. 330). Nevertheless, as Reisch and Sommerfeld suggest, "The emphasis on service delivery and its frequently associated efficiency-based evaluation orientation threatens to erode some of the distinctive features that have characterized the nonprofit sector ... even a long-standing advocacy organization remarked that it is less involved in advocacy these days and more focused on training" (2003, p. 42).

As discussed in the case study of suburban day labor presented in Chapter 4, if through the facilitation of CBOs, immigrant newcomers receive the human services and resources they need to "get started" in suburbia – and if regulatory agencies adopt policies that seemingly appease these groups – why would constituents bother becoming politically active, attending PTA or neighborhood association meetings, applying for citizenship, registering to vote, or casting a ballot on election day? In other words, to what extent do CBOs risk being silenced when they form interdependent relationships? This does not seem to have occurred for one large Latino- and immigrant-serving CBO, CASA de Maryland. Prior to establishing a sister organization called CASA in Action in 2010 (a registered 501(c)4) to engage in direct political action and also endorse candidates, CASA de Maryland (a registered 501(c)3) rallied thousands of both legal and undocumented immigrants to lobby elected officials in the Maryland state capitol and in Washington, DC, on behalf of several immigrants' rights issues. CASA led some of the largest immigrant rights marches during the height of the 2006 comprehensive immigration reform debate, lobbying for the Maryland DREAM Act, low-wage workers' rights, and legal justice for immigrants.

Yet, one might see CASA as blurring the lines between nonprofit and interest group. The positive responses it receives from the government despite the relentless pressure it places on both state and local governments in Maryland (publicly bringing to task state and local leaders on behalf of immigrant workers and families) is unprecedented. The hand of CASA seemingly extends its reach into nearly all aspects of Latino and immigrant rights and concerns in the state. Elected officials listen to CASA and support its efforts because it holds a unique set of resources that the state and local governments need to access to get things done in the face of rapidly changing demographics. CASA and a few other select CBOs in the region can leverage their strong background in immigrant social service work, cultural and linguistic connection to newcomers, and ability to help officials identify needs and provide service delivery. What is more, CASA's ability to galvanize thousands to rally on the steps of the state capitol or on Capitol Hill give it political power to drive social change that extends far beyond the financial resources it receives from the public sector.

Academics, policy makers, and community-based groups increasingly underscore that local partnerships between elected, bureaucratic, and non-profit officials may serve as a springboards toward greater understanding, collaborative efforts, and even civic and political incorporation of minorities. These factors are important given the history of racial and economic sub-urban exclusion, as well as other negative by-products of fifty-plus years of metropolitan fragmentation. Ideally, public-nonprofit partnerships can have broader effects: the social capital built through interdependent relationships in suburbia can be stored to later produce minority elected officials, push for diverse representation on community boards, get out the vote, or mobi-lize immigrant and historically disenfranchised or disenchanted groups in other ways.

Minority suburbanization has traditionally been assumed to raise minori-ties' social status, increase their contact with European Americans and middle-to upper-income groups, and improve their life chances (Massey & Denton, 1988a, 1993). These gains are assumed to translate into social and economic incorporation in society, and promote civic/political representation and incor-poration. Yet these groups still face many challenges on their road to civic and political incorporation. The final section offers a brief discussion of the civic/political implications of the changing demographics and future of racial poli-tics in American suburbs.

The Civic/Political Implications of Minority Suburbanization

Greater research is needed to address the prospects for the civic and politi-cal advancement of suburban newcomers. Political participation is broadly defined as participation in formal political activities such as voting, volun-teering for and contributing to political campaigns, and becoming mem-bers of explicitly political organizations. Political participation "provides the mechanism by which citizens can communicate information about their interests, preferences, and needs and generate pressure to respond" (Verba, Schlozman, & Brady, 1995, p. 1).

Since the early twentieth century, an exhaustive body of research has examined the social, economic, and political consequences of immigrant and African American migrant settlement in urban areas. Much of this work has focused on civic and political participation or the effect of particular government-sponsored social programs and policies. Still unanswered is to what extent civic and political life for recent immigrant and ethnic minority suburbanites is similar to or different from that of their urban predecessors at the turn of the twentieth century.

In a participatory democracy, civic and political engagement is voluntary. The choice to participate may be constrained by time, money, and skills but also by factors such as political interest, information, knowledge, and efficacy (Verba et al., 1995). As noted, the focus group discussions reveal that major factors impeding neighborhood interactions are lack of time and desire, as well as linguistic and cultural barriers. The same factors also likely impede active involvement in civic or political affairs.

In the study of suburban jurisdictions, greater attention must be paid to the social, economic, and cultural contexts of civic and political participation. The clustering of immigrant and ethnic minority groups in specific areas may have reduced their prospects for civic and political participation, despite their suburban street addresses. Given the historical legacy of structural and institutional constraints on them, U.S. racial/ethnic groups have made immigration and migration decisions from a severely constrained set of choices. In many cases, they land in ailing suburbs on the fringes of central cities. Thus, one cannot assume that all suburban residents enjoy the same level of opportunity for civic and political engagement.

Huckfeldt was among the first scholars to call for the study of neighborhood social contexts, stating, "Political activity seldom occurs in individual isolation; as a result the social context is an important determinant of the extent to which individuals participate in politics" (1979, p. 579). Some scholars contend that the fragmentation of municipal government structures created by post–World War II suburbanization may be "undermining the health of American democracy" (Oliver, 1999, p. 206). In *Bowling Alone*, Putnam (2000) contends that metropolitan fragmentation and suburban sprawl are major causes of the decline in community and civic participation. As Oliver observes, "By creating politically separated pockets of affluence, suburbanization reduces the social needs faced by citizens with the most resources to address them; by creating communities of homogeneous political interests, suburbanization reduces the local conflicts that engage and draw the citizenry into the public realm" (1999, p. 205). He also argues that "municipal competition may empower some people to shop as consumers, but it immobilizes and isolates them as citizens in the democratic process" (p. 206).

In *Democracy in Suburbia* (2001), Oliver explores the civic effects of economic segregation along municipal boundaries. Unlike earlier pioneers of social context research such as Huckfeldt, Oliver does not find support for the long-standing contention that the affluent participate in politics at greater levels. Instead, using data from the 1990 Citizen Participation Study and the 1990 census, he finds a curvilinear relationship in suburbia: participation is lowest in the most affluent jurisdictions, slightly higher in the poorest areas, and highest in the middle-income locales. Oliver suggests that affluent cities have fewer social needs that drive citizen action. Moreover, heterogeneous cities have more competition for public goods, which stimulates citizen interest and participation (also see Putnam, 2000).

Within the contemporary American metropolis, economic composition is a major determinant of the level of interest in local politics. At the upper end of the economic spectrum, wealth and social homogeneity keep affluent suburbs from facing the problems or conflicts that make local politics lively. Cities with relatively homogenous and affluent populations have few social needs. Presumably, citizens in affluent cities also share a consensus about exclusionary government politics that keep their property values high and taxes low. Between the absence of social problems and the overwhelming political consensus, few local issues are engaging to the citizenry. At the low end of the economic scale, poverty and social homogeneity reduce conflict, limit local capacity, and discourage citizen involvement because people tend to focus on meeting their immediate basic needs (Oliver, 2001, pp. 203–204).

Historically, those groups marginalized from formal avenues of representation, such as mainstream party politics, have had to resort to informal means, such as protesting, picketing, and civil unrest, to express their interests publicly (Piven & Cloward, 1971, 1977). Recognizing the biases against them that operate in the local political arena, such groups have tended to eschew mainstream politics and mobilize through "extra-institutional" means. As Frasure and Williams (2009) contend,

for people of color, civil society has been dual. There has been the external civil society, which has more often than not marginalized them and their interests, and there has been the internal civil society that people of color have built themselves to contest their marginalization. It is in these internal civil societies that people of color have built networks of reciprocity and trust, which have facilitated the development of forms of collective action that clearly contested existing policies or practices directly affecting their communities. [Therefore] concern with civic disparities is concern with marginalization and contestation.

The literature on race, ethnicity, class, and social context (which has largely been conducted within urban settings) reveals the detrimental effects of economic and racial concentration, particularly for lower-income populations. Although many studies have examined the political behaviors of various racial and ethnic groups in the United States, much of this research has examined only one racial or ethnic group (often in comparison to non-Hispanic whites) or has focused on groups residing largely in urban areas.[1]

Much of the recent scholarship on political participation in suburbs has focused disproportionately on cities versus suburbs rather than on the differences and persistent disparities (racial/ethnic or class related, etc.) across suburban jurisdictions (Gainsborough, 2001, 2005; McKee & Shaw, 2003). Party identification remains an important predictor of political participation in the United States overall (Rosenstone & Hansen, 1993; Wong, 2000) and among immigrant populations specifically (Cain, Kiewiet, & Uhlaner, 1991; Uhlaner et al., 1989; Wong, 2000). In the 1950s and 1960s, some of the literature published in the fields of political science and sociology sought to explain shifts in party identification in suburbs. Specifically, these studies examined whether populations (largely white and working or middle class) who moved to American suburbs during the post–World War II era shifted their loyalties from the Democratic to the Republican Party, why these shifts occurred, and the extent to which they were stable or simply representative of nationwide trends during a given election season (Bell, 1969; Campbell et al., 1964; H. Hirsch, 1968; Manis & Stine, 1959; Wirt, 1965, 1975; Wood & Truman, 1959; Zikmund, 1973). Little is known about the extent to which partisanship influences political participation across various types of suburbs, particularly when accounting for other factors such as socioeconomic status. We do know that political parties currently are less effective in mobilizing their bases in American suburbs than political parties were in mobilizing urban constituents during the era of machine politics (Erie, 1988; Jones-Correa, 2001; Wong, 2000, 2006).

Unfortunately, the study of suburban political behavior took a several-decade hiatus before reawakening during recent election cycles (Gainsborough, 2001, 2005; McKee & Shaw, 2003; Oliver, 2001; W. Schneider, 1992). Some recent studies of suburban voting behavior during presidential elections (Gainsborough, 2001, 2005; McKee & Shaw, 2003) have examined differences in voter choice and party identification between central city and suburban residents. Using data from the 1992, 1996, and 2000 presidential elections, Gainsborough (2005) found that although the individual-level characteristics of voters are important in informing their political decisions, so is their location. In short, place matters, and all else being equal, voters in cities were more likely than their suburban counterparts to support Democrats.

Fast-forward only eight years, and American suburbs were regarded as the "anchors of the new Democratic surge" (Frey & Teixeira, 2008, p. 1). Unlike Al Gore in 2000 and John Kerry in 2004, Obama won the suburbs by a margin

---

[1] See, for example, Alex-Assensoh and Assensoh, 2001; Arvizu and Garcia, 1996; Bobo and Gilliam, 1990; Calvo and Rosenstone, 1989; de la Garza, 1992; de la Garza and DeSipio, 1999; Jones-Correa, 1998, 2001; Lien, 2000; Rosenstone and Hansen, 1993; Shingles, 1981; Tate, 1993; Uhlaner, Cain, and Kiewiet, 1989; Verba and Nie, 1972; and Verba et al., 1995.

of fifty to forty-eight (Gore lost the suburbs by five points and Kerry lost the suburbs by two points; Frey and Teixeira (2008). President Obama's historic victory was cemented by suburban voters as well as racial/ethnic minority, young (particularly black youth aged eighteen to twenty-four years), and college-educated voters (U.S. Census Bureau, 2008).[2] The accounts of suburbanites turning out in droves and standing in line for hours to elect the first African American president of the United States are quite remarkable.

At the county level, Obama won Montgomery County with 71.58 percent of the vote in 2008 and 70.92 percent of the vote in 2012 (Montgomery County Board of Elections, 2008, 2012). Virginia, traditionally viewed as conservative and Republican, is considered a battleground state shifting from a Republican stronghold in 2004 to being much more competitive by 2008. Obama received 52 percent of the vote in this state, which no Democratic nominee had carried since 1964 (Lang, Sanchez, & Levy, 2008). In 2004, John Kerry was the only presidential candidate to carry Fairfax County since Lyndon B. Johnson won 64 percent of the vote in 1964 (Conroy, 2012; Jackman, 2012). However, G. W. Bush won the state of Virginia by a slim margin with 53.68 percent of the vote. In 2005, Democratic gubernatorial candidate Tim Kaine carried Fairfax County with 60 percent of the vote, helping him to secure the state's governorship with 51.7 percent of the vote (Conroy, 2012).

Republicans began distinguishing northern Virginia from the "real Virginia," calling it a peculiar part of the state because of its proximity to the DC metropolitan area. Thus, they intensified their outreach efforts in parts of the state believed to be more Southern in political orientation (Conroy, 2012; Hoppock, 2008). This shift toward more Democratic Party leanings has been attributed to Fairfax County's population increase and the consequent increased political leverage in the state. Six of the 100 fastest-growing counties from 2000 to 2007 lie in northern Virginia (B. Lewis, 2008). In 2012, Fairfax County was the most populous jurisdiction in the Washington metro area, accounting for 19.8 percent of its population (U.S. Census Bureau, 2013).

During the 1968 presidential election 100,000 votes were cast in Fairfax County, compared to 524,034 votes in 2008. During the 2008 national election, Republican strategists expressed concern about the political implications of a more diverse northern Virginia due to the increase in minorities and

---

[2] Between 2004 and 2008, African American voter turnout increased by 4.9 percent (2 million more African Americans voted), Latino turnout increased by 2.7 percent (2 million more Latinos voted), and Asian American turnout increased by 2.4 percent (about 600,000 more Asian Americans voted than in 2004). White voter turnout decreased by 1.1 percent. Voters aged eighteen to twenty-four were the only age group to show a statistically significant increase in turnout, at 49 percent in 2008 compared with 47 percent in 2004 (Lopez & Taylor, 2009; U.S. Census Bureau, 2008). Black youth had the highest voter turnout among voters aged eighteen to twenty-four, a first in our nation's history (Lopez & Taylor, 2009; U.S. Census Bureau, 2008). African American youth turnout jumped eight percentage points, from 47 percent in 2004 to 55 percent in 2008.

out-of-state transplants without cultural identification with Old South norms (Conroy, 2012).

There are signs of an increasing split between the views and political behaviors of northern Virginia voters compared to the rest of the Virginia. Although Obama lost rural Virginia, he won the inner suburbs of Fairfax County and the "new growth" outer suburbs of Prince William and Loudoun Counties. The "emerging suburbs" and "exurbs" of northern Virginia garnered the largest percentage gains for Obama in 2008. During his presidential campaign, Obama regularly visited Prince William County in northern Virginia, where the nonwhite population had grown by thirteen percentage points since 2000. Obama's visits there on the first and last days of the general election campaign paid dividends, as he carried this suburban outer county with almost 58 percent of the vote – thirteen points more than former presidential candidate Al Gore earned in 2000. In these outer suburbs, "a growing number of nonwhite residents, particularly Latinos, are diminishing what has been a big source of votes for Republican candidates. Loudoun, Prince William and Stafford counties and Manassas and Manassas Park have all experienced double-digit increases in the percentage of nonwhite residents since 2000. And in each of these locations, Democrats' share of the vote increased proportionally" (Craig & Agiesta, 2008).

In 2009 Republican candidate Bob McDonnell won Fairfax County with 57 percent of the vote and went on to win the state and succeed Democrat Tim Kaine as governor (Jackman, 2012). In that year, the GOP swept statewide executive offices; in 2010, Republicans picked up three congressional seats; and in 2011 made gains in the Virginia Senate and House of Delegates. Yet by 2012 Virginia was widely considered a battleground state, with northern Virginia proving pivotal in giving Democratic candidates an edge. Obama won Virginia by 50.8 percent to Mitt Romney's 47.8 percent, securing thirteen electoral votes. In Fairfax County, Obama won 57.3 percent of the vote versus 41.1 percent for Mitt Romney. Obama also won Prince William County (by 57.4 percent to 41.4 percent) as well as Loudoun County (by 51.6 percent to 47.1 percent). Governor Bob McDonnell noted, "To win twice in a row as a Democrat in Virginia is a historic achievement … this was certainly a setback after three very good years of Republican gains in Virginia." He further commented, "overall, we've got work to do up in the Northern Virginia beltway area. I was fortunate to do well up there in 2009, but those are the greatest number of independent voters who will vote the issue and vote the person as opposed to the party, and we're losing the exchange up there as you see in Fairfax, Prince William and Loudoun…. We've got to do a better job in explaining to people why the conservative view of America is better for them and their pocketbook, and we apparently didn't do it well enough, but we'll get better" (Meola, 2012).

Republican leaders in Fairfax have expressed concern about the political and social consequences of recent demographic shifts eroding support for the

GOP (Khoury, 2008). However, in parts of the county voters remain affluent and very concerned about potential tax increases or the redirection of county resources to fund immigrants, particularly those perceived to be undocumented and/or undeserving. Therefore policy issues such as immigration reform, public education, language access, and more recently voting rights have become highly contentious issues as demographics have changed.

Much of the research on suburban political participation has focused on voter turnout or candidate choice; nonvoting political participation (e.g., volunteer work for political and civil action organizations, political donations, protest/activist activities for a political cause) remains understudied but important for understanding the socialization processes leading to who votes and for which candidate, particularly in U.S. suburbs. Massey and Denton describe suburbanization as "a political creation brought about by the division of urban space into mutually exclusive units of local government" (1988a, p. 596). In this space, local municipal opportunities for choice and participation (exit and voice) are important components of a well-functioning suburban civil society. As political fragmentation meets suburban heterogeneity head on, we are forced to examine how diversity (racial/ethnic, class, cultural, religious, civic, and political) inhibits voice – access, representation, and influence – in the American political process. This is particularly important for minority newcomers, who may lack the resources or efficacy to voice their grievances, or the financial wherewithal to readily exit particular jurisdictions when their needs are not met. These factors underscore the need for policy analysts, and others in the public, private, and nonprofit sectors concerned with the well-being of immigrant and ethnic minority groups, to continue the examination of minority suburbanization, including its socioeconomic, cultural, and political implications.

Appendix A

Focus Group Protocols and Data Collection Procedures

The focus group data presented in this analysis were collected in collaboration with Michael Jones-Correa (Cornell University) in research funded by the Russell Sage Foundation. In summer 2005, we conducted five two-hour-long focus groups of immigrant and racial/ethnic minorities in suburban Washington, DC, one with each of the following groups: Latino, black, Chinese, Korean, and Iranian. The Latino and black focus groups took place in Montgomery County and Prince George's County, Maryland; the remaining three were held in Fairfax County, Virginia.

We contracted with a Washington, DC–based consulting firm, Rivera Qualitative Research, to assist in the respondent selection and facilitation of each focus group. Each group consisted of nine to twelve adults, ages twenty-five to sixty-four years and representing immigrant as well as domestic migrants to suburbia (see Table A.1). The focus groups were conducted in the respondents' native languages: English for blacks, Mandarin for Chinese, Korean for Koreans, Spanish for Latinos, and Farsi for Iranians. Prior to each focus group, facilitators were trained using the protocol Jones-Correa and I developed (see later).

Focus Group Discussion Protocol

- **Introduction of Moderator**
- **Objectives of Study and Purpose of Focus Group Session**
  - The purpose of this study is to find out more about life in suburbia and how the experiences of living in suburbia may differ between various immigrant and ethnic groups. During this discussion we would like you to share your honest feelings about your experiences, positive or negative, following your move to ____ County. Everything that you say here will be kept confidential, and your names or any other identifying information will not be used in any report coming from this research.

TABLE A.1. *Demographics of Focus Group Participants*

	Number of Participants	Focus Group Location	Gender Breakdown	Income Range
Black	12	Media Network, Inc. Broadcasting company, Silver Spring, MD	7 males 5 females	3 low: < $25k 9 med: $25k–$50k 0 high: >$50k
Chinese	10	Library, Fairfax, VA	5 females 5 males	2 low: < $25k 6 med: $25k–$50k 0 high: >$50k 2 retired
Iranian	9	Iranian residence in Fairfax, VA	3 males 6 females	2 low: < $25k 4 med: $25k–$50k 3 high: >$50k
Korean	10	Korean church, Fairfax, VA	5 females 5 males	1 low: < $25k 6 med: $25k–$50k 1 high: >$50k 2 retired
Latino/a	12	Media Network, Inc. Broadcasting company, Silver Spring, MD	5 males 7 females	5 low: < $25k 7 med: $25k–$50k 0 high >$50k

- **Organization of Session**
  - [We detail the consent form before beginning and obtain signatures.]
- **Now I want to tell you how the session will be organized. Today we will discuss the following topics (briefly highlight here):**

  - How you chose your current neighborhood and why you chose to live there;
  - Your interactions with neighbors and other [co-ethnics];
  - Your personal experiences with the local government and the services the local government provides, such as schools, police, health services, etc.

Before we get started here are a few things to remember, our sort of ground rules:

- We have a limited amount of time, so I might have to interrupt from time to time to keep things moving.
- There are no wrong answers to any questions, and we would like to hear from everyone. We are interested in your personal views, so don't feel like you have to agree with anyone else.

- Please talk one at a time and please do not have side conversations. Are there any questions? Do you fully understand everything said to you today? Well, we are ready to begin.

Warm-up Question

- Although you have a card with your first name in front of you, please go around the room and introduce yourselves using first names only, and tell how long you have lived in _____ County.

Section I: Discussion Related to Residential Selection

- How did you come to live in _____ County? Share with us some specific reasons that led you to live in _____ County.
- If you moved to _____ County from somewhere else, could you name one important difference between your previous place of residence and where you live now? Tell us why that difference is important to you.
- Do you think that living in _____ County has improved your life? If so, in what ways? If not, why not?

Section II: Discussion Related to Neighborhood Interactions

- Would you describe your current neighborhood as racially/ethnically diverse, or are people pretty much all alike? Is this something you chose? Or did this happen by chance?
- How well would you say you know the people in your neighborhood? Do you do things together with your neighbors? What are some examples of the kinds of things you do? Have you ever gotten together formally or informally to address common issues or problems in your neighborhood?
- How about people who share your race/ethnicity [alternatively: from _____ country/race]: do you do things together with other people from _____ [country/race]? Where do you get together? For what kinds of events? How often?
- Do you volunteer or take part in the activities of [_____ country] civic groups, religious groups, schools, etc.? What about groups like the PTA or neighborhood associations? In what ways have you gotten involved with them?
- How do you keep up with events related to people of _____ country/race] in the DC area? Through word of mouth, by listening to the radio, by reading a newspaper, by e-mail?

Section III: Discussion Related to County/Municipal Government Interactions

- The government of _____ County and municipalities like _____ take care of providing and administering services like schools, policing, libraries, etc. What has been your most positive experience of local government?

- What has been your most negative experience of local government? Do you think this was race related?
- Do you think that local government officials are responsive or care about your concerns (why or why not, how much, how little)? Have you ever tried to contact a local government agency to express your concerns or ask for changes in service? If so, how? And if not, why not?
- [For non-black groups only:] Have you ever encountered language difficulties in communicating with local officials? If yes, when did this happen?

Section IV: Iranians

- Have your encounters with government changed at all after 9/11?
- Have your experiences/encounters with other people changed at all since 9/11?
- Did 9/11 have an impact on the sense of community among Iranians? If so, how?

Debriefing

- We would like to thank you for your participation. We also want to restate that what you have shared with us is confidential. No part of our discussion that includes names or other identifying information will be used in any report coming from this research. We want to provide you with a chance to ask any questions that you might have about this research. So, do you have any questions?

Appendix B

In-Depth Interview Protocol for Chapters 3, 4, and 5

Questions for Elected Officials

General Questions

- (warm-up) Tell us how you became interested in political leadership.
- (warm-up) Please tell us a little about your role as ____.
- Were there any individual or group/organizational efforts undertaken to increase the representation of ____ (group) or minority representation generally in your campaign? What were some of the strategies or resources provided to you?
- Were these efforts focused on ____ (group) candidates (example: Latino women candidates or minorities generally)?
- What factors or candidate characteristics, other than race, have been responsible for efforts focused on some ____ candidates over others?
- Have there been any obstacles to increasing ____ (group) – or minority – representation in elected office in ____ County, if so what are they?

Now, I would like to ask you some questions about policy issues or concerns facing immigrant and ethnic minority groups in ____ County.

- What specific issues or group constituencies did your electoral campaign focus on?
- What policy issues were/are you most concerned about? How has this changed or developed during your time as ____ (elected office)?
- Have you initiated any policies or programs related to a specific issue?
- Have you received any support or opposition from white members or other oppositional forces for your policy initiatives relating to ____ (issue)?
- What about specific support or opposition from other minority elected or appointed officials or seeming proponents of your cause(s)?

Questions related to programs and policies targeted toward immigrants and ethnic minorities in each county:

- What groups or organizations helped facilitate these programs/policies and their implementation?
- How effective have these programs been in closing the gap between white and immigrant/ethnic minority groups in _____ County?
- What remains some of the obstacles in closing the gap between these groups?
- What remain some of the obstacles for you as an elected official?
- What if I were to ask about "political action" that didn't take place through electoral politics – say, attending meetings, lobbying, etc. Is there this kind of involvement on the part of new immigrants and racial minorities in the county?
- What can be done to increase such involvement?
- Do you think that involvement by racial/ethnic minorities in _____ County differs much from other counties in the area, either by intensity of involvement, organization, or issue areas?

Questions for Non-elected Officials/Leaders

- (warm-up) So how long have you been at _____ (organization/unit/department)?
- (warm-up) Tell me a little about your role in this _____ (organization/unit/department).
- Talk a little about the program/services/support your organization offers.
- Which populations would you say you primarily serve? On average, how many people participate in programs/support/services offered here?
- What areas/counties do they generally come from? Would you say you draw people from all over the Washington, DC, metropolitan area, or just this county? [If from all over the area, or all over the county, ask:] How do your clientele find out about the services you offer, and how do they access them?
- If there are several regional associations in _____ (DC, county, etc.), how do you divide organizational responsibilities by region?
- How do new immigrants know if there is an association?
- So, do you feel that community organizations/units/departments like _____ can help immigrants and ethnic minorities get involved in the community? If so, how?
- When/how, if at all, would residents become politically involved? In what ways would they begin to act? Can you provide some instances/examples of political action?
- What if I were to ask about "political action" that didn't take place through electoral politics – say, attending meetings, lobbying, etc. Is there this kind of involvement on the part of new immigrants and racial minorities in the county?

• Do you think that involvement by racial/ethnic minorities in ＿＿＿ County differs much from other counties in the area, either by intensity of involvement, organization, or issue areas?

Education Questions: For English for Speakers of Other Languages (ESOL), Talented and Gifted/Magnet, and No Child Left Behind Program Officials

• Please talk a little about the programs/services/support offered to immigrant and ethnic minority students and families by ＿＿＿ (organization/department).
• Which populations would you say you primarily serve? On average, how many people participate in programs/support/services offered here? Which programs/services are most utilized?
• In the face of competing claims on the county budget, how did these programs get established in the first place? What was their rationale? Who made the initial decision and why?
• As these counties' minority/immigrant populations grew, and again, with competing claims on the budget, how did these programs continue to grow? Was there a sense that these programs were competing against other claims for resources, or was the logic for their expansion so compelling that these claims seemed irrelevant?
• Has the case for these programs come under pressure with the budget pressures of the past couple of years?

References

Abramitzky, R., Boustan, L. P., & Eriksson, K. (2012). Have the Poor Always Been Less Likely to Migrate? Evidence from Inheritance Practices during the Age of Mass Migration. *Journal of Development Economics*, 102, 2–14.

Alba, R. D., & Logan, J. R. (1991). Variations on Two Themes: Racial and Ethnic Patterns in the Attainment of Suburban Residence. *Demography*, 28(3), 431–453.

Alba, R. D. (1992). Analyzing Locational Attainments. *Sociological Methods & Research*, 20(3), 367–397.

(1993). Minority Proximity to Whites in Suburbs: An Individual-Level Analysis of Segregation. *The American Journal of Sociology*, 98(6), 1388–1427.

Alba, R. D., Logan, J. R., & Stults, B. J. (2000). The Changing Neighborhood Contexts of the Immigrant Metropolis. *Social Forces*, 79(2), 587–621.

Alba, R. D., Logan, J. R., Stults, B. J., Marzan, G., & Zhang, W. (1999). Immigrant Groups in the Suburbs: A Reexamination of Suburbanization and Spatial Assimilation. *American Sociological Review*, 64(3), 446–460.

Alex-Assensoh, Y., & Assensoh, A. B. (2001). Inner-City Contexts, Church Attendance, and African-American Political Participation. *The Journal of Politics*, 63(3), 886–901.

Alexander, J. (2000). Adaptive Strategies of Nonprofit Human Service Organizations in an Era of Devolution and New Public Management. *Nonprofit Management & Leadership*, 10, 287–303.

Alexander, J., Nank, R., & Stivers, C. (1999). Implications of Welfare Reform: Do Nonprofit Survival Strategies Threaten Civil Society? *Nonprofit and Voluntary Sector Quarterly*, 28, 452–475.

Alfisi, K. (2009). Language Barriers to Justice. *Washington Lawyer* (April).

Allard, S. W. (2004). *Access to Social Services: The Changing Urban Geography of Poverty and Service Provision Survey Series.* Washington, DC: Brookings Institution.

Alonso, A. D. (2007). From Congress to the Suburbs: Local Initiatives to Regulate Immigration in the United States. *Migración y Desarrollo*, 2, 65–82.

APALRC. (2009, September 1). Asian American Language Access Project. http://www.apalrc.org/dp/node/54.

Arvizu, J. R., & Garcia, F. C. (1996). Latino Voting Participation: Explaining and Differentiating Latino Voting Turnout. *Hispanic Journal of Behavioral Sciences,* 18(2), 104–128.

Axelrod, R. (1984). *The Evolution of Cooperation.* New York: Basic Books.

AYUDA. (2013). Community Legal Interpreter Bank. Washington, DC and Falls Church, VA. http://www.ayudainc.org/index.cfm/community-legal-interpreter-bank.

Bachrach, P., & Baratz, M. (1962). Two Faces of Power. *The American Political Science Review,* 56(4), 947–952.

Baldassare, M. (1986). *Trouble in Paradise: The Suburban Transformation in America.* New York: Columbia University Press.

(1992). Suburban Communities. *Annual Review of Sociology,* 18, 475–494.

Bandoh, E. (2003). Outsourcing the Delivery of Human Services. *Welfare Information Network,* 7(12), 1–12.

Bass, F., & Homan, T. R. (2011, October 19). Beltway Earnings Make U.S. Capital Richer than Silicon Valley. *Bloomberg Business.*

Baxandall, R. F., & Ewen, E. (2000). *Picture Windows: How the Suburbs Happened.* New York: Basic Books.

Bell, C. (1969). A New Suburban Politics. *Social Forces,* 47(3), 280–288.

Birnbaum, M. (2010a, August 24). Jerry Weast, superintendent of Montgomery schools, to retire in June. *Washington Post.*

(2010b, May 12). Montgomery schools set to act against council. *Washington Post.*
(2010c, August 25). Weast says he'll step down in '11. *Washington Post.*

Bish, R. L. (1971). *The Public Economy of Metropolitan Areas.* Chicago, IL: Markham Publishing Company.

Bishaw, A. (2012). *Poverty: 2010 and 2011 American Community Survey Briefs* (pp. 1–8). Washington, DC: U.S. Census Bureau.

Bobo, L., & Gilliam, F. D., Jr. (1990). Race, Sociopolitical Participation, and Black Empowerment. *The American Political Science Review,* 84(2), 377–393.

Bobo, L., & Hutchings, V. L. (1996). Perceptions of Racial Group Competition: Extending Blumer's Theory of Group Position to a Multiracial Social Context. *American Sociological Review,* 61(6), 951–972.

Bobo, L., & Zubrinsky, C. (1996). Attitudes on Residential Integration: Perceived Status Differences, Mere In-group Preference, or Racial Prejudice? *Social Forces,* 74(3), 883–909.

Bond, J. (2004, March 19). Roundtable to Fund Itself to Help Students Move into Work Force. *The Gazette.*

Boustan, L. P. (2007). Were Jews Political Refugees or Economic Migrants? Assessing the Persecution Theory of Jewish Emigration, 1881–1914. In T. J. Hatton, K. H. O'Rourke, and Alan M. Taylor (Eds.) *The New Comparative Economic History, Essays in Honor of Jeffrey G. Williamson.* Cambridge, MA: MIT Press, 267–290.

Brewington, K. (2007, December 20). Day-labor center opens: Project designed to curb loitering, offer jobs, training. *Baltimore Sun.*

Brown, M. C., & Halaby, C. N. (1987). Machine Politics in America, 1870–1945. *The Journal of Interdisciplinary History,* 17(3), 587–612.

Browning, R. P., Marshall, D. R., & Tabb, D. H. (1984). *Protest Is Not Enough: The Struggle of Blacks and Hispanics for Equality in Urban Politics.* Berkeley: University of California Press.

Buchanan, J. M. (1965). An Economic Theory of Clubs. *Economica*, 32(125), 1–14.
(1971). Principles of Urban Fiscal Strategy. *Public Choice*, 11, 1–16.
Burgess, E. W. (1925). The Growth of the City: An Introduction to a Research Project. In R. E. Park, E. W. Burgess, & R. D. McKinzie (Eds.), *The City*. Chicago, IL: University of Chicago Press.
Cain, B. E., Kiewiet, D. R., & Uhlaner, C. J. (1991). The Acquisition of Partisanship by Latinos and Asian-Americans. *American Journal of Political Science*, 35(2), 390–422.
Calderon, J. Z., Suzanne, F., & Rodriguez, S. (2005). Organizing Immigrant Workers: Action Research and Strategies in the Pomona Day Labor Center. In E. C. Ochoa and G. L. Ochoa (Eds.) *Latino Los Angeles: Transforming, Communities, and Activism*. Tucson: University of Arizona Press.
Calvo, M. A., & Rosenstone, S. J. (1989). *Hispanic Political Participation*. San Antonio, TX: Southwest Voter Research Institute.
Campbell, A., Converse, P. E., Miller, A. H., & Stokes, D. E. (1964). *The American Voter: An Abridgment*. New York: Wiley.
Cantor, G. (2010). Struggling for Immigrants' Rights at the Local Level: The Domestic Workers Bill of Rights Initiative in a Suburb of Washington, DC. *Journal of Ethnic & Migration Studies*, 36(7), 1061–1078.
CASA de Maryland. (2003, 2013). Homepage. http://wearecasa.org/
(2010). Annual Report 2010. http://wearecasa.org/resources/reports-publications/
(2012). Annual Report 2012. http://wearecasa.org/resources/reports-publications/
(2013). CASA de Maryland English at Night Flier, English and Spanish Versions.
Castaneda, R., & Miranda, S. (2011, May 17). Johnson, ex-county executive in Prince George's, pleads guilty to taking bribes. *Washington Post*.
Castaneda, R., & Thomas, A. (2010, November 12). Prince George's County executive Jack B. Johnson arrested. *Washington Post*.
Chandler, M. A. (2008, May 13). Predicted ESOL savings debated: 760 students left Pr. William Schools. *Washington Post*.
Chandler, M. A., & Kravitz, D. (2010, January 8). Fairfax County Schools chief proposes dramatic budget cuts. *Washington Post*.
Charles, C. Z. (2000). Neighborhood Racial-Composition Preferences: Evidence from a Multiethnic Metropolis. *Social Problems*, 47(3), 379–407.
(2001). Processes of Residential Segregation. In A. O'Connor, C. Tilly, & L. Bobo (Eds.), *Urban Inequality: Evidence from Four Cities*. New York: Russell Sage Foundation.
(2003). The Dynamics of Racial Residential Segregation. *Annual Review of Sociology*, 29(1), 167–207.
Childress, S., Doyle, D. P., & Thomas, D. (2009). *Leading for Equity*. Cambridge, MA: Harvard Education Press.
Childress, S., & Goldin, A. (2009). *The Turnaround at Highland Elementary School. Harvard University Public Education Leadership Project*. A Joint Initiative of the Harvard Graduate School of Education and Harvard Business School. PEL-O61: September 10.
Chong, D. (1991). *Collective Action and the Civil Rights Movement*. Chicago, IL: University of Chicago Press.
City of Gaithersberg. (2002) *Minutes of Regular City Council Meeting*, 1–12.

(2004) *Minutes of Regular City Council Meeting*, 1–7.

Clark, W. A. V. (1991). Residential Preferences and Neighborhood Racial Segregation: A Test of the Schelling Segregation Model. *Demography*, 28(1), 1–19.

(1992). Residential Preferences and Residential Choices in a Multiethnic Context. *Demography*, 29(3), 451–466.

(2006a). Ethnic Preferences and Residential Segregation: A Commentary on Outcomes from Agent-Based Modeling. *Journal of Mathematical Sociology*, 30(3–4), 319–326.

(2006b). Race, Class, and Space: Outcomes of Suburban Access for Asians and Hispanics. *Urban Geography*, 27(6), 489–506.

Clark, W. A. V., & Blue, S. A. (2004). Race, Class, and Segregation Patterns in U.S. Immigrant Gateway Cities. *Urban Affairs Review*, 39(6), 667–688.

Cohn, D. V., & Morin, R. (2008). Who Moves? Who Stays Put? Where's Home? Pew Research Center. A Social & Demographic Trends Report. December 17. pp. 1–45.

Conley, J. P., & Wooders, M. H. (1997). Equivalence of the Core and Competitive Equilibrium in a Tiebout Economy with Crowding Types. *Journal of Urban Economics*, Vol. 41, pp. 421–440.

Conroy, S. (2012, June 13). Northern Virginia edge could be pivotal for Obama. http://www.realclearpolitics.com/articles/2012/06/13/northern_virginia_edge_could_be_pivotal_for_obama_114458.html.

Cornwell, E. E., Jr. (1964). Bosses, Machines, and Ethnic Groups. *Annals of the American Academy of Political and Social Science*, 353(1), 27–39.

Craig, T., & Agiesta, J. (2008, November 30). Democrats make most of shifts in Va. electorate; demographic changes put party in optimal position. *Washington Post*.

Dahl, R. A. (1961). *Who Governs? Democracy and Power in an American City*. New Haven, CT: Yale University Press.

Danielson, M. N. (1976). *The Politics of Exclusion*. New York: Columbia University Press.

Dawson, M. (1994). *Behind the Mule: Race and Class in African-American Politics*. Princeton, NJ: Princeton University Press.

de la Garza, R. O. (1992). *Latino Voices: Mexican, Puerto Rican, and Cuban Perspectives on American Politics*. Boulder, CO: Westview Press.

de la Garza, R. O., & DeSipio, L. (1999). *Awash in the Mainstream: Latino Politics in the 1996 Elections*. Boulder, CO: Westview Press.

de Graauw, E. (2008). Nonprofit Organizations: Agents of Immigrant Political Incorporation in Urban America. In S. K. Ramakrishnan and I. Bloemraad (Eds.), *Civic Hopes and Political Realities: Immigrants, Community Organizations, and Political Engagement* (pp. 323–350). New York: Russell Sage Foundation.

de Graauw, E., Gleeson, S., & Bloemraad, I. (2013). Funding Immigrant Organizations: Suburban Free-Riding and Local Civic Presence. *American Journal of Sociology*, 119(1), 75–130.

de Leon, E., Maronick, M., De Vita, C. J., & Boris, E. T. (2009). Community-Based Organizations and Immigrant Integration in the Washington, D.C., Metropolitan Area: Urban Institute. Center on Nonprofits and Philanthopy.

de Vise, D. (2009, July 28). It's been 10 years' worth of on-the-job learning for Montgomery's Jerry Weast. *Washington Post*.

del Carmen Fani, N. (2005). *Equality Works: Protecting Low-Wage Workers in the State of Maryland: A Study Conducted by the Maryland Latino Coalition for Justice*: Maryland Latino Coalition for Justice.

de Parle, J. (2009, April 19). Struggling to rise in suburbs where failing means fitting in. *New York Times*.

Department of Health and Human Services. (2013). Temporary Assistance for Needy Families (TANF). http://www.hhs.gov/recovery/programs/tanf/.

Department of Justice. (2013). Commonly asked questions and answers regarding Executive Order 13166. http://www.justice.gov/crt/about/cor/Pubs/lepqa.php.

Department of Neighborhood and Community Services. (2011). 2010 Census Summaries Fairfax County, Virginia. http://www.fairfaxcounty.gov/demogrph/decennialcensus.htm.

Dinan, S. (2012, Februrary 14). Casa de Maryland faces challenge over tax-exempt status. *Washington Times*.

Dobriner, W. M. (1958). *The Suburban Community, ed. by William M. Dobriner*. New York, Putnam.

Dowding, K., Dunleavy, P., King, D., Margetts, H., & Rydin, Y. (1999). Regime Politics in London Local Government. *Urban Affairs Review*, 34(4), 515–545.

Downs, A. (1957). *An Economic Theory of Democracy*. New York: Harper.

Dreier, P., Mollenkopf, J. H., & Swanstrom, T. (2004). *Place Matters: Metropolitics for the Twenty-first Century* (2nd ed.). Lawrence: University Press of Kansas.

DSMHS, (2004). An account of day laborers in Fairfax County: Report of the findings from the Fairfax County, Day Laborer Survey. Department of Systems Management for Human Services, pp. 1–36.

Dwyer, T. (2005, December 13). Where Herndon day laborers go: The dogged Minutemen will follow; Herndon Minutemen to observe new site. *Washington Post*.

El, A. (2007, March 4). *Outsourcing to CBOs (Community Based Organizations): Collaborations or catastrophes*. Special Education Teacher, Second Opportunity School, Queens Outreach http://groups.yahoo.com/group/nyceducationnews/message/2141.

Erie, S. P. (1988). *Rainbow's End: Irish-Americans and the Dilemmas of Urban Machine Politics, 1840–1985*. Berkeley: University of California Press.

Espenshade, T. J., & Calhoun, C. A. (1993). An Analysis of Public Opinion toward Undocumented Immigration. *Population Research and Policy Review*, 12(3), 189–224.

Fairfax County. (2011). Behind the trendline: Trends and implications for county residents. Prepared by Fairfax County Department of Neighborhood & Community Services (May 2011) http://www.fairfaxcounty.gov/demogrph/pdf/behind_the_headline.pdf.

(2013). Chairman Sharon Bulova's biography. http://www.fairfaxcounty.gov/chairman/biography.htm.

Fairfax Democrats. (2013). Homepage. http://www.fairfaxdemocrats.org/.

Farley, R. (1970). The Changing Distribution of Negroes within Metropolitan Areas: The Emergence of Black Suburbs. *American Journal of Sociology*, 75(4), 512–529.

(1978). Chocolate City, Vanilla Suburbs: Will the Trend toward Racially Separate Communities Continue? *Social Science Research*, 7(4), 319–344.

Federal Register. (2000). *The President Executive Order 13166 – Improving Access to Services for Persons with Limited English Proficiency*. Department of Justice Enforcement of Title VI of the Civil Rights Act of 1964 – National Origin Discrimination against Persons with Limited English Proficiency. http://www.justice.gov/crt/cor/Pubs/eolep.pdf.

Feiock, R. C. (2009). Metropolitan Governance and Institutional Collective Action. *Urban Affairs Review*, 44(3), 356–377.

Feiock, R. C., In Won, L., Hyung, J., & Park Lee, K. H. (2010). Collaboration Networks among Local Elected Officials: Information, Commitment, and Risk Aversion. *Urban Affairs Review*, 46(2), 241–262.

Fenno, R. F. (1973). *Congressmen in Committees*. Boston, MA: Little, Brown.

(1978). *Home Style: House Members in their Districts*. Boston, MA: Little, Brown.

Fiorina, M. P. (1977). *Congress, Keystone of the Washington Establishment*. New Haven, CT: Yale University Press.

Fischel, W. (2001). *The Homevoter Hypothesis: How Home Values Influence Local Government Taxation, School Finance, and Land-Use Policies*. Cambridge, MA: Harvard University Press.

Fishman, R. (1987). *Bourgeois Utopias: The Rise and Fall of Suburbia*. New York: Basic Books.

Fix, M., & Passel, J. (2002). The Scope and Impact of Welfare Reform's Immigrant Provisions. Assessing the New Federalism: An Urban Instritute Program to Assess Changing Social Policies. Discussion Papers. Washington, DC: Urban Institute, pp. 1–44.

Ford, C. B., & Montes, S. (2007, March 21). Police worry about growing distrust among immigrants. *The Gazette*.

Fossett, M. (2006). Ethnic Preferences, Social Distance Dynamics, and Residential Segregation: Theoretical Explorations Using Simulation Analysis. *Journal of Mathematical Sociology*, 30(3–4), 185–273.

(2011). Generative Models of Segregation: Investigating Model-Generated Patterns of Residential Segregation by Ethnicity and Socioeconomic Status. *Journal of Mathematical Sociology*, 35(1–3), 114–145.

Frasure, L. (2005). "We won't turn back: The political economy paradoxes of immigrant and ethnic minority settlement in suburban America" (Doctoral dissertation). University of Maryland, College Park.

Frasure, L., & Jones-Correa, M. (2010). The Logic of Institutional Interdependency: The Case of Day Laborer Policy in Suburbia. *Urban Affairs Review*, 45(4), 451–482.

Frasure, L., & Williams, L. F. (2009). Racial, Ethnic, and Gender Disparities in Political Participation and Civic Engagement. In B. T. Dill & R. E. Zambrana (Eds.), *Emerging Intersections: Race, Class, and Gender in Theory, Policy, and Practice* (pp. 316–356). New Jersey: Rutgers University Press.

Frasure-Yokley, L. (2012). Holding the Borderline: School District Responsiveness to Demographic Change in Orange County, California. In E. Frankenberg & G. Orfield (Eds.), *The Resegregation of Suburban Schools: A Hidden Crisis in American Education*. Cambridge, MA: Harvard Education Press.

Frasure-Yokley, L., & Greene, S. (2013). Inter-group Relations, Neighborhood Context and African American Views toward Undocumented Immigration. In L. Pulido & J. Kun (Eds.), *Black and Brown Los Angeles: A Contemporary Reader*. Berkeley: University of California Press.

Freeman, J., & Minow, M. (2009). *Government by Contract Outsourcing and American Democracy*. Cambridge, MA: Harvard University Press.

Freund, D. M. (2007). *Colored Property: State Policy and White Racial Politics in Suburban America*. Chicago, IL: University of Chicago Press.

Frey, W. H. (1995). Immigration and Internal Migration "Flight" from US Metropolitan Areas: Toward a New Demographic Balkanisation. *Urban Studies*, 32(4–5), 733–757.

(2003a). Melting Pot Suburbs: A Study of Suburban Diversity. In B. Katz & R. Lang (Eds.), *Redefining Urban and Suburban America: Evidence from Census 2000*. Washington, DC: Brookings Institution.

(2003b). *Metropolitan Magnets for International and Domestic Migrants: The Living Cities Survey Series*. Center on Urban and Metropolitan Policy. Washington, DC: Brookings Institution, pp. 1–23.

(2011). Melting Pot Cities and Suburbs: Racial and Ethnic Change in Metro America in the 2000s. Metropolitan Policy Program. Washington, DC: Brookings Institution, pp. 1–16.

Frey, W. H., Berube, A., Singer, A., & Wilson, J. H. (2009). *Getting Current: Recent Demographic Trends in Metropolitan America*. Metropolitan Policy Program. Washington, DC: Brookings Institution, pp. 1–23.

Frey, W. H., & Speare, A. (1988). *Regional and Metropolitan Growth and Decline in the United States*. New York: Russell Sage Foundation.

Frey, W. H., & Teixeira, R. (2008). *A Demographic Breakthrough for Democrats*. Washington, DC: Brookings Institution.

Frohlich, N., & Oppenheimer, J. A. (1978). *Modern Political Economy*. Englewood Cliffs, NJ: Prentice-Hall.

Gainsborough, J. F. (2001). *Fenced Off: The Suburbanization of American Politics*. Washington DC: Georgetown University Press.

(2005). Voters in Context: Cities, Suburbs, and Presidential Vote. *American Politics Research*, 33(3), 435–461.

Gale, D. E. (1987). *Washington, D.C.: Inner-City Revitalization and Minority Suburbanization*. Philadelphia, PA: Temple University Press.

Gans, H. J. (1967). *The Levittowners: Ways of Life and Politics in a New Suburban Community*. New York: Pantheon Books.

GAO, U. G. A. O. (1995). Community Development: Comprehensive Approaches Address Multiple Needs but Are Challenging to Implement. GAO /RCED/ HEHS-95-69. Washington, DC: U.S. General Accounting Office. February 22, pp.1–81.

(2002). Worker Protection: Labor Efforts to Enforce Protections for Day Laborers Could Benefit from Better Data and Guidance. *Report to the Honorable Luis V. Gutierrez House of Representatives*. GAO-02-925. Washington, DC: U.S. General Accounting Office. September 26, pp. 1–53.

(2010). Revitalization Programs: Empowerment Zones, Enterprise Communities, and Renewal Communities. GAO-10-464R. Washington, DC: U.S. General Accounting Office. March 12, pp. 1–57.

Garcia Bedolla, L. (2012). Latino Education, Civic Engagement, and the Public Good. *Review of Research in Education*, 36(1), 23–42.

Ghaffarian, S. (1998). The Acculturation of Iranian Immigrants in the United States and the Implications for Mental Health. *Journal of Social Psychology*, 138(5), 645–654.

Gilchrist Center for Cultural Diversity. (2011). Annual Report FY 2011 (pp. 2–11).

Gordon, J., & Cornell, A. (2008). Suburban Sweatshops: The Fight for Immigrant Rights. *Industrial & Labor Relations Review*, 61(3), 429.

Grant-Thomas, A., & Sarfati, Y. (2009). *African American-Immigrant Alliance Building Efforts across the United States*. Kirwan Institute for the Study of Race and Ethnicity, Ohio State University.

Griffin, J. D., & Newman, B. (2007). The Unequal Representation of Latinos and Whites. *Journal of Politics*, 69(4), 1032–1046.

Grimshaw, W. J. (1992). *Bitter Fruit: Black Politics and the Chicago Machine, 1931–1991*. Chicago, IL: University of Chicago Press.

Guest, A. M. (1978). Suburban Social Status: Persistence or Evolution? *American Sociological Review*, 43(2), 251–264.

Hakimzadeh, S., & Dixon, D. (2006). Spotlight on the Iranian foreign born. Washington, DC: Migration Policy Institute. June 1.

Hamilton, B. W. (1975). Zoning and Property Taxation in a System of Local Governments. *Urban Studies*, 12(2), 205–211.

Hardin, R. (1982). *Collective Action*. Baltimore, MD: Johns Hopkins University Press.

Harris, D. R. (1999a). All Suburbs Are Not Created Equal: A New Look at Racial Differences in Suburban Location. *Population Studies Center Research Report* 99–440. Ann Arbor: University of Michigan. September.

(1999b). "Property Values Drop When Blacks Move in, Because...": Racial and Socioeconomic Determinants of Neighborhood Desirability. *American Sociological Review*, 64(3), 461–479.

(2001). Why Are Whites and Blacks Averse to Black Neighbors? *Social Science Research*, 30(1), 100–116.

Haus, M., & Klausen, J. E. (2011). Urban Leadership and Community Involvement: Ingredients for Good Governance? *Urban Affairs Review*, 47(2), 256–279.

Haynes, B. D. (2001). *Red Lines, Black Spaces: The Politics of Race and Space in a Black Middle-Class Suburb*. New Haven, CT: Yale University Press.

Help Save Maryland. Homepage. http://www.helpsavemaryland.org.

Hero, R. E. (2005). Crossroads of Equality: Race/Ethnicity and Cities in American Democracy. *Urban Affairs Review*, 40(6), 695–705.

Higley, S. (2010). Washington DC: African-Americans Find Success, but Separate and Not Financially Equal. http://higley1000.com/archives/272.

Hirsch, H. (1968). Suburban Voting and National Trends: a Research Note. *Political Research Quarterly*(21), 508–514.

Hirsch, A. (1983). *Making the Second Ghetto: Race and Housing in Chicago 1940–1960*. Chicago, Il: University of Chicago.

(2005). *Blockbusting. The Electronic Encyclopedia of Chicago*. Chicago Historical Society.

Hirsch, M. (2012, February 21). Poverty has a new address: Suburbia. *Fiscal Times*.

Hirschman, A. O. (1970). *Exit, Voice, and Loyalty: Responses to Decline in Firms, Organizations, and States*. Cambridge, MA: Harvard University Press.

Hobbins, M. B. (2006). The Day Laborer Debate: Small Town, U.S.A. Takes on Federal Immigration Law Regarding Undocumented Workers. (April 21). *bepress Legal Series*. Working Paper 1278.

Hopkins, D. J. (2010). Politicized Places: Explaining Where and When Immigrants Provoke Local Opposition. *American Political Science Review*, 104(1), 1–21.

Hoppock, J. (2008, October 20). McCain Adviser Says Northern Virginia Not "Real" Virginia. http://blogs.abcnews.com/politicalpunch/2008/10/mccain-adviser.html.

Hoyman, M., & Faricy, C. (2009). It Takes a Village: A Test of the Creative Class, Social Capital, and Human Capital Theories. *Urban Affairs Review*, 44(3), 311–333.

HPRP & Casa de Maryland. (2004). *Baltimore's Day Laborer Report: Their Stolen Sweat.* Baltimore, MD: Homeless Persons Representation Project and CASA de Maryland.

Huckfeldt, R. (1979). Political Participation and the Neighborhood Social Context. *American Journal of Political Science*, 23(3), 579–592.

Huckfeldt, R., Plutzer, E., & Sprague, J. (1993). Alternative Contexts of Political Behavior: Churches, Neighborhoods, and Individuals. *Journal of Politics*, 55(2), 365–381.

Iceland, J. (2004). Beyond Black and White: Residential Segregation in Multiethnic America. *Social Science Research*, 33(2), 248–271.

Iceland, J., & Wilkes, R. (2006). Does Socioeconomic Status Matter? Race, Class, and Residential Segregation. *Social Problems*, 53(2), 248–273.

Ihrke, D. K., & Faber, C. S. (2012). *Geographical Mobility Report: 2005 to 2010*. U.S. Census Bureau.

Imbroscio, D. L. (2006). Shaming the Inside Game: A Critique of the Liberal Expansionist Approach to Addressing Urban Problems. *Urban Affairs Review*, 42(2), 224–248.

Izadi, E. (2010, June 24). Casa of Maryland moves into historic Langley Park mansion. *The Gazette.*

Jackman, T. (2012, July 12). Will Fairfax County determine the next president? *Washington Post.*

Jackson, K. T. (1985). *Crabgrass Frontier: The Suburbanization of the United States.* New York: Oxford University Press.

Jayasundera, T., Silver, J., Anacker, K., & Mantcheva, D. (2010). Foreclosure in the Nation's Capital: How Unfair and Reckless Lending Undermines Homeownership. *NCRC Disparities in Lending Series* Washington, DC: National Community Reinvestment Coalition.

Johnson, V. (2002). *Black Power in the Suburbs: The Myth or Reality of African-American Suburban Political Incorporation.* Albany: State University of New York Press.

Jones-Correa, M. (1998). *Between Two Nations: The Political Predicament of Latinos in New York City.* Ithaca, NY: Cornell University Press.

(2001). *Governing American Cities: Interethnic Coalitions, Competitions, and Conflict.* New York: Russell Sage Foundation.

(2008). Immigrant Incorporation in Suburbia: The Role of Bureaucratic Norms in Education. In D. Massey (Ed.), *New Faces in New Places* (pp. 308–340). New York: Russell Sage Foundation.

Judd, D. R., & Swanstrom, T. (1994). *City Politics: Private Power and Public Policy.* New York: HarperCollins.

Junn, J. (2007). From Coolie to Model Minority: U.S. Immigration Policy and the Construction of Racial Identity. *Du Bois Review: Social Science Research on Race*, 4(02), 355–373.

Katz, C., & Baldassare, M. (1992). Using the "L-Word" in Public: A Test of the Spiral of Silence in Conservative Orange County, California. *Public Opinion Quarterly*, 56(2), 232–235.

Katznelson, I. (1973). *Black Men, White Cities: Race, Politics, and Migration in the United States, 1900–30 and Britain, 1948–68.* London and New York: Oxford University Press.

(1982). *City Trenches: Urban Politics and the Patterning of Class in the United States.* Chicago, IL: University of Chicago Press.

Khoury, J. (2008, November 5). Even in GOP strongholds, Republicans are worried. *Haaretz.*

Kleinberg, B. (1995). *Urban America in Transformation: Perspectives on Urban Policy and Development.* Thousand Oaks, CA: Sage.

Kneebone, E., & Garr, E. (2010). The Suburbanization of Poverty: Trends in Metropolitan America, 2000 to 2008. *Metropolitan Opportunity Series.* Washington DC: Brookings Institution.

Koles, M., & Muench, D. (2002). Why People Are Moving to Suburbia (and Beyond): Examining the Pull Factor in the Fox Valley. *Journal of Extension,* 40(6).

Korean Community Service Center of Greater Washington. (2013). KCSC Affiliate Organizations. http://www.kcscgw.info/e-sub6-1.php.

Lagdameo, A., & Ortiz, A. (2009). A Fresh Start: Renewing Immigrant Integration for a Stronger Maryland. Report of the Maryland Council for New Americans. Submitted to Governor Martin O'Malley. pp. 1–70.

Lang, R. E., Sanchez, T. W., & Levy, L. C. (2008). *The New Suburban Swingers: How America's Most Contested Suburban Counties Could Decide the Next President.* 2008 Election Brief, Metropolitan Institute, Virginia Tech.

Lassiter, M. D. (2007). *The Silent Majority: Suburban Politics in the Sunbelt South.* Princeton, NJ: Princeton University Press.

Lazo, A. (2008, August 5). Citgo giving $1.5 million to Maryland charity. *Washington Post.*

Lee, K. (2009, March 19). Maryland Council for New Americans, Government Access Working Group, Bethel Korean Presbyterian Church. Meeting Minutes Draft.

LEP Leadership Team. (2011). *Annual Report on Language Access Implementation (FY2011).* Montgomery County, Maryland.

LeRoux, K. (2007). Nonprofits as Civic Intermediaries: The Role of Community-Based Organizations in Promoting Political Participation. *Urban Affairs Review,* 42(3), 410–422.

Lewis, B. (2008, September 26). Virginia presidential contest hinges on DC exurbs. *USA Today.*

Lewis, P. G., & Ramakrishnan, S. K. (2007). Police Practices in Immigrant-Destination Cities: Political Control or Bureaucratic Professionalism? *Urban Affairs Review,* 43(6), 874–900.

Lewis, V. A., Emerson, M. O., & Klineberg, S. L. (2011). Who We'll Live With: Neighborhood Racial Composition Preferences of Whites, Blacks and Latinos. *Social Forces,* 89(4), 1385–1407.

LGLAC. (2008) Local Government Language Access Coordinators, Mission Statement, (November).

Lien, P.-T. (2000). Who Votes in Multiracial America? An Analysis of Voting and Registration by Race and Ethnicity, 1990–96. In Y. M. Alex-Assensoh & L. J. Hanks (Eds.), *Black and Multiracial Politics in America* (pp. 199–224). New York: New York University Press.

Lipsitz, G. (1998). *The Possessive Investment in Whiteness: How White People Profit from Identity Politics.* Philadelphia: Temple University Press.

Listokin, D., Lahr, M. L., & Heydt, C. (2012). *Third Annual Report on the Economic Impact of the Federal Historic Tax Credit*. Historic Tax Credit Coalition Report. Center for Urban Policy Research, Edward J. Bloustein School of Planning and Public Policy, Rutgers, State University of New Jersey, New Brunswick, New Jersey.

Logan, J. R. (2003). Ethnic Diversity Grows, Neighborhood Integration Lags. In B. Katz & R. Lang (Eds.), *Redefining Urban and Suburban America: Evidence from Census 2000* (vol. 3). Washington, DC: Brookings Institution.

Logan, J. R., & Alba, R. D. (1993). Locational Returns to Human Capital: Minority Access to Suburban Community Resources. *Demography*, 30(2), 243–268.

Logan, J. R., & Molotch, H. L. (1987). *Urban Fortunes: The Political Economy of Place*. Berkeley: University of California Press.

Logan, J. R., & Schneider, M. (1982). Governmental Organization and City-Suburb Income Inequality, 1960–1970. *Urban Affairs Quarterly*, 17, 303–318.

Logan, J. R. (1984). Racial Segregation and Racial Change in American Suburbs, 1970–1980. *American Journal of Sociology*, 89(4), 874–888.

Logan, J. R., & Stearns, L. B. (1981). Suburban Racial Segregation as a Nonecological Process. *Social Forces*, 60(1), 61–73.

Logan, J. R., Stults, B. J., & Farley, R. (2004). Segregation of Minorities in the Metropolis: Two Decades of Change. *Demography*, 41(1), 1–22.

Logan, J. R., Zhang, W., & Alba, R. D. (2002). Immigrant Enclaves and Ethnic Communities in New York and Los Angeles. *American Sociological Review*, 67(2), 299–322.

Londoño, E. (2007, July 22). Day-laborer center draws protest. *Washington Post*.

Lopez, M. H., & Taylor, P. (2009). Dissecting the 2008 Electorate: Most Diverse in U.S. History. Washington, DC: Pew Research Center.

Lowi, T. J. (1964). *At the Pleasure of the Mayor: Patronage and Power in New York City, 1898–1958*. New York: Free Press of Glencoe.

Luna, L. (2006). Outsourcing in State and Local Governments: A Literature Review and a Report on Best Practices. Nashville-Davidson County Metropolitan Government, Office of Metropolitan Social Services (pp. 1–46).

Maher, K. H. (2003). Workers and Strangers – The Household Service Economy and the Landscape of Suburban Fear. *Urban Affairs Review*, 38(6), 751–786.

Manis, J. G., & Stine, L. C. (1958). Suburban Residence and Political Behavior. *Public Opinion Quarterly*, 22(4), 483–489.

Manning, R. D. (1998). Multicultural Washington, DC: The Changing Social and Economic Landscape of a Post-Industrial Metropolis. *Ethnic and Racial Studies*, 21(2), 328–355.

Mapp, K., Thomas, D., & Cheek, C. T. (2006a). *Race, Accountability, and the Achievement Gap (A) Case PEL-043. Harvard University Public Education Leadership Project*. A Joint Initiative of the Harvard Graduate School of Education and Harvard Business School (August, 29).

Mapp, K. (2006b). *Race, Accountability, and the Achievement Gap (B) Case PEL-044. Harvard University Public Education Leadership Project*. A Joint Initiative of the Harvard Graduate School of Education and Harvard Business School (August 31).

Marietta, G. (2010). Lessons for PreK–3rd from Montgomery County Public Schools. FCD Case Studies: Foundation for Child Development.

Marrow, H. B. (2009). Immigrant Bureaucratic Incorporation: The Dual Roles of Professional Missions and Government Policies. *American Sociological Review*, 74(5), 756–776.

Marschall, M. J., Rigby, E., & Jenkins, J. (2011). Do State Policies Constrain Local Actors? The Impact of English Only Laws on Language Instruction in Public Schools. *Publius: The Journal of Federalism*, 41(4), 1–24.

Marwell, N. P. (2004). Privatizing the Welfare State: Nonprofit Community-Based Organizations as Political Actors. *American Sociological Review*, 69(2), 265–291.

Maryland State Department of Education. (2010). Maryland State Department of Education Fact Book, 2008–2009. Baltimore, MD: Department of Education.

Massey, D. S. (1985). Ethnic Residential Segregation: A Theoretical Synthesis and Empirical Review. *Sociology and Social Research*, 69, 315–350.

(2007). *Categorically Unequal: The American Stratification System.* New York: Russell Sage Foundation.

Massey, D. S., & Denton, N. A. (1988a). The Dimensions of Residential Segregation. *Social Forces*, 67(2), 281–315.

Massey, D. S. (1988b). Suburbanization and Segregation in U.S. Metropolitan Areas. *American Journal of Sociology*, 94(3), 592–626.

(1993). *American Apartheid: Segregation and the Making of the Underclass.* Cambridge, MA: Harvard University Press.

Massey, D. S., & Fischer, M. (1999). Does Rising Income Bring Integration? New Results for Blacks, Hispanics, and Asians in 1990. *Social Science Research*, 28(3), 316–326.

Masuoka, N., & Junn, J. (2013). *The Politics of Belonging: Race, Public Opinion, and Immigration.* Chicago, IL: University of Chicago Press.

Mayhew, D. R. (1974). *Congress: The Electoral Connection.* New Haven, CT: Yale University Press.

McClain, P. D., Carter, N. M., DeFrancesco Soto, V. M., Lyle, M. L., Grynaviski, J. D., Nunnally, S. C., ... & Cotton, K. D. (2006). Racial Distancing in a Southern City: Latino Immigrants' Views of Black Americans. *Journal of Politics*, 68(3), 571–584.

McGirr, L. (2001). *Suburban Warriors: The Origins of the New American Right.* Princeton, NJ: Princeton University Press.

McGovern, S. J. (2009). Mobilization on the Waterfront: The Ideological/Cultural Roots of Potential Regime Change in Philadelphia. *Urban Affairs Review*, 44(5), 663–694.

McKee, S. C., & Shaw, D. R. (2003). Suburban Voting in Presidential Elections. *Presidential Studies Quarterly*, 33(1), 125–144.

MCPS (2003). FY2003 The Citizens Budget. Montgomery County Public Schools, pp. 1–31.

Meier, K. J., & O'Toole, L. J. (2006). Political Control versus Bureaucratic Values: Reframing the Debate. *Public Administration Review*, 66(2), 177–192.

Meier, K. J., Stewart, J., Jr., & England, R. E. (1991). The Politics of Bureaucratic Discretion: Educational Access as an Urban Service. *American Journal of Political Science*, 35(1), 155–177.

Meola, O. (2012, November 8). Virginia 2012 voting results show Obama domination of population centers. *Richmond Times-Dispatch*.

Miller, G. J. (1981). *Cities by Contract: The Politics of Municipal Incorporation.* Cambridge, MA: MIT Press.

Mladenka, K. R. (1980). The Urban Bureaucracy and the Chicago Political Machine: Who Gets What and the Limits to Political Control. *American Political Science Review*, 74(4), 991–998.

(1981). Citizen Demands and Urban Services: The Distribution of Bureaucratic Response in Chicago and Houston. *American Journal of Political Science*, 25(4), 693–714.

Montes, S. (2007, May 4). Fire set at day-laborer center near Shady Grove. *The Gazette.*

Montgomery Coalition for Adult English Literacy. (2009, 2013b). MCAEL History Highlights. http://www.mcael.org/mission-and-history.

(2013a). MCAEL announces $650,000 in grants to support adult English literacy. http://www.mcael.org/news-announcements/id/43/mcael-announces–grants-support-adult-english-literacy.

Montgomery County. (2009). Limited English proficiency (LEP) policy and expectations. http://www.montgomerycountymd.gov/leptmpl.asp?url=/Content/exec/lep/lep.asp – EO.

(2011). Language access for individuals with limited English proficiency. http://www6.montgomerycountymd.gov/leptmpl.asp?url=/Content/exec/lep/teamlist.asp.

Montgomery County Board of Elections. (2008). Election Summary Report Presidential General Election. http://www.montgomerycountymd.gov/Elections/Resources/Files/htm/pastelections/2008/presidentialgeneral/jurisdiction/jurisdiction widepplabs1provabs2.htm.

Montgomery County (2012). Election Summary Report Presidential General Election. http://www.montgomerycountymd.gov/Elections/Resources/Files/htm/2012/generalelection/canvass/EPCompleteResults111912.htm.

Montgomery County News Release. (2005). Duncan announces new Wheaton day laborer site. Release ID: 05-030, (January 31).

Montgomery County Planning Department. (2012). Montgomery County snapshots council district by the numbers. www.MontgomeryPlanning.org.

Montgomery, D. (2011, July 14). Head of CASA is a man with a plan. *Washington Post.*

Mossberger, K., & Stoker, G. (2001). The Evolution of Urban Regime Theory: The Challenge of Conceptualization. *Urban Affairs Review*, 36(6), 810–835.

Musgrave, R. A. (1939). The Voluntary Exchange Theory of Public Economy. *Quarterly Journal of Economics*, 53(2), 213–237.

Navarro, N. (2013). Nancy Navarro Biography. http://www.nancynavarro.org/archive/biography.htm.

Nichols, R. (2010, December). The pros and cons of privatizing government functions. *Governing States and Localities* (online).

Nicolaides, B. M., & Wiese, A. (2006). *The Suburb Reader.* New York: Routledge.

Nightingale, D. S., & Pindus, N. M. (1997). Privatization of Public Social Services: A Background Paper. Prepared for the U.S. Department of Labor, Office of the Assistant Secretary for Policy. Washington, DC: Urban Institute

Niskanen, W. A. (1971). *Bureaucracy and Representative Government.* Chicago, IL: Aldine, Atherton.

Office of Budget and Management. (2002). Assessment of the Total Benefits and Costs of Implementing Executive Order No. 13166: Improving Access to Services for Persons with Limited English Proficiency. Washington, DC: U.S. Office of Budget and Management.

Office of the County Executive. (2013). Isiah (Ike) Leggett Biography. http://www .montgomerycountymd.gov/exec/bio/ike_leggett.html.

Oliver, J. E. (1999). The Effects of Metropolitan Economic Segregation on Local Civic Participation. *American Journal of Political Science*, 43(1), 186–212.

(2001). *Democracy in Suburbia*. Princeton, NJ: Princeton University Press.

(2003). Suburbanization and Sense of Community. In D. Levison & K. Christensen (Eds.), *The Encyclopedia of Community: From the Village to the Virtual World*. Thousand Oaks, CA: Sage.

Oliver, J. E., & Ha, S. E. (2007). Vote Choice in Suburban Elections. *American Political Science Review*, 101(3), 393–408.

Olson, M. (1965). *The Logic of Collective Action: Public Goods and the Theory of Groups*. Cambridge, MA: Harvard University Press.

(1969). The Principle of "Fiscal Equivalence": The Division of Responsibilities among Different Levels of Government. *American Economic Review*, 59(2), 479–487.

Orfield, M. (2002). *American Metropolitics: The New Suburban Reality*. Washington, DC: Brookings Institution.

Osterling, J. P., & McClure, S. (2008). Dystopia in Virginia: The 2008 Immigration Debate. *Mosaic, a Journal of Original Research on Multicultural Education, Teaching and Learning*, 1(1), 11–21.

Ostrom, E. (1990). *Governing the Commons: The Evolution of Institutions for Collective Action*. Cambridge and New York: Cambridge University Press.

Ostrom, V., Tiebout, C. M., & Warren, R. (1961). The Organization of Government in Metropolitan Areas: A Theoretical Inquiry. *American Political Science Review*, 55(4), 831–842.

Owens, M. L., & Yuen, A. (2011). The Distributive Politics of "Compassion in Action": Federal Funding, Faith-Based Organizations, and Electoral Advantage. *Political Research Quarterly*, 65(2), 422–442.

Pandya, C., McHugh, M., & Batalova, J. (2011). Limited English Proficient Individuals in the United States: Number, Share, Growth, and Linguistic Diversity. Washington, DC: Migration Policy Institute.

Park, R. E. (1926). The Urban Community as a Spatial Pattern and a Moral Order. In Edward W. Burgess (Ed.), *The Urban Community*. Chicago, IL: University of Chicago Press.

Parks, R. B., & Ostrom, E. (1981). Complex Models of Urban Service Systems. In T. N. Clark (Ed.), *Urban Policy Analysis: Directions for Future Research, Urban Affairs Annual Reviews* (vol. 7, pp. 171–199). Beverly Hills, CA: Sage.

Peterson, P. E. (1981). *City Limits*. Chicago, IL: University of Chicago Press.

Pierson, J. (2013, July 17). How big government co-opted charities. *Wall Street Journal*.

Pinderhughes, D. M. (1987). *Race and Ethnicity in Chicago Politics: A Reexamination of Pluralist Theory*. Chicago, IL: University of Chicago Press.

Piven, F. F., & Cloward, R. A. (1971). *Regulating the Poor: The Functions of Public Welfare*. New York: Pantheon Books.

Piven, F. F. (1977). *Poor People's Movements: Why They Succeed, How They Fail*. New York: Pantheon Books.

Price, M., & Singer, A. (2008). Edge Gateways: Immigrants, Suburbs, and the Politic of Reception in Metropolitan Washington. In A. Singer, S. W. Hardwick, & C. Brettell (Eds.), *Twenty-first-century Gateways: Immigrant Incorporation in Suburban America*. Washington, DC: Brookings Institution.

Putnam, R. D. (2000). *Bowling Alone*. New York: Simon and Schuster.

Qi, L. (2013). Practitioner's corner: Doing more with less on language access. Washington, DC: Migration Policy Institute.

Rafii, R., & Soroya, F. (2003). *Strength in Numbers: The Relative Concentration of Iranian Americans across the Nation Iran Census Report*: National Iranian Action Council (NIAC).

Ramakrishnan, S. K., & Bloemraad, I. (2008). Making Organizations Count: Case Studies in California. In S. K. Ramakrishnan & I. Bloemraad (Eds.), *Civic Roots and Political Realities: Immigrants, Community Organizations, and Political Engagement*. New York: Russell Sage Foundation.

Ramakrishnan, S. K. (2011). *Civic Hopes and Political Realities: Immigrants, Community Organizations, and Political Engagement*. New York: Russell Sage Foundation.

Ramakrishnan, S. K., & Wong, T. K. (2007). Immigration Policies Go Local: The Varying Responses of Local Governments to Undocumented Immigration. University of California Riverside, Working Paper, pp. 1–29.

Ramakrishnan, S. K. (2010). Partisanship, Not Spanish: Explaining Municipal Ordinances Affecting Undocumented Immigrants. In M. Varsanyi (Ed.), *Taking Local Control: Immigration Policy Activism in U.S. Cities and States*. Palo Alto, CA: Stanford University Press.

Reisch, M., & Sommerfeld, D. (2003). Welfare Reform and the Future of Nonprofit Organizations. *Nonprofit Management & Leadership*, 14(1), 19–43.

Robbins, L. (2010, July 15). Foreclosures in Prince George's County again lead Maryland. *Washington Post*.

Rogers, R. R. (2004). Race-Based Coalitions among Minority Groups: Afro-Caribbean Immigrants and African-Americans in New York City. *Urban Affairs Review*, 39(3), 283–317.

Rosenstone, S. J., & Hansen, J. M. (1993). *Mobilization, Participation, and Democracy in America*. New York: Macmillan Publishing Company.

Ross, B. H., & Levine, M. A. (2005). *Urban Politics: Power in Metropolitan America* (7th ed.). Belmont, CA: Thomson Wadsworth.

Ruark, E. (2009). English Learners and Immigration: A Case Study of Prince George's County, Maryland. Federation for American Immigration Reform (FAIR) (November).

Rusk, D. (1999). *Inside Game/Outside Game: Winning Strategies for Saving Urban America*. Washington, DC: Brookings Institution.

Salamon, L. M. (1995). *Partners in Public Service: Government (Nonprofit Relations in the Modern Welfare State)*. Baltimore, MD: Johns Hopkins University Press.

(1999). *America's Nonprofit Sector: A Primer*. New York: Foundation Center.

(2002). *The Resilient Sector: The State of Nonprofit America*. Washington, DC: Brookings Institution.

Salamon, L. M., Hems, L. C., & Chinnock, K. (2000). *The Nonprofit Sector: For What and for Whom? (Working Papers of the Johns Hopkins Comparative Nonprofit Sector Project No. 37)*. Baltimore, MD: Johns Hopkins Center for Civil Society Studies.

Salisbury, R. H. (1969). An Exchange Theory of Interest Groups. *Midwest Journal of Political Science*, 13(1), 1–32.

Samuelson, P. A. (1954). The Pure Theory of Public Expenditure. *Review of Economics and Statistics*, 36(4), 387–389.

Sanders, H. T., & Stone, C. (1987a). Competing Paradigms. *Urban Affairs Review*, 22(4), 548–551.

Sanders, H. T. (1987b). Developmental Politics Reconsidered. *Urban Affairs Quarterly*, 22(4).

Sandler, T., & Tschirhart, J. T. (1980). The Economic Theory of Clubs: An Evaluative Survey. *Journal of Economic Literature*, 18(4), 1481–1521.

Sassen, S. (1999). *Globalization and Its Discontents: Essays on the New Mobility of People and Money*. New York: New Press.

(2000). Informalization: Imported through Immigration or a Feature of Advanced Economies? *Working USA: The Journal of Labor & Society*, 3(6), 6–26.

Schachter, J. (2001a). *Geographical Mobility: Population Characteristics*. Washington, DC: Bureau of the Census.

(2001b). *Why People Move: Exploring the March 1998 to March 2000 Current Population Survey*. Washington, DC: Bureau of the Census.

Schachter, J. P. (2004). *Geographical Mobility Report: 2002 to 2003*. Washington, DC: Bureau of the Census.

Schelling, T. C. (1971). Dynamic Models of Segregation. *Journal of Mathematical Sociology*, 1(2), 143–186.

Schneider, M. (1989a). *The Competitive City: The Political Economy of Suburbia*. Pittsburgh, PA: University of Pittsburgh Press.

(1989b). Intermunicipal Competition, Budget-Maximizing Bureaucrats, and the Level of Suburban Competition. *American Journal of Political Science*, 33(3), 612–628.

Schneider, M., & Logan, J. R. (1982). The Effects of Local Government Finances on Community Growth Rates: A Test of the Tiebout Model. *Urban Affairs Review*, 18(1), 91–105.

Schneider, M., & Phelan, T. (1993). Black Suburbanization in the 1980s. *Demography*, 30(2), 269–279.

Schneider, W. (1992, July). The Suburban Century Begins. *The Atlantic Online*, 270(1), 33–44.

Seper, J. (2007, May 7). Guide Coaches Illegals on Raids: CASA Explains Job-Site Rights. *Washington Times*.

Serwer, A. (2009, September 17). Why can't Tom Perez get confirmed. *American Prospect*.

Sfikas, P. (2002). Senate Bill 265. State Government Access to State Agencies – Persons with Limited English Proficiency. Assigned to Education, Health, and Environmental Affairs Committee (January 23).

Shefter, M. (1978). The Electoral Foundations of the Political Machine. In J. H. Silbey, A. G. Bogue, W. H. Flanigan, & L. Benson (Eds.), *The History of American Electoral Behavior*. Princeton, NJ: Princeton University Press.

Shingles, R. D. (1981). Black Consciousness and Political Participation: The Missing Link. *American Political Science Review*, 75(1), 76–91.

Sicola, K. (2004). Reaching out to non-native speakers of English. Fairfax County Division of Solid Waste Collection & Recycling. (July 15). PowerPoint Presentation to Metropolitan Washington Council of Governments.

Simpson, J. (2011). CASA de Maryland: The Illegals' ACORN. Accuracy in Media. (September 20).

Singer, A. (2003). *At Home in the Nation's Capital: Immigrant Trends in Metropolitan Washington*. Washington, DC: Brookings Institution.

(2004). *The Rise of Immigrant Gateways*: Washington, DC: Brookings Institution.

(2009). Language Access in the District: Five Years in the Making. Washington, DC: Brookings Institution.

(2012). Metropolitan Washington: A New Immigrant Gateway. In E. S. Pumar (Ed.), *Hispanic Migration and Urban Development: Studies from Washington DC* (vol. 17, pp. 3–24). United Kingdom: Emerald Group Publishing Limited.

Singer, A., Friedman, S. R., Cheung, I., & Price, M. (2001). *The World in a Zip Code: Greater Washington, D.C. as a New Region of Immigration*. Washington, DC: Brookings Institution.

Singer, A., Hardwick, S. W., & Brettell, C. B. (2008). *Twenty-First Century Gateways*. Washington, DC: Brooking Institution.

Singer, A., & Wilson, J. H. (2006). Polyglot Washington: Language Needs and Abilities in the Nation's Capital. Washington, DC: Brookings Institution.

Singer, A., Wilson, J. H., & DeRennzis, B. (2009). Immigrants, politics, and local response in suburban Washington. Washington, DC: Brookings Institution.

South, S. J., & Crowder, K. D. (1997). Residential Mobility between Cities and Suburbs: Race, Suburbanization, and Back-to-the-City Moves. *Demography*, 34(4), 525–538.

Squires, G. D., Friedman, S. R., & Saidat, C. E. (2002). *Experiencing Residential Segregation: A Contemporary Study of Washington, D.C.* Washington, DC: Center for Washington Area Studies, George Washington University.

Stevens, J. B. (1993). *The Economics of Collective Choice*. Boulder, CO: Westview Press.

Stiglitz, J. (1982). The Theory of Local Public Goods Twenty-Five Years after Tiebout: A Perspective. NBER Working Paper Series. National Bureau of Economic Research.

Stone, C. (1989). *Regime Politics: Governing Atlanta, 1946–1988*. Lawrence: University Press of Kansas.

(1993). *Urban Regimes and the Capacity to Govern: A Political Economy Approach. Journal of Urban Affairs*, 15 (1), 1–28.

(1998). Urban Regimes: A Research Perspective. In D. R. Judd and P. P. Kantor (Eds.), *Politics of Urban America: A Reader, 2nd Edition*. New York: Pearson.

(2005). Looking Back to Look Forward: Reflections on Urban Regime Analysis. *Urban Affairs Review*, 40(3), 309–341.

(2011). Beyond the Equality-Efficiency Tradeoff. In C. Hayward & T. Swanstrom (Eds.), *Justice and the American Metropolis*. Minneapolis: University of Minnesota Press.

Suro, R., Wilson, J. H., & Singer, A. (2011). *Immigration and Poverty in America's Suburbs. Metropolitan Opportunity Series*. Washington, DC: Brookings Institution.

Swanstrom, T. (1988). Semisovereign Cities: The Politics of Urban Development. *Polity*, 21(1), 83–110.

Tate, K. (1993). *From Protest to Politics: The New Black Voters in Elections*. Cambridge, MA: Harvard University Press.

Taylor, A. L. (2010, March 10). Leggett signs language access executive order. *The Gazette*.

Thomas, G. S. (1998). *The United States of Suburbia: How the Suburbs Took Control of America and What They Plan to Do with It.* Amherst, NY: Prometheus.

Tiebout, C. M. (1956). A Pure Theory of Local Expenditures. *Journal of Political Economy,* 64(5), 416–424.

Torbat, A. E. (2002). The Brain Drain from Iran to the United States. *Middle East Journal,* 56(2), 272–295.

(2008). *Political Monopolies in American Cities: The Rise and Fall of Bosses and Reformers.* Chicago, IL: University of Chicago Press.

Trounstine, Jessica (2010). Representation and Accountability in Cities. *Annual Review of Political Science,* 13, 407–423.

Turque, B. (2006, October 31). New group is sought to run labor center. *Washington Post.*

Turque, B., & Brulliard, K. (2006, October 1). Police enforcement of immigration laws raises worry: Foreigners without documents say they may leave out of fear. *Washington Post.*

Uhlaner, C. J., Cain, B. E., & Kiewiet, D. R. (1989). Political Participation of Ethnic Minorities in the 1980s. *Political Behavior,* 11(3), 195–231.

U.S. Census Bureau. (2008). Current Population Survey: Voting and Registration Supplement 2008. Washington, DC: Bureau of the Census.

(2010a). 2010 Homeownership Rate for Maryland's Jurisdictions. Washington, DC: Bureau of the Census.

(2010b). Census Counts for Iranian Write-In Groups/Terms Alone, or Alone or in Any Combination, for the United States, Regions, and States. Washington, DC: Bureau of the Census.

(2010c). Profile of General Population and Housing Characteristics: 2010 Prince George's County, Maryland. Washington, DC: Bureau of the Census.

(2013). Fairfax County, Virginia. Washington, DC: Bureau of the Census.

U.S. Dept. of Housing and Urban Development. (2013). Fair housing laws and presidential executive orders. http://portal.hud.gov/hudportal/HUD?src=/program_offices/fair_housing_equal_opp/FHLaws.

Valenzuela, A. (1999). Day laborers in Southern California: Preliminary findings from the day labor survey. Los Angeles: Center for the Study of Urban Poverty, Institute for Social Science Research, University of California, Los Angeles.

(2000). Working on the margins: Immigrant day labor characteristics and prospects for employment. Center for Comparative Immigration Studies, University of California, San Diego.

(2006). On the corner: Day labor in the United States. Los Angeles: Center for the Study of Urban Poverty, Institute for Social Science Research, University of California, Los Angeles.

Valenzuela, A., & Meléndez, E. (2003). Day labor in New York: Findings from the NYDL survey. New York, Los Angeles, CA: Community Development Research Center, Milano Graduate School of Management and Urban Policy, New School University.

Varian, H. R. (1993). Markets for Public Goods? *Critical Review: A Journal of Politics and Society,* 7(4), 539–557.

Varsanyi, M. (2010). *Taking Local Control: Immigration Policy Activism in U.S. Cities and States.* Stanford, CA: Stanford University Press.

Verba, S., & Nie, N. H. (1972). *Participation in America: Political Democracy and Social Equality.* New York: Harper & Row.

Verba, S., Schlozman, K. L., & Brady, H. E. (1995). *Voice and Equality: Civic Voluntarism in American Politics*. Cambridge, MA: Harvard University Press.

Virginia Politics Northern Virginia Style. (2011, May 10). Virginia politics, northern Virginia style. *Washington Post*.

Wagner, C. (1982). Simpson's Paradox in Real Life. *American Statistician*, 36(1), 46–48.

Waldinger, R. D. (1986). *Through the Eye of the Needle: Immigrants and Enterprise in New York's Garment Trades*. New York: New York University Press.

Waldinger, R. D., & Lichter, M. I. (2003). *How the Other Half Works: Immigration and the Social Organization of Labor*. Berkeley: University of California Press.

Walker, K. E., & Leitner, H. (2011). The Variegated Landscape of Local Immigration Policies in the United States. *Urban Geography*, 32(2), 156–178.

Wang, T. (2009). Eliminating Language Barriers for LEP Individuals: Promising Practices from the Public Sector (pp. 1–36): Grantmakers Concerned with Immigrants and Refugees (GCIR).

Weast, J. (2009). Beyond "Heroes and Sheroes": The Success of Montgomery County Schools. *Learning First Alliance*. http://www.learningfirst.org/stories/MontgomeryCounty.

Weir, M. (Ed.) (1998). *The Social Divide: Political Parties and the Future of Activist Government*. Washington, DC: Brookings Institution.

Werker, E., & Ahmed, F. Z. (2008). What Do Organizations Nongovernmental Do? *American Economic Association*, 73–92.

Whyte, W. H. (1956). *The Organization Man*. New York: Simon and Schuster.

Williams, L. F. (1998). Race and the Politics of Social Policy. In M. Weir (Ed.), *The Social Divide: Political Parties and the Future of Activist Government* (pp. 417–463). Washington, DC: Brookings Institution.

(2003). *The Constraint of Race: Legacies of White Skin Privilege in America*. University Park: Pennsylvania State University Press.

Wilson, W. J. (1980). *The Declining Significance of Race: Blacks and Changing American Institutions*. Chicago, IL: University of Chicago Press.

Winders, J. (2012). Seeing Immigrants: Institutional Visibility and Immigrant Incorporation in New Immigrant Destinations. *The ANNALS of the American Academy of Political and Social Science*, 641(1), 58–78.

Wirt, F. M. (1965). The Political Sociology of American Suburbia: A Reinterpretation. *Journal of Politics*, 27(3), 647–666.

(1975). Suburbs and Politics in America. *Publius: The Journal of Federalism*, 5(1), 121–144.

Woldoff, R. A., & Ovadia, S. (2009). Not Getting Their Money's Worth. *Urban Affairs Review*, 45(1), 66–91.

Wong, J. (2000). The Effects of Age and Political Exposure on the Development of Party Identification among Asian American and Latino Immigrants in the United States. *Political Behavior*, 22(4), 341–371.

(2006). *Democracy's Promise: Immigrants & American Civic Institutions*. Ann Arbor: University of Michigan Press.

Wood, R. C. (1959). *Suburbia, Its People and Their Politics*. Boston, MA: Houghton Mifflin.

Wood, R. C., & Truman, D. B. (1959). Suburbia: Its People and Their Politics. *American Political Science Review*, 53(3), 824–826.

Yinger, J. (1995). *Closed Doors, Opportunities Lost: The Continuing Costs of Housing Discrimination*. New York: Russell Sage Foundation.

Zikmund, J. (1973). Suburbs in State and National Politics. In L. H. Masotti & J. K. Hadden (Eds.), *The Urbanization of the Suburbs*. Beverly Hills, CA: Sage.

Zubrinsky, C., & Bobo, L. (1996). Prismatic Metropolis: Race and Residential Segregation in the City of the Angels. *Social Science Research*, 25(4), 335–374.

Index

Note: An *f* following a page number indicates a figure; an *n* following a page number indicates a note; a *t* following a page number indicates a table.

blacks (*cont.*)
   as percentage of suburban residents, 4
   relations with Latinos, 62–63, 70, 131
   views on undocumented immigrants
      by, 62
   voter turnout, 2004–2008, 143*n*2
   See also demographics, school district;
      residential selection case study
blockbusting, 24
blockbusting (panic-peddling), 24, 26
block grants, 135
Bobo, L., 62
Browning, R. P., 89
budgetary line items, 32
Bulova, Sharon, 39*n*12
bureaucratic agencies, and SII, 33, 37–38
Bush, George H. W., 31
Bush, George W., 112, 143

California
   English Only Law in, 113
   language access policy in, 113
   LEP population in, 110
   Proposition 187, 6, 6*n*5
   Proposition 209, 75
Cambodian immigrants, intra-group language/
      cultural barriers among, 110
CAP (Community Action Program), 29–30
CASA de Maryland, 1, 2
   and establishment of first day labor site,
      103–104
   evening ESOL program, 126*f*5.2
   and funding controversy, 96, 97
   growth of, 96
   hate crime against, 96–97
   and increased access to resources, 95,
      96–99
   and language access complaint against DC
      law enforcement, 113–114*n*4
   and McCormick-Goodhart Mansion
      renovation, 97–98
   and New Americans Initiative, 114
   opposition to, 107–108
   organization of, 96
   origins of, 96
   positive response from government,
      138–139
   and Welcome Center/Day Laborer ESOL
      program, 125
   and zoning policy, 103, 104
CASA in Action, 108, 138
CASA-NAACP alliance, 137

Central Americans, reasons for settling in DC
      metro area, 52
centralized *vs.* fragmented/decentralized
      government structures, 9–11
   autonomy issues, 9–10
   and federally funded redistributive
      programs, 10–11
   and political/electoral incorporation of
      immigrants, 10
Charles, C. Z., 43, 44, 48, 51, 70
Charles Gilchrist Center for Cultural
      Diversity, 122
Chicago School, 45
Chinese
   communication issues with law enforcement
      officers, 122–123
   and language access, 84, 122, 123–124
   neighborhood interactions, 45
   and suburban neighborhood interactions, 66
   See also residential selection case study
Chong Ho Yuk, 124
citizenship, 105, 114–115, 122
City of Gaithersburg, 82
civic cooperation, 28
civic/political implications of minority
      suburbanization, 139–145
   and factors impeding engagement, 140
   and mobilization through extra-institutional
      means, 141
   and party identification, 142–145
   and social context of neighborhood,
      140–141
Civil Rights Act (1964), 25
Clark, William, 48
Clickstein, Gregg, 97
Clinton, Bill/administration, urban policy
      of, 30–31
collective action model of Olson, 35–37
common-pool resources (CPRs), 36–37
Community Action Program (CAP), 29–30
community-based initiatives, origins
      of, 29–30
community-based organizations (CBOs),
      nonprofit
   advantages of, 133, 135, 136, 139
   competition among, 136–137
   concerns/challenges, 136
   disadvantages of, 134
   donor satisfaction *vs.* beneficiary welfare,
      137–138
   effect of poverty on client increase, 134–135
   framework for successful, 136